HATELAND

HATELAND

A LONG, HARD LOOK AT AMERICA'S

EXTREMIST HEART

DARYL JOHNSON

PB Prometheus Books

59 John Glenn Drive
Amherst, New York 14228

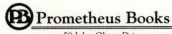

Published 2019 by Prometheus Books

Cover design by Liz Mills
Cover image of man holding torch © Pressmaster/Shutterstock
Cover image of man wearing bandana © ArtOfPhotos/Shutterstock
Cover image of tiki torch © FashionStock.com/Shutterstock
Cover image © Prometheus Books

Inquiries should be addressed to
Prometheus Books
59 John Glenn Drive
Amherst, New York 14228
VOICE: 716–691–0133 • FAX: 716–691–0137
WWW.PROMETHEUSBOOKS.COM

23 22 21 20 19   5 4 3 2 1

Library of Congress Cataloging-in-Publication Data

Names: Johnson, Daryl, 1969- author.
Title: Hateland : a long, hard look at America's extremist heart / by Daryl Johnson.
Description: Amherst, New York : Prometheus Books, 2019. | Includes index.
Identifiers: LCCN 2018061153 (print) | LCCN 2019009020 (ebook) |
    ISBN 9781633885172 (ebook) | ISBN 9781633885165 (hardback)
Subjects: LCSH: Radicalism—United States. | Domestic terrorism—United States. | Political violence—United States. | Political culture—United States. | BISAC: SOCIAL SCIENCE / Violence in Society. | POLITICAL SCIENCE / Political Freedom & Security / Terrorism.
Classification: LCC HN90.R3 (ebook) | LCC HN90.R3 J63 2019 (print) |
    DDC 303.48/4—dc23
LC record available at https://lccn.loc.gov/2018061153

Printed in the United States of America

CONTENTS

PART IV: UNCIVIL WAR

THE SECRET EXTREMISTS

On July 7, 2016, a twenty-five-year-old African American man with a neatly trimmed beard called out to his mom, "I'm going into Dallas. There's a march tonight."

"What kind of march?"

"Two days ago the cops shot a black man down in Louisiana. They killed another one yesterday up in Minneapolis. They got it on video. Mom—you gotta watch the news."

"Just stay out of trouble, baby."

"I will."[1]

With that, Micah Johnson walked out the front door of the suburban house in Mesquite, Texas, where he was raised and still lived with his mother, Delphine, and his younger sister. Johnson worked from home as well, providing care to his learning-disabled younger brother through a local social services agency. He played basketball at the school down the street and was described by his neighborhood friends as "chill." He had no criminal record and was not a member of any violent groups.

To the casual observer, there was little that set Johnson apart—politically or otherwise—from tens of thousands of other young African American men. And there was certainly no reason for Delphine to suspect that this was the last conversation she would have with her son.

Johnson headed into Dallas, driving west on I-30, and parked his Chevy SUV on Lamar Street, a block from Dealey Plaza, where John Kennedy was assassinated. By 8:58 p.m., as the peaceful march was winding down, he had dressed in tactical gear, armed himself with a Saiga AK-47 and a Glock 19 handgun, and begun firing at police.

After the shooting, an army buddy of Johnson's said, "I loved him to death, but that guy was not really a good soldier."[2] But the veteran had been training hard recently to make up for his deficiencies. While attacking the cops, he used advanced tactics, shooting and moving, luring officers in one direction with gunfire, then flanking them on the opposite side. By the time the police cornered him on the second floor of a community college, Johnson had killed five of them and wounded another nine.

During negotiations, Johnson taunted the cops, sang, and laughed. Eventually, the police decided to deliver a bomb to Johnson with a mobile robotic unit that was normally used to dispose of explosives. As soon as the robot rolled into the area where Johnson had holed up, the bomb detonated, killing Johnson instantly.

Johnson's mass shooting and suicide was a tragedy. But it was also an odd sort of murder mystery: the perpetrator was easily caught, but no one recognized him as the person who committed those hateful crimes. Micah Johnson's friends, family, and acquaintances were left with a burning question: what possessed this sensitive young man to go down such a dark antisocial path?

It turned out this was not an isolated case. Something similar had happened in a suburb of Chattanooga, Tennessee, almost exactly a year earlier. Tall, friendly, handsome, and athletic, twenty-four-year-old Muhammad Abdulazeez had been a champion wrestler and a good student at Red Bank High School. He'd gone on to earn an engineering degree from the University of Tennessee at Chattanooga and worked at a company that made cabling for the telecommunications industries. He lived at his parents' home in Colonial Shores, a suburb with large, well-tended yards, where his neighbors knew him as polite. Like Johnson, Abdulazeez had no criminal record and didn't belong to gangs or other violent groups.

Outside of work, his interests were unremarkable for a male in his twenties: fast cars, mixed martial arts, and guns. Abdulazeez joked that he was a "Muslim Redneck."[3] He'd taught his friend James Petty how to shoot an AR-15 in the Tennessee woods, but lots of Americans owned assault rifles.

Like many other people in their twenties, Abdulazeez sometimes partied too hard. On the morning of July 16, 2015, he woke up with a horrible hangover and lay in bed, texting back and forth with a friend while he nursed his headache. Then, around ten that morning, he walked out to his rented Ford Mustang, tore out of Colonial Shores and across the Tennessee River toward central Chattanooga.

Ten minutes later, Abdulazeez turned into the parking lot of a strip mall and pulled up outside a US Army recruiting station next to a Cricket Wireless store. Armed with an AK-47, a Saiga 12 shotgun, and a 9mm handgun, Abdulazeez fired a few dozen rounds at the station but didn't kill anyone. Just before the police arrived, he sped off to a nearby US Navy Reserve center, rammed through the security gate, and jumped out with his weapons. He sprayed bullets as he charged through a reception building and out into the parking lot, killing five people. When Abdulazeez ran back into the building, police fatally shot him.

The incident was eerily similar to Johnson's. A seemingly normal middle-class young man drove out of his suburban neighborhood for the last time, armed with a cache of military-grade weapons and determined to kill as many of a specific group of people as possible. Back in Colonial Shores, the reaction to Muhammad Abdulazeez's mass shooting was the same as Johnson's: nobody saw it coming.

It didn't stop there, though. There had been another such incident in South Carolina just a month earlier. On the morning of June 17, 2015, a black sedan drove on the backroads outside of Columbia, South Carolina, headed for the local swimming hole. Inside, twenty-one-year-old Joe Meek, his girlfriend, Lindsey, and little brother, Jacob, were already in their swimsuits, ready to escape the humid air by jumping into Lake Murray. At the wheel was Joe's old middle-school friend, Dylann Roof, who had recently gotten back in touch via Facebook. Sometimes Roof stayed with the three of them in Meek's mom's trailer, set back in the woods off Platt Springs Road.

In the back, Jacob Meek dropped his Big Gulp, spilling ice on Roof's black backpack.

"Watch it!" yelled Roof. "There are magazines in there."

"Pornos?" joked Meek, as he brushed the ice off.

"No, man. Not pornos."[4]

They pulled up at the lake a few minutes later, and everyone except the driver hopped out.

Roof told them he was going to check out *Jurassic World*. He was a ravenous consumer of movies, including *Titanic*, which he'd watched repeatedly. Roof was also studious, spending a lot of time writing and online at the library. Again, he had no known affiliations with violent groups. Roof said that he would meet up with his friends again back at Joe's mom's trailer unless he went to his own mom's house.

At 8:00 p.m., surveillance cameras showed Roof walking into an African American church in central Charleston, South Carolina, about two hours from Columbia. For about forty-give minutes, he sat down in a Bible study circle with a dozen parishioners. As everyone joined hands together and closed their eyes to pray, Roof pulled out a Glock .45 caliber handgun from his fanny pack and began methodically shooting the other people in the room while yelling racial epithets. He stood over some of the fallen victims, shooting them repeatedly as they helplessly lay on the floor. After killing nine people, Roof tried to shoot himself in the head, but realized he was out of ammo and fled the scene.

In the space of thirteen months, three relatively normal young men had killed a total of nineteen people. They hadn't known their victims or stolen anything. There were neither precipitating arguments nor evidence of gang affiliation. They didn't fit the profile of serial killers. And, in each case, the family and friends were at a loss to explain why they had committed their crime. What was causing this epidemic?

The official answer was to label the young men "violent extremists." But this answer created more questions. For example, if extremists are, by definition, outside the borders of mainstream society, how do we explain Abdulazeez's wrestling coach describing him as "All American" and "one of the nicest kids we trained"? Or his friend saying he was "very positive about people"?[5] Or his neighbors, in what the *New York Times* called his "movie-set version of American suburbia," remembering him as a friendly young man who jumped into front-yard whiffle ball games?[6] This was an extremist? He sounded more like a double agent.

Johnson had perpetrated the deadliest terror attack on police since 9/11. But how did his hatred of law enforcement square with the young man who had joined the Junior ROTC in high school, hoping one day to serve his country? Or with the fact that he had been vocal about his mainstream Christian faith while stationed in Afghanistan? How did Johnson, described by an army friend as "goofy" or by his mother as so sensitive that he got upset when their car hit a squirrel, fit into the profile of an extremist who gunned down five cops?[7] In what way did his apparently racially motivated violence intersect with the young man who went next door to buy Girl Scout cookies from his white neighbors? The descriptions of Johnson by the people who knew him best did not square with someone on the fringes of American society.

Roof's attack was racially motivated but, to the people who knew him best, little had suggested that such a violent turn was imminent. He had grown up with black and biracial classmates, some of whom came over for middle school sleepovers. At the time of the shooting, a surprisingly large percentage of Roof's Facebook friends were African American. Roof had reportedly expressed admiration for Rev. Martin Luther King after watching a documentary on him. Both his mother and father claimed they raised him to respect all people and that he'd never showed any aversion to being around people of other races. In a note written the day of the shooting, Roof himself wrote that "I was not raised in a racist home or environment."[8]

Most confounding, just a week before the shooting, Roof and his friend Joe had invited over Joe's African American neighbor, Christon Scriven, to party with pot, cocaine, and cheap vodka. Scriven later claimed that Roof "never said anything racist, never treated me any different," adding that Roof "had no intention of harming those people in that church."[9]

It was undeniable that the men had committed acts of extreme violence. But, up to that point, they had flown under the radar, well inside the boundaries of mainstream America. Were they a new breed of extremist Manchurian Candidate? And what was meant by extremism?

PART I

WHAT IS EXTREMISM?

CHAPTER ONE

WE WANT THE BROKEN TOYS

Despite their relatively mainstream, middle class existence, Micah Johnson, Muhammad Abdulazeez, and Dylann Roof were closer to extremism than most people suspected. This was not, however, because of some previously unknown revelation about their lives, but simply because everybody is. The idea that there is a firm barrier between any one person and an alternate, extremist version of them is a misconception. There is no us and them. It is an uncomfortable reality, but understanding that one fact is critical to understanding how extremism operates.

Radicalization, meaning the process by which any "normal" person becomes an "extremist," is complex, but it has two primary components. The first elements are internal, the backgrounds, individual traits, and psychology that make up personalities. Within everybody, an internal battle exists between destabilizing factors, like drug abuse or anger, and grounding inhibitors, such as strong personal relationships or patience. Imagine this ongoing conflict as a kind of personal safety net. Destabilizers, such as ignorance, bias, stubbornness, rebellion, alienation, grievance, and isolation, fray and weaken the net. Curiosity about other belief systems resulting from destabilizing influences can also cause deterioration. Inhibitors—careers, faith, family ties, education, and social networks—increase the net's thickness, strength, and flexibility.

Everyone moves through an unpredictable world, but each navigates it with different equipment. Faced with, say, the stress of losing a house or job or the trauma of losing a loved one, everyone reacts differently. Some people become angry, others depressed, while still others hold themselves together much better. In general terms, the more grounding inhibitors that exist, the stronger the network support and the better the chance of dealing with stress healthily. The weaker the net, the more likely people are to seek revenge, sink into depression, commit suicide—or be sucked into an extremist universe.

The second element of the radicalization process is exposure to external radicalizing forces, such as leaders, ideologies, conspiracy theories, social groups, propaganda, and personal relationships. There's nothing resembling an exact calculus on how the process plays out but, generally speaking, people with weakened safety nets who come into contact with extremist rhetoric and ideology are most likely to accept or latch onto extremist ideas. This is the initial step in the radicalization process.

Simply by being human in a world full of extremist ideologies and theories, everyone is possibly capable of radicalization, the process of becoming what we call an "extremist." As the 1993 documentary *Skinheads USA: Soldiers of Hate* so forcefully reveals, the genius of William E. Davidson, better known as Bill Riccio, was to lure in boys whose safety nets were already tattered.

An infamous former Klan leader, Riccio was best known for bringing the neo-Nazi movement that flourished during the 1980s in the inland Pacific Northwest to the South. He set up his WAR house, short for White Aryan Resistance, on a compound tucked away in the woods southeast of Birmingham, Alabama. It served as a crash pad, clubhouse, and recruitment center for teenage boys eager to escape their own lives. *Skinheads USA* portrays these boys shouting "Sieg Heil!" while watching a hardcore band and giddily shaving each other's heads in the bathroom. Late at night, they ruminate drunkenly on a 1930s Nazi propaganda video: "Everyone had jobs," one kid explains to the camera. "Our government had to fuck it up . . . I really wish [Hitler] had won."[1]

WAR house may seem like a summer camp for malcontents, but it soon became clear why these boys ended up as Riccio's acolytes. Many came from broken homes, places where they were physically and emotionally abused. Few excelled at school; many had dropped out. Some of the teenagers had been in trouble with the law. Drug and alcohol addiction were common. When Riccio tells the camera, "We want the broken toys,"[2] it's nonclinical language describing kids with active destabilizers—anger, ignorance, crisis, alienation, isolation—and often virtually no grounding inhibitors, including family ties, faith, education, future goals, and social networks.

At WAR house, the boys found the community they desperately needed, but it was intertwined with a vicious extremist ideology. So, they began down the path of radicalization, not because they had a strong desire to resurrect Hitler's agenda in 1990s Alabama, but it was impossible for them to separate the rewards of the social network without Riccio's rhetoric. Being a neo-Nazi skinhead was, in fact, what bound them. At WAR house, "White Power" was a greeting and space filler in conversations. Throughout *Skinheads USA*, the boys have almost nothing to hold on to, other than the ideology that Riccio has offered.

Riccio sought out angry, adrift youth because they were the most likely to buy into his celebration of Hitler in a country where Nazis are usually shorthand for evil. But there was likely a secondary reason he was seeking out "broken toys." In one scene in the documentary, Riccio prays to Odin to protect his youth, but in recent years, several former WAR house residents came forward to report multiple cases of sexual abuse.

Ronnie Painter, then a fifteen-year-old alcoholic addicted to painkillers when he met Riccio, told authorities he fled to WAR house to get away from his mother's physically abusive boyfriend, but his escape was short-lived. Painter said that Riccio had sexually exploited him at least four times while he lived under his roof. "I'd get extremely drunk and ride off in the car with him; then he'd perform oral sex on me."[3] His brother, Lonnie, told a similar story.

This is not to suggest that all recruiters for white supremacy—or other types of extremism—are sexual predators. But it does serve to highlight how much the two groups share in common in terms of targeting and recruitment techniques. Both look for young people in need of love and attention. Both know that it's much easier to groom a child who has a missing or abusive parent. Both frequent places like playgrounds, parks, malls, arcades, and sports fields. Undeterred by the allegations against him, Riccio himself says he continues to look for disaffected youth to join his white supremacist movement at "shopping malls, concerts, and swimming holes."[4] As repugnant as the neo-Nazi ideology embraced by the teenagers was, they were also victims.

Do the activities at a neo-Nazi compound in the 1990s have anything in common with the possible radicalization of Micah Johnson, Muhammad Abdulazeez, and Dylann Roof? On the surface, perhaps not much is similar. Roof and Abdulazeez both abused alcohol and drugs, but none of the three were runaways, belonged to any extremist social groups, had shaved heads or any other telltale extremist appearance. However, digging a little deeper reveals fraying inhibitions and growing destabilization.

Inspired by his high school Junior ROTC experience, Johnson had been excited to serve his country when he shipped off to Afghanistan with his engineering unit in 2013. He had a bunch of friends in his unit, including a girl he'd had a crush on since high school. They weren't a couple, but she and Johnson had been close for years. She bought his mom, Delphine, presents on her birthday and Christmas, and had spent the night at the Johnson household several times.

In Afghanistan, though, things fell apart in short order. From the beginning, Johnson was traumatized by the daily explosion of mortar shells. Then Johnson's crush got involved with an officer, and he angrily confronted her. Soon afterward, Johnson was caught in possession of a pair of her underwear that he'd stolen from the laundry. A search of his room found illegal weapons.

As a result, Johnson's army-issued gun was taken away, and he was put under twenty-four-hour escort before being discharged and sent home. Johnson's military lawyer suggested the punishment was unusually harsh—normally soldiers would be sent to counseling for such a first-time offense—but for whatever reasons, his plea fell on deaf ears.

His mother said Johnson wasn't the same after he returned. He had spent every Sunday in church as a child; now he claimed he'd lost faith in God. He continued to play basketball at the neighborhood school, but his friends would later say he didn't joke around like he used to. What's more, what had long been his future goal—a career in the army—was over and done with.

In short, Johnson came back to Dallas physically intact, but his pre-Afghanistan understanding of the world was being pelted by destabilizers on all sides. He was smart but overwhelmed by his grievances against the army and his former girlfriend. He had some degree of PTSD, a result of the constant shelling of his base in Afghanistan. By 2016, he was known to be angered by perceived police harassment of him as well as the highly publicized shootings of African American men around the country. Somewhere between Bagram Air Base and the night he killed six cops, Johnson's inhibitors completely gave out.

Muhammad Abdulazeez's once golden life was also collapsing as the clock ran down to his shooting spree. Following the loss of his job at a nuclear power plant, the intelligent, successful Abdulazeez seems to have suffered an existential crisis. His heavy drinking worried his parents. Because their health insurance refused to pay for an inpatient abuse program, they sent him to live in Jordan with his straight-laced businessman uncle for a few months. When he returned, however, he started using drugs and drinking again.

In the days leading up to the attack, Abdulazeez called in sick to work and spent most of his time writing depressing journal entries about how his life felt like a prison. He was also increasingly angered by the deaths of Muslims as a result of the ongoing US wars in the Middle East.

Dylann Roof checked nearly all the boxes for destabilizers. He was stubborn in many ways, including his insistence that his mom give him the same bowl haircut for years. He spent hours in isolation. Much of what social time he had was spent drinking and doing drugs. Dylann had quit his job with his dad's landscaping business a few months before the shooting and had no career prospects. His parents were divorced, although he was in touch with both of them. He was intelligent but had dropped out of high school. He was also believed to carry a grievance after being rejected by a romantic interest in favor of an African American male. And, perhaps most importantly, he seemed to have no coherent plan for his life going forward.

In all three cases, a significant number of inhibitors had either long been frayed or were weakening while destabilizers multiplied. The men's safety nets were less likely to keep them from falling into the orbit of extremist ideologies or theories.

But, while those conditions may have explained the three men's individual psychological susceptibilities to extremism, it didn't explain from where they got their radical ideologies. America has always been full of disaffected youth. Plenty of kids come from unhappy homes, and feel put upon, lack direction, abuse alcohol, and act restless and rebellious. If this was the sum total of the formula for radicalization, "extremists" would pop up around every bend.

At the WAR house, Riccio played the ever-present "charismatic leader" for his acolytes. Sometimes, he was the cool dad, dispensing endless cans of Hamm's beer. Other times, he was a fascist scout leader, teaching the boys how to shoot guns and leading his group in sieg-heiling.

In one telling scene from the documentary, Riccio produces a swastika cake to honor Hitler's birthday.

"Okay," he says as he begins to slice, "everybody grab a napkin."[5]

"Thanks, Dad!" a teenage skinhead responds.

But Johnson, Abdulazeez, and Roof never had nearly that kind of close personal contact with extremist ideas. So from where did the external radicalizing forces come?

After he returned from Afghanistan, Johnson attended some Pan-African events at a Dallas bookstore and went to a Malcolm X film festival. People who remember meeting him described him as a polite young man. Perhaps more relevantly, Johnson also attended meetings of the New Black Panther Party, which is listed as a hate group by the SPLC and has been disowned by members of the original Black Panther Party that started in the 1960s. But that's it. Johnson had limited personal involvement with one or two extremist groups, and Abdulazeez and Roof are not known to have had any.

Roof did, however, leave a clue about what could have radicalized him in lieu of real-world connections. In a lengthy manifesto he wrote before his attack on the church-goers in Charleston, Roof described searching Google for the terms "black on white crime," a term he had picked up in online discussions during the national debate following George Zimmerman's 2012 shooting of African American teenager Trayvon Martin. The search brought Roof to the website of the Council of Concerned Citizens, a white supremacist group formerly known as the White Citizens Council. The site apparently sparked his interest in white supremacist ideologies. "I've never been the same since that day,"[6] wrote Roof.

Roof also claimed to have found inspiration in popular culture. At another point in the manifesto, he (mis)quoted a neo-Nazi character in the movie *American History X*: "I see all this stuff going on and I don't see anyone doing anything about it. And it pisses me off."[7]

Johnson also spent time on Black Nationalist websites, like Black Riders Liberation Army. One site—the African American Defense League—explicitly called for violence against cops.

Abdulazeez is also reported to have spent time in his bedroom watching videos by Anwar al-Awlaki—an American-Yemeni Imam often described as "the bin Laden of the internet."[8] Al-Awlaki's videos explicitly call for Muslims to kill Americans.

Compared to living at the WAR house, spending time online seems pretty tame. Is it possible that clicking through websites and social media replaced the radicalizing function served by living and socializing with other extremists, hardcore shows, charismatic leadership, and cause-based group activities?

As ugly as the swastika cake is—or the racist ideology and violent rhetoric that Johnson, Abdulazeez, and Roof found online—it is not illegal. In the United States, at least, all of those activities are protected by the Constitution. What's more, extremist ideas by themselves don't create criminal activity, much less violence.

However, all the elements discussed thus far—inhibitors, destabilizers, and a range of external radicalizers—do propel a select few further and further into what is known as the cone of radicalization. As someone becomes more radicalized, they rise into an increasingly smaller and rarified space at the tip of the cone. These people may be more likely to cross over into violent behavior, although most don't. So, what separates those whose extremist ideology and rhetoric remain legal and those who go beyond the law?

The story of Paul Jennings Hill suggests an answer. By 1994, the forty-year-old Hill had established himself as one of the most radical voices in the anti-abortion extremist movement. He had appeared on both *Donahue* and ABC's *Nightline* to defend killing abortion providers. He had put in his time locally as a regular protestor at a Pensacola, Florida, abortion clinic called the Ladies Center. In short, his activity was very extreme—and completely legal.

Hill was, however, also increasingly frustrated. He had spent day after day, month after month, year after year picketing and protesting outside the Ladies Center. Yet no one was listening to him. No one seemed deterred by his warnings and pictures of aborted fetuses. People still walked in and out of the clinic, as they did elsewhere, every day to access abortion services.

Worse, Hill was being ostracized by his colleagues for his radical views. In 1993, he was even excommunicated from the church where he had served as pastor for several years.[9] The board members were all staunchly anti-abortion, but they couldn't support Hill's extreme stance.

Hill's bitterness at the perceived ineffectualness of his actions is common to dedicated extremists. It's known as hitting the "Wall of Frustration." As an extremist's desire for radical action crystallizes, he usually collides with a barrier created by some combination of forces—including society, laws, friends, family, teachers, or religious groups. As was the case with Hill, the radicalizing communities and groups themselves will sometimes resist such action, due to ideological conflicts, public ridicule, or concern about law enforcement attention. However it happens, the Wall of Frustration suppresses an extremist's desire to undertake dangerous, illegal action.

This is the critical moment in the radicalizing process. At the Wall, they face a stark decision. Some will accede to the barrier, swallow their frustration, and continue legal activities. Others become disillusioned and drop out of the orbit of their cause or ideology altogether. But a very small fraction of those with the necessary motivation will push through.

There are often additional, nonideological factors in extremists' decisions to turn violent. They may plan attacks as a misguided attempt at revenge or to confirm a messianic vision of themselves. In other words, extremist ideologies do not themselves cause violence. They do, however, encourage an actor to focus what may otherwise be an incoherent sense of grievance on a specific target. They can create a narrative, supplying a sense of purpose and mission to the extremist's actions. Finally, ideology may help define the triggering incident that precedes the attack.

The other factor in violent acts is more logistical: having the means to carry them out. But for people carrying out a mass shooting in the United States, this is not much of a barrier. Assault weapons are not only easy to procure, but so widespread that owning them isn't remarkable. It's these people, with the motivation to push through the Wall and means to carry out attacks, who are on the path toward violence.

Paul Hill chose to push through. On the morning of June 29, 1994, he went to the abortion clinic to set up white crosses around the perimeter as he often did. A little while later, Dr. John Britton arrived at the Ladies Clinic and asked Hill to move his picket signs and white crosses so he and his bodyguard, James Barrett, could drive into the parking lot. Hill did as requested, then pulled out a 12-gauge shotgun and shot both men in the head before they could even exit their vehicle. As they bled to death, Hill put down his weapon and waited to be arrested.

Assuming that Johnson, Abdulazeez, and Roof were in fact deeply radicalized before their attacks, did the final part of their journeys look anything like Hill's?

At one meeting of New Black Panther Party, Johnson was so insistent that the group stockpile more ammunition and guns that he was banned from future meetings. This could have been his Wall of Frustration. Afterward, he became convinced that nobody else was going to take action and began training for the Dallas attacks. His attack also came immediately following two widely publicized fatal police shootings of African American men, likely his immediate trigger for the specific day.

Roof was also frustrated by small acts of resistance. His friend Joe Meek claimed he refused to take a photo of Roof burning the US flag. During a drug and alcohol binge a week before the shooting with Meek and Christon Scriven, Roof began talking about doing "something big" at the College of Charleston.[10] He didn't describe the attack as racially motivated. Though they doubted Roof would carry out any kind of threat, Meek and Scriven broke into Roof's car and hid his gun. Unfortunately, Meek returned it after his girlfriend reminded him possessing a firearm violated his probation for a burglary.

In his manifesto, Roof also appeared to have a sense of heroic messianism, writing, "No one [is] doing anything but talking on the internet. Well someone has to have the bravery to take it to the real world, and I guess that has to be me."

In the days leading up to his attack, Abdulazeez similarly painted himself as a lonely warrior without support from the rest of the world. He began making self-comparisons to the seventh-century companions of an Islamic prophet, who he believed had to commit jihad. As apparent proof of his commitment, Abdulazeez bought ammunition at Walmart on July 11, 2015, five days before the shooting. Hours before his attack on the military targets, Abdulazeez was having a religious and philosophical discussion with a friend via text in which he quoted an Islamic verse that read, "Whosoever shows enmity to a friend of mine, then I have declared war against him."

In short, each young man had his own personal problems. Each of their safety nets—constructed out of inhibitors and worn down by destabilizers—was at least somewhat frayed. Individually, they came into contact with violent, extremist rhetoric. Finally, their frustration with perceived inaction led them to seize upon a narrative of heroic, self-sacrificing violence—the ultimate contribution to their radical cause.

If that journey explains the motivation behind those young men's killing sprees, then the difficulty of predicting who becomes a violent extremist helps to explain why they were able to fly under the radar. The combination of inhibitors, destabilizers, and external radicalizing forces is a general diagnostic tool, not a crystal ball. In hindsight, the model describes the three men's path to extremism fairly well, but their general profiles match those of tens of thousands of young men, somewhat adrift and aggrieved.

In fact, the known markers of extremism are so common that it is a huge challenge for law enforcement and intelligence analysts to target specific individuals for potential radicalization. In a 2016 article, the *New York Times* described prediction as a "murky science [that] seems to imply that nearly anyone is a potential terrorist."[11]

This isn't because intelligence analysts need to design a better tool. As Chip Berlet, a longtime chronicler of right-wing extremism, claims: "There is no recent social science evidence showing that people who join the Patriot movement (or any social movement on the right or left) are mentally ill, suffer from paranoid delusions, or are more or less uneducated, ignorant or stupid than people in a surrounding batch of zip codes. They tend to be just like their neighbors."[12] This statement seems to describe Johnson, Abdulazeez, and Roof quite well.

One final clue to what motivated these murders came in the Southern Poverty Law Center's annual *Year in Hate and Extremism* reports.

In 2016, the SPLC recorded the highest number of right-wing hate groups in the thirty years since they began keeping records, a spike that began in 2008. The Ku Klux Klan remained the single largest entity, representing 21 percent of all hate groups, but heavily armed, conspiracy-minded, and anti-government "Patriot" groups had also recently hit record highs. In 2008, there were 149 such groups; by 2015, there were 998, nearly a seven-fold increase.

During this same time period, attacks by domestic Islamic extremists continued unabated. A year after Abdulazeez's attack, twenty-nine-year-old Omar Mateen, an American citizen who had pledged allegiance to ISIS, killed forty-nine people at a nightclub in Orlando, Florida. Five months later, Rizwan Farook and Tashfeen Malik killed fourteen and wounded twenty-two in a mass shooting attack at an office holiday party held at the Inland Regional Center in San Bernardino, California.

The most unexpected trend between 2008 and 2016 was the growth of violent Black Nationalism. Groups embracing black separatism, nationalism, and related ideologies had experienced the largest growth of any hate group over the previous ten years. By 2016, a segment that had not been considered a serious threat since the 1970s represented a fifth of the entire hate sector.

Broadly speaking, the process of radicalization was very similar for the three young men, even though they ended up associated with very different brands of extremism: Black Nationalist, Islamic extremist, white supremacist. But, historically, the numbers and level of activity for each of those groups has tended to rise and fall at different times. In the 1960s and 70s, left-wing and black militant groups were considered the biggest threats. While those groups waned in the 1980s and 90s, right-wing extremist groups had surges of activity. It wasn't until the 1990s that terrorism related to Islamic extremists became a top concern. But, by the time of the attacks in 2015 and 2016, there was an alarming increase in hate-driven radicalization in the United States across the political spectrum.

So, perhaps Johnson, Abdulazeez, and Roof's acts could also be explained as part of a tidal wave of radical, ideological hate. But, if so, that asked an even bigger question: why was extremism expanding so rapidly across the political spectrum?

CHAPTER TWO

A RADICAL ECHO, IGNORED

On the morning of September 29, 1983, the president and the chief loan officer of Buffalo Ridge State Bank, Rudolf Blythe, Jr., and Deems Thulin, drove out to an abandoned dairy farm in southwest Minnesota. The property had been foreclosed on three years previously and, in the stark economic climate, Blythe and Thulin were having trouble unloading it. Unfortunately for them, the people they were meeting had no intention of buying the farm.

James and Steve Jenkins, the bankrupt farm's previous owners, were waiting for them with shotguns. Full of angry despair at their shattered existence, the two men shot the bankers to death and fled south. Three days later, the younger Jenkins turned himself in to authorities in Paducah, Texas. He then took them to an abandoned farm where his father, Steve, lay dead. He'd shot himself in the head.

The father-son murderers terrified farm families across the Midwest, but many of them were also facing the same sort of financial disasters as the Jenkins. By 1983, American farmers were losing their land at a rate unseen since the dustbowl of the 1920s and 1930s. Economic factors drove the farm crisis, including high debt for new, expensive machinery, overproduction, falling commodity prices, high oil prices and a strong dollar. But the worst costs were personal. In many areas, rates for alcoholism, divorce, and child abuse shot up, while the suicide rate among ex-farmers increased so rapidly that a system of rural prevention networks were set up.

Psychologist Glen Wallace was a primary counselor on call for a suicide hotline run by a group called Ag-link. At the peak of the farm crisis, Wallace was being sent into the field to talk down suicidal farmers at a rate of nearly two hundred a year—and that was just in the state of Oklahoma. Some days, Wallace had to handle up to four farm suicide emergencies hundreds of miles apart.

His extraordinary efforts were chronicled by a journalist named Joel Dyer. Dyer had begun traveling around with Wallace in an attempt to understand the high rate of suicides among the farm families, and its links to the ongoing crisis in the rural American economy. But he also, unintentionally, ended up getting a front row seat to the beginnings of a massive wave of radicalization across the country's heartland.[1] Dyer's analysis of why right-wing extremism spiked in the 1980s and 90s might give us some insight into how extremism began rising across the political spectrum two decades later.

The crisis-level rates of suicide and alcoholism reflected the disillusion of the famers' families, employment, social networks, and future expectations during the 1980s. They often felt guilty, blaming themselves for their economic plight, even though it was rarely ever that simple.

In this weakened, confused, and angry state, Wallace saw people choosing one of three options: counseling, suicide, or shifting their guilt to blame some other group. The Jenkinses, for example, had shifted blame to the bankers. The elder Jenkins had then committed suicide.

Wallace was there to encourage farmers to accept his professional help. But during their farm visits, both Wallace and Dyer noticed other groups showing up. These people, including Christian Identitarians and the Posse Comitatus, were there to assuage the ex-farmers' crushing feelings of guilt by shifting blame to others via their extremist ideologies.

The Christian Identitarian theology begins with a familiar story: "The Lord God formed man of the dust of the ground, and breathed into his nostrils the breath of life; and man became a living soul." But, in their racist reinterpretation of the original Hebrew, the narrative quickly heads into unfamiliar territory.

As Christian Identitarians have it, the Garden of Eden, is already crowded with "Negroid," "Oriental," and "Mongoloid" peoples before

Adam is created. They had, in fact, already been in the garden for at least fifty thousand years. In this telling, Adam was no longer the first man; he was the original Caucasian—and thus the first person created in the image of God, who was apparently white. Because the pre-Adamic, non-white people were not intelligent enough to cultivate or store foods, they survived as hunters and gatherers. Adam retained the title as the first person to till the earth.

Another well-known starting point veers further into hateful territory: "And the rib, which the Lord God had taken from man, made he a woman, and brought her unto the man." But, due to a reinterpretation of words including "eat" and "touch," Eve was said to be seduced by Satan, who impregnated her. Eve then convinced Adam to have sexual relations with Satan. Not surprisingly, Adam and Eve were cast out by an angry God. Several days later, Adam impregnated Eve.

Nine months after that, Eve gave birth to two boys, Cain and Abel. But they were half brothers: Cain was the son of Satan, while Abel was Adam's true son. As such, the brothers represented two bloodlines, one evil and one righteous. Cain eventually killed Abel, was cursed by God, and went off to the land of Nod where he began his own family. Cain's progeny were said to be the first Jews, making all Jews the literal spawn of Satan. Meanwhile, Eve gave birth to Seth, a Caucasian and, according to Christian Identitarians, a true Hebrew.

This alternate Garden of Eden narrative is called "dual-seed" theory by its Christian Identity adherents but can't be described as the official theology of that religion. There is not any one unifying document or scripture. What all branches of Christian Identity, or CI, do share in common is racism and, even more so, a virulent anti-Semitism. Even for "single-seed" theorists, the more figuratively Satanic Jews control the New World Order with the intention of killing or imprisoning God's real chosen people: whites.

Christian Identity has never had a huge number of dedicated followers. It isn't even considered Christianity by almost every other church. But it has been extremely influential on the radical right, and its adherents include leaders of the Ku Klux Klan, some neo-Nazis, and prominent figures in militias. In the 1980s, Christian Identitarians were actively recruiting among the desperate Midwestern farm families.

Another group looking for new members at the same time and place was the Posse Comitatus. While many of its members also harbored anti-Semitic and white supremacist views, they were particularly distinguished by their extreme hostility toward legal authority, especially that exercised by the federal government. The founder of the Sheriff's Posse Comitatus, Henry Lamont Beach, declared grandiosely that government officials who violated oaths of office should be taken to the "most populated intersection of town and, at high noon, be hung by the neck, the body remaining until sundown as example of those who would subvert the law."

Although no such frontier justice hangings have been recorded, both the Posse and Christian Identitarians have been linked to multiple violent encounters and fatalities. In the early 1980s, at the same time as the Posse were recruiting farm families, a former Posse member and Christian Identitarian named Gordon Kahl killed two federal marshals and a sheriff. Another Identitarian, David Tate, killed a Missouri State Highway Patrol officer while trying to reach a compound called The Covenant, The Sword, and the Arm of the Lord.

Of course, when Posse members or representatives of Christian Identity approached the victims of the 1980s farm crisis, they didn't start by spouting off about the New World Order or bizarre racial theories—much less killing police officers. The extremists visited the stressed farmers and assured them their problems weren't their fault. They'd invite them to community events, dinners, prayer groups, kids' activities. Like Bill Riccio's Alabama skinheads, the families were angry and full of despair—not ready-made extremists. Most probably had zero interest in anti-Semitic reinterpretations of the second and third chapters of Genesis. But, throughout the 1980s, Christian Identitarians and Posse Comitatus ended up being remarkably effective at radicalization.

Skip forward to the early 1990s and the worst of the previous decade's farm crisis had passed, but the anger and despair across the heartland had not. Coupled with a new economic recession, membership in right-wing, anti-government groups exploded. As many as three million Americans were involved in some sort of extremist activity, in groups ranging from the Constitutionalists, Sovereign Citizens, militias, the Freemen, neo-Nazis, and various anti-immigrant groups along the Mexican border.

The movement climaxed when Timothy McVeigh, a Gulf War veteran who had spent years immersed in conspiratorial, white supremacist, and anti-government communities, blew up the Oklahoma City Alfred P. Murrah Federal Building, killing 168 people, including the 15 children in the building's day care center.

After the 1995 bombing, author Joel Dyer set out across the farm belt again, this time looking for explanations for the spike in right-wing activity. Remembering how many victims of the farm crisis were being actively recruited by extremist groups, Dyer got back in touch with the families he had met the previous decade. The groups' membership drives turned out to have been shockingly successful. Roughly 80 percent of the people Dyer had met on suicide watch during the farm crisis were now affiliated with some kind of extremist group.[2]

Without realizing it at the time, Dyer had been witness to a classic radicalization process, but on a massive scale. First, the farmers' economic and personal hardship had weakened or destroyed their inhibitors, including family, employment, social networks, and future goals. Many were affected by destabilizers, including anger, grievances, and isolation. In this state of personal crisis—weak inhibitors, strong destabilizers—they were extremely vulnerable to radicalization.

By creating social events, personal relationships, and exposing farm families to propaganda and charismatic leaders, the Identitarians, Posse Comitatus, and other groups proved strong radicalizing forces. Eventually, as a good number of the ex-farmers became more radical, they had a new way of understanding their problems. They'd shift blame for their problems to blacks, Jews, immigrants, the Zionist Occupation Government (ZOG), international banking cartels, or other extreme right-wing bogeymen.

Dyer even described the process as a funnel, an inverted cone. A huge number of nonradicalized "normal" people entered the broad top. At the funnel's bottom, a much smaller number of radicalized extremists dropped out.

But Dyer's funnel had another dimension. While he still saw the personal psychological element described in the cone of radicalization— "some combination of stress, anger, misinformation, religion, fear and blame-shifting"—the process was initiated and driven by external factors that reached across huge numbers of people simultaneously.[3] In this case, the economy was the biggest force manipulating the inhibitors and destabilizers of millions of people.

At the time of their attacks, Johnson, Abdulazeez, and Roof each faced their own individual employment problems, losing preferred jobs or not working at all. But none of them was facing bankruptcy or complete financial collapse. What's more, in a depressed economy, people are more likely to take lower paying jobs, less meaningful work, or be unemployed. They go into debt more often and only see dim career prospects in their future. In short, an economic catastrophe negatively affects resistance to radicalization on a massive scale.

Again, radicalization is too complex to make specific predictions. For example, the people who suffered the worst economically are not necessarily the most likely to embrace extremist ideas. But a catastrophe that destroys families and careers while frequently leaving people angry, confused, despondent, and aggrieved will certainly increase the overall chances of radicalization across a whole population or country.

This exactly describes what happened to thousands of farm families across the country in the 1980s. External economic factors were influencing the internal psychological process of radicalization, eroding personal inhibitors on a massive scale. Though it was not the only factor, the economic devastation of the 1980s farm crisis sowed the seeds of the rage that blossomed in the early 1990s.

In April of 2009, the Department of Homeland Security (DHS) released a report entitled *Rightwing Extremism: Current Economic and Political Climate Fueling Resurgence in Radicalization and Recruitment.* As the title suggests, the report warned that many of the same macro-conditions that led to extremist activity in the 1990s were evident in 2009.

The document specifically warned that the "economic downturn" might play a similar role in present day right-wing radicalization as it did in the 1990s. Additionally, it pointed to a unique political event—"the election of the first African American president"—as another factor that could spur radicalization among members of the racist far right.[4] Other potential drivers for radicalization included the return of veterans from Iraq and Afghanistan "facing significant challenges reintegrating into their communities,"[5] and the anticipation among some people that President Obama, who had said he supported "common sense" gun laws, was going to crack down on Second Amendment rights. Together, the report concluded, these factors—economic, political, and societal—"present unique drivers for right-wing radicalization and recruitment."[6]

Because the report was a warning about possible future activity, most of the threats were largely theoretical. But DHS did cite a recent example. On April 4, 2009, two police officers in Pittsburgh, Pennsylvania, responded to a domestic dispute between Margaret Poplawski and her twenty-two-year-old son Richard. The dispute began after the son's pit bulls had peed on Margaret Poplawski's carpet and she told him to get out of her house. But when the police arrived, the younger Poplawski, lying in wait with a bullet-proof vest, shot both police officers at the door.[7] Those two officers, as well as a third officer who responded to the call, bled to death on the ground while Poplawski held law enforcement at bay for four hours with his AK-47 and several handguns.

Richard Poplawski had a troubled background. Aside from a combative relationship with his mother, he had been kicked out of the Marines and was upset after recently losing his job at a glass factory. He had also apparently come into contact with some conspiratorial extreme right-wing propaganda. According to a friend who Poplawski called during the shootout, the gunman was unhappy about "the Obama gun ban that's on the way,"[8] a baseless idea propagated by right-wing extremists including the burgeoning militia and Patriot groups. Over nine pages, the DHS report focused on two possibilities: that this tragic incident was spurred by the unique political and economic factors that the country was confronting, and that it might not be the last such event.

For DHS analysts, the warning seemed prudent and evidence-based. The correlation between broad economic and political trends and radicalization was well-established among experts who monitor extremist groups. In hindsight, the warnings accurately predicted a sustained spike in right-wing extremism. At the time, however, the report was met with scorn and fierce resistance from conservatives.

Writing in the *Washington Times*, syndicated columnist and Fox News contributor Michelle Malkin referred to the "piece of crap report" as a "sweeping indictment of conservatives."[9] For her, the fact that these far-right extremist threats were not specifically linked to named organizations—e.g., Ku Klux Klan or Ohio Defense Force militia—meant that the DHS report could be used to target any group with "right-wing" ideologies.

She claimed the report "demonizes the very Americans who will be protesting in the thousands on Wednesday for the nationwide Tax Day Tea Party."[10] As a sarcastic rebuttal, Malkin suggested that attendees make signs for the Tea Party event reading: "Honk if you're a radicalized right-wing extremist" and "Guilty of right-wing extremist chatter."[11]

Malkin wasn't done, nor was she alone. Because the report warned about the danger posed by skinheads and violent neo-Nazis learning the art of warfare in US armed forces, Malkin accused the authors of left-wing antimilitary bias. She was joined by numerous prominent Republicans, including House minority leader, John Boehner, who described the report as offensive and demanded that the agency apologize to veterans. "To characterize men and women returning home after defending our country as potential terrorists is offensive and unacceptable," he said.[12] It was not, however, unfounded.

The Aryan Nations compound was established in the 1970s by white supremacist, Christian Identity adherent, and pioneering American neo-Nazi Richard Butler. Set in a semi-rural, wooded area north of Coeur d'Alene, Idaho, it had a summer camp look to it: low-slung buildings sat under towering pine trees. The fingers of nearby Hayden Lake stretched off toward the surrounding green hills.

Butler used the compound as a center of his white supremacist operations for two decades. In the early 1980s, he invited farmers who lost their land in the farm crisis to live there in exchange for their participation in his movement. Much like at Riccio's Alabama WAR house, Butler's twenty acres was also home for teenagers and other young men who became neo-Nazi skinheads. In the mid-1980s, Butler also hosted some of the most important figures in the extreme right, including Klansman Louis Beam, Christian Identitarian Gordon Mohr, and white supremacist Robert E. Miles.

Idaho, in which less than one percent of the population is African American, was a popular destination for other white supremacists and far-right extremists. In the 1990s, James "Bo" Gritz, an impassioned anti-Semite, built a housing community called Almost Heaven about three hours south of the Hayden Lake compound.[13] About an hour north of Butler's operations base sat Randy Weaver's house in Ruby Ridge—a location that, following a 1990s standoff with law enforcement, became a right-wing rallying slogan.

It also turned out that Gritz, Weaver, Beam, Mohr, and Miles had all served in the military. Likewise, Klansman, neo-Nazi, and number two in the Posse Comitatus, August Kreis, served on a Navy vessel during Vietnam.[14]

What's more, the two most infamous right-wing extremist attacks of the 1990s were carried out by military veterans. Oklahoma City bomber Timothy McVeigh was a Gulf War veteran. And Eric Rudolph, whose series of bombings between 1996 and 1998 injured over 120 people and killed 2, had served in the army in the late 1980s.

In fact, extremist right-wing groups made no secret of their recruitment of military personnel. At the 2004 Hate Rock festival in Phoenix, Arizona, white supremacist Tom Metzger enjoined the crowd to covertly infiltrate military and law enforcement. "Don't operate like a battleship," he said. "Operate like a Nazi submarine."[15]

Metzger's strategy made sense. Wars are by nature destructive and traumatic. One in four veterans has a service-connected disability. What's more, veterans of the First Gulf War were three times more likely to have post-traumatic stress disorder (PTSD), which can disrupt family life and social networks, increase isolation, and limit employment options. Targeting any one veteran as an extremist solely based on their military service is wasteful profiling. But the destabilizing conditions of war make veterans, as a whole, more susceptible to radicalization. Additionally, military veterans have advanced tradecraft including knowledge of guns, explosives, and tactics. If they were radicalized and committed violence, they would be more likely to do huge amounts of damage than a civilian.

A government survey of 17,080 soldiers that found 3.5 percent of soldiers have, in fact, been contacted for recruitment by an extremist organization. There are over two million Americans serving in the military and National Guard, which means extremist organizations have approached more than seventy thousand active duty military. More than twice that number, 7.1 percent, said they knew another soldier who was actually part of an extremist organization.

Despite the abuse directed at its "left-wing" bias, the DHS report's warning was anchored in solid analysis, data, and historical examples. In the aggregate, it was reasonable that the steady stream of soldiers returning from an increasingly unpopular series of wars were more likely to be radicalized. And at least one of them, Micah Johnson, did in fact go on a killing spree.

The suggestion that an election of a Democratic president might be used as a recruitment device by right-wing "Patriot" and militia groups was also grounded in historical example. Membership in those extremist groups had, in fact, been as predictable as the tides over the past two decades. Patriot and militia groups first emerged and rose when a Democrat, Bill Clinton, was elected president. Their numbers fell when a Republican, George W. Bush, replaced Clinton. By 2001, the SPLC was in a rare position: heralding the near death of a once powerful extremist movement, in this case, the seven-year-old Patriot and militia groups.[16]

There were several reasons for the rapid rise and fall of the movement. First, militias and Patriot groups are typified by a conspiratorial and antagonistic view of the government, including a widespread belief that a federal program of weapons confiscation is imminent. Clinton, in fact, did sign into law two pieces of meaningful gun control in the early 1990s: the Brady Bill, which created a waiting period on gun purchases, and the assault weapons ban, which made a certain number of military-grade rifles illegal. Although nowhere close to a widespread confiscation of weapons, the new laws initially triggered a paranoia and excitement that helped recruitment. Membership in the movement began a downward slide following the 1995 Oklahoma City bombing. First, the tragedy led to a federal crackdown on right-wing extremist groups. Second, there was a splintering within the ranks as some militias tried to distance themselves from white supremacist groups. There was a certain amount of disillusionment that a promised revolution never came, including a revolt that was meant to be kicked off by the Y2K catastrophe.[17] But it was the 2000 election of a Republican president that stamped out the militia and Patriot movements of the 1990s.

Given the significant similarities between the early 1990s and 2009, it was also reasonable to assume that the election of a president who was a Democrat and had spoken favorably of "common sense" gun laws might drive an increase in militia recruitment.

Unfortunately, in 2009, critics like Malkin won the day. The Obama White House decided that the staunch conservative resistance to the report made it politically toxic. So, in the face of claims that the report was too politicized, DHS took two remarkable actions. First, the agency rebuked its own analysis about the potential for a rise in right-wing extremism. The prescient report was, essentially, killed.

Then, to make absolutely certain that conservatives were placated, DHS also reduced its meager resources dedicated to monitoring right-wing extremists. To put this in context, in 2009, as many as forty analysts at DHS's Office of Intelligence and Analysis tracked domestic Islamic threats. Just six people were dedicated to investigating domestic terrorism, which includes environmental radicals, black nationalists, anti-abortion extremists, white supremacists, and militias.

By this time, data had already showed that this resource allocation was not proportionate to the threats the nation faced. Over the previous eight years, right-wing groups had proved to be a bigger domestic threat than any extreme Islamic or radical left-wing activity. In the face of denunciations of the report, however, DHS actually cut back resources for right-wing analysis.

If there was one particular way in which the disowned DHS report did come up short, it was that rather than seeing a replay of the right-wing extremism of the 1990s, 2008–2016 was much worse. During that period, the number of active militia, Ku Klux Klan, and other hate groups grew steadily and for longer than they had in the 1990s, all reaching record highs.

One reason for this unprecedented explosion of hate was simple: the economic and political conditions that drove it were also unprecedented. For example, in the thirty years between 1986 and 2016, the US Gross Domestic Product (GDP) experienced negative growth just three times. The first was in 1991, around the same time that 1990s right-wing extremism was expanding. The second and third were in 2008 and 2009, and both were much deeper.[18]

Similarly to the 1980s farm crisis, unemployment and foreclosures had a dramatic personal impact. As a result of financial stress, people were statistically less likely to have kids or get divorced while, at the same time, there was a substantial spike in domestic abuse.[19] Meanwhile, the suicide rate exploded, reaching a thirty-year high by 2016. It was particularly pronounced among middle-aged white males, shooting up by 40 percent between 2006 and 2016.

During this era, one European study actually suggested a very specific relationship between these sorts of broad economic downturns and extremism: a one percent decline in economic growth results in a one percent increase in the vote share for far-right or nationalist parties.[20]

In his 2016 article "The New Harvest of Rage," Dyer also stressed how economic conditions in 2016 were more severe and widespread than what he had seen in the 1980s or 1990s. "The gap between the rich and poor," he wrote, "has gotten much wider in the past quarter century." Over this period of time, people have lost their homes to mortgage crisis and their "manufacturing jobs to cheap overseas labor."

So, clearly the harsh economic environment played some important role in the spate of extremism between 2008 and 2016. What that didn't explain was how extremist groups continued to expand even as the economy steadily improved from about 2009. The recession-driven radicalization of the 1980s and 90s had tapered off as the economy improved. Clearly, macroeconomics couldn't explain everything that was going on between 2008 and 2016.

The divisive role of politics might partially explain the unprecedented expansion of extremism. In February 2010, an attendee at a GOP conference in Boca Raton, Florida, left a hard copy of the Republican Party's plan to raise money for the upcoming elections. The discarded document, which was found and leaked to the press, revealed an incredibly cynical fundraising strategy.

The party was in a tough spot, the presentation began. The GOP, which controlled neither the presidency nor Congress, had little to offer the big money donors who paid tens of thousands of dollars for access, networking opportunities, and ego trips. So the party proposed two changes. First, they would focus their fundraising efforts on smaller money donors. Second, they would seek to exploit these donors by "visceral" appeals based on fear, reactionary instincts, and negative feelings toward the current administration.

The presentation asserted that millions of these middle and lower level voters could be whipped into frenzy by calls like "save the country from trending towards socialism!" The authors suggested propaganda, like images of President Obama as comic book villain The Joker and Speaker of the House Nancy Pelosi as Cruella de Vil. In short, the GOP fundraising strategy was to demonize the other side with all the subtlety of a fifth grader.

That same year, the GOP's minority leader, Mitch McConnell,

declared that "Our top political priority over the next two years should be to deny President Obama a second term."[21] They were not alone in this game, however. Democrats were also becoming increasingly addicted to negative politics. As the parties bickered and demonized each other, Americans' confidence in government fell to new lows.

This strategy did get some people elected, while other times it backfired, but it was always playing with fire. When the primary fundraising or political tactic of the two major parties is to demonize the other, overall trust in the system is bound to degrade. Indeed, trust in the federal government reached historic lows. In the late 1950s, 77 percent of Americans reported that they trusted the federal government "always" or "most of the time," according to a Pew Research Center poll. In 1974, with the nation slouching toward defeat in Vietnam, in the midst of an economic recession and Richard Nixon fending off the Watergate scandal, 68 percent of respondents still reported trusting the federal government at least most of the time. But by November 2015, confidence had dropped precipitously: just 19 percent of Americans reported that they trusted the federal government either "always" or "most of the time."[22]

Support for Congress was also dismal post-2009. In a yearly Gallup poll, Americans were asked "Do you approve or disapprove of the way Congress is handling its job?" Between 1976 and 2006, approval for Congress only fell below 25 percent twice. Once was briefly in 1979 and the second time was in 1990–1994, during the rise in extremist activity.[23] Between 2010 and December 2016, however, Congress' approval rating didn't get *over* 25 percent even once.

This lack of trust in government can play a role in encouraging extremism and even violence. If the official system seems useless, people are more likely to look for other options to create political and societal change—including violence. As researcher Mark Littler puts it, "Attitudes towards politics may frame assessments of not just political participation but also support for terrorism."[24]

It turned out that Americans were less willing to put trust in institutions other than the federal government as well. Another Gallup poll asked Americans how much confidence they had in different mainstream institutions, including organized religion, the medical system, presidency, Supreme Court, organized labor, justice system, TV news, newspapers, big business, military, police, and Congress. In 1994, a relatively low average of 36 percent of Americans claimed either "a great deal" or "quite a lot" of faith across the institutions. Those percentages rebounded, climbing as high as 43 percent in 2004.[25]

By early 2009, that number was down to 36 percent again and the public's faith in virtually all its major institutions has continued dropping, surpassing the historically low numbers of the early 1990s. By 2016, it reached an unprecedented 32 percent. That year, Americans only awarded two institutions, the military and police, with above 50 percent confidence. In other words, less than half of Americans trusted mainstream religion, organized labor, media, and the medical and legal systems.[26]

Americans also reported being less optimistic about the future. In quarterly polls between 1997 and 2003, at least half of respondents believed that the country was "headed in the right direction." In virtually every period since late 2003, less than half the country has seen it as "headed in the right direction." But it got even worse between 2008 and 2016. By 2013, that level of approval fell again, never getting above 40 percent.

Perhaps the only thing more remarkable than the complete collapse of confidence in American institutions and the political system was that it was, in large part, engineered by the national political parties themselves. For these groups, viciously divisive partisanship was not a problem, but a fundraising strategy.

However, the most ominous development over this time period is not how politicians have played a role in persuading Americans to intensely dislike other politicians and institutions, but each other. An official strategy of creating fear, paranoia, and hatred has also made people more agitated, scared, and paranoid. The predictable result: 40 percent of registered Democrats and Republicans today report that they are "afraid of" the other party.[27]

In 1995, a Florida militiaman named Donald Beauregard claimed that, while eating breakfast one morning, he discovered a secret plan to turn the United States into a biosphere. The New World Order had mistakenly printed it on his box of Trix.[28]

In 2002, the New Black Panther Party's Malik Zulu Shabazz invoked a crowd to: "Kill every goddamn Zionist in Israel! Goddamn little babies, goddamn old ladies! Blow up Zionist supermarkets!"[29]

A message on a deep ecology internet group suggested offering a prize to "the high school student who comes up with the best plan to bring about the destruction of civilization without seriously harming the biosphere."[30]

It's reassuring to think of these groups as the face of extremism. But, not only is every American capable of radicalization, America's two largest political parties have actively encouraged radicalization. The crumbling faith in mainstream America and the metrics showing broad divisiveness and fear play a role in the spread of extremism.

This is because what we call the personal portion of the radicalization process is not necessarily internal. Images of Nancy Pelosi as Cruella de Vil are designed to create anger. A lack of trust in religion, news, business, and other institutions can spur feelings of isolation and alienation from society. The machinations of the mainstream were, in fact, encouraging "normal" people to be more susceptible to extremist ideas.

At close to midnight on November 4, 2008, President-elect Barack Obama stood behind a lectern in Chicago's Grant Park. "As Lincoln said to a nation far more divided than ours," the president-elect exhorted the ecstatic crowd, "we are not enemies but friends. Though passion may have strained, it must not break our bonds of affection."[31]

That same night in New York City, an African American teenager was attacked by four men wielding a bat and chanting "Obama!" The next day in Snellville, Georgia, a white boy walked up to a nine-year-old African American girl on their school bus. "I hope Obama gets assassinated," he said. A spike in racist incidents continued to be reported in every corner of the country over the following weeks. In Maine, black figures hung from nooses. In New Jersey and Pennsylvania, crosses were burned in Obama supporters' front yards. In Idaho, second and third graders chanted "Assassinate Obama!" on their school bus.[32]

In his speech, Obama made plays for unity, for hard work, for coming together as a truly "United States of America." But over his eight years in office, the exact opposite happened. Americans became more partisan and intolerant. The president comfortably won a second term in 2012, but extremism across the country was still exploding.

By 2016—and in the face of a steadily improving economy—none of the classic drivers of radicalization could fully explain the massive increase of extremism and hate groups across the political spectrum. If America was a house divided in 2008, it was a house on fire by the time Obama left. What other forces were at work?

PART II

THE AIR HATE BREATHES

CHAPTER THREE

THE GREATEST THING TO EVER HAPPEN TO HATE

A few days after Barack Obama's 2008 election, David Duke—the long-time face of American white nationalism—co-hosted an international conference of white nationalists in a flea-bag motel outside Memphis. The event had originally been planned to run for three days at a nearby resort, but the venue had canceled on them days earlier. Undeterred, a smaller number of attendees reduced the event to one day and met at the only place that would have them. After a few speeches in the dingy setting, they declared the meeting a success.

Over his prodigious five-decade career, Duke had constantly courted both publicity and controversy. He had stints as a campus neo-Nazi, Grand Wizard of the Knights of the Ku Klux Klan (KKK), Louisiana state representative, talk-show guest, failed presidential candidate, and professional anti-Semite on the lecture circuit.

Duke had endured plenty of criticism from within his movement as well. The highest profile incident occurred in 1979 when Duke's second in command at the Knights of the KKK, Tom Metzger, left the group, accusing his boss of being a fraud, egomaniac, and rip-off artist.[1] In 2002, Metzger—by then a well-known neo-Nazi—was vindicated when Duke was convicted of tax evasion, mail fraud, and embezzlement. A few months after the 2008 Memphis motel meeting, Duke would be arrested, deported, and banned from Germany for his open anti-Semitism and Holocaust denial, a crime in some European countries.[2]

Over the years, Duke had developed a tough hide. Like many of his compatriots, he was inured to the difficulties of representing what most Americans considered repulsive, backward, and wrongheaded racist ideologies. KKK groups could march in public, but were almost always surrounded by police and groups of counter demonstrators many times their size. It was hard to sell and distribute their literature or advertise their events.

This was exactly what had happened in Memphis. Duke's original bookings had been canceled after resort staff discovered the nature of his event. Or, perhaps more accurately, after local anti-racist activists found out about the white supremacist convention and informed the hotel. There was, however, a place where hateful extremists weren't confronted by public repulsion and protest: the internet, with its rapidly expanding number of websites, chat rooms, and other virtual venues.

Back in the 1980s, the fledgling internet's potential to spread widely the message of the marginalized had been quickly seized on by the pioneers of hate sites, as researcher Chip Berlet explains in "When Hate Went Online."[3] In 1984, a publisher of racist and anti-Semitic literature named George Dietz used a 5MB Apple IIe computer and a dial-up connection to launch a small computer bulletin board system (BBS) blandly named "Info International." In doing so, Dietz had achieved a dubious milestone: the first white supremacist in cyberspace.

Digital bulletin board systems, crude precursors to the World Wide Web popularized in the 1990s, allowed people to post messages and documents for other members of their communities to access. Dietz's BBS carried sections entitled "The Jew in Review" and "On Race and Religion"—as well as a more commercially focused section titled "WVA Real Estate Bargains."[4] Because he had been printing hard copies of neo-Nazi material for over a decade, Dietz also used the new medium as an opportunity to republish back issues.

Dietz was a pioneer, but only by a few months. Later in 1984, thirty-eight-year-old Louis Beam launched the Aryan Liberty Net from Richard Butler's Aryan Nations compound in northern Idaho. Beam was a fiery apostle of the radical racist right. During his 1983 address to the Aryan World Congress, he warned: "If you don't help me kill the bastards, you're going to be required to beg for your child's life, and the answer will be no."[5]

Beam was equally adamant about the promise of new computer-enhanced telecommunications, speaking of the technology with an evangelical zeal. "American know-how," he prophesized, "has provided the technology which will allow those who love this country to save it from an ill-deserved fate."[6]

At the time, the future of what would become today's omnipresent internet was still uncertain. The first personal computers had been widely available for only a few years, while BBS's were just emerging from the domain of universities, computer clubs, and hobbyists. But Beam was euphoric that these early advances in telecommunications had allowed him to get around other countries' bans on his literature.

In August of 1984, he had circulated a flyer inviting people to access his white supremacist material. A year later, he was bragging that he had effectively ended Canadian censorship of his materials. He was even more convinced that "those who love God and their Race and strive to serve their nation will be utilizing some of the advanced technology available heretofore only to those in the ZOG [Zionist Occupation Government] government and others who have sought the destruction of the Aryan people." Soon, other extremists wanted in on the technology, too.

Tom Metzger, the neo-Nazi who had a falling out with David Duke in the late 1970s, also believed the internet would have a prominent role in his cause. Metzger never shied away from publicly advertising his extremist politics. In 1980, for example, the forty-two-year-old had led his own renegade group called the California Knights of the Ku Klux Klan into an armed brawl with anti-Klan protestors. Later that same year, he won the Democratic nomination for Congress in a conservative California district.

But, after he was trounced in the general election, Metzger began focusing on adopting various new technologies to spread his message. At the time, local cable access stations were required to allow local programming. Metzger was soon hosting a show called "Race and Reason," which eventually reached sixty-one cities in twenty-one states. He also created a telephone hotline with recorded messages like ". . . advocate more violence than both world wars put together."[7]

Soon thereafter, Metzger jumped at the chance to get online. In 1985, he set up his own network in Southern California on a Commodore 64. Metzger's board joined Beam's Aryan Nations Bulletin Board System (BBS) in Idaho, and Klan systems in both Dallas, Texas, and Raleigh, North Carolina. With nothing more than mid-80s Radio Shack technology, the telecommunications pioneers could link all of the networks together. A June 1985 message on Aryan Liberty Net system heralded the event in all caps: "ALL OF THE GREAT MINDS OF THE PATRIOTIC CHRISTIAN MOVEMENT LINKED TOGETHER AND JOINED INTO ONE COMPUTER."[8]

Beam and Metzger had become among the first non-academics to organize not just an extremist group, but any national group via BBS. These early steps gave a leg up to the racist radical right, which has long been "[w]idely recognised as being amongst the first to exploit the transformative organisational and recruitment potential of the internet."[9]

Beyond being able to bypass national borders and network remotely, the radical right's leadership in this area had another advantage: most Americans didn't see the internet as a serious threat. Home computers were becoming more commonplace, but few Americans had a modem—much less the knowledge or desire to access a BBS. As a result, extremists could circulate their materials without much pushback. It took a full year for a website to be set up to challenge the message of a growing number of right-wing extremist BBSs.

Chip Berlet, the chronicler and activist opponent of the extremist right, recalls traveling to his public speeches in the 1980s lugging around a computer, printer, and a hundred feet of telephone line. During his speeches, he would download and print the material from white supremacist BBSs in real time. Afterward, he'd ask people to grab a few feet of the print-outs and go home and read it to their kids. That, Berlet said, finally made people aware about the volumes of vile messages available to anyone on the early internet.[10]

Through the 1980s and into the early 1990s, white supremacist sites continued to spread, communicate, and share information via BBS from sites all across the country. Decentralized, low-cost, and anonymous, the technology had huge advantages for child molesters, pornographers, extremists—and any other group forced by law or society to keep a low profile. But the pioneers of online hate weren't even close to leveraging this architecture to its full capacity. To them, the technology was primarily about cyber flyering and teleconferences. Hate hadn't yet migrated to the much larger and accessible World Wide Web, but it soon would.

The co-host of the ill-fated 2008 white nationalist conference in Memphis was a fifty-five-year-old man named Don Black. He had succeeded Duke as Grand Wizard of the Knights of the KKK in the 1980s and remained his close friend, as well as marrying Duke's former wife, Chloe.[11] In March of 1995, Black registered a new website, stormfront.org. Although the racist far right had been pioneers in developing the technology, Black was disappointed with the quality of other sites at the time. "I could only find three worthwhile sites to link to," he recalled.[12] Change, though, was waiting right around the corner.

The mid-1990s was when the impact of internet-based companies began reverberating loudly throughout the economy. Amazon sold its first book in mid-July of 1995, but the startup got the attention of consumers and massive competitors soon thereafter. In 1997, Barnes & Noble sued Amazon for claiming it was the world's largest bookstore. The following year, Walmart sued the company for allegedly stealing trade secrets.[13] None of that slowed Amazon's growth. In 1999, CEO Jeff Bezos was named *Time*'s Person of the Year.

As the value and glamor of the web grew, so did its dark side. The same era that the technology came to be seen as essential for business growth was also the tipping point for online extremism. In September 1997, the Simon Wiesenthal Center reported that there were over six hundred hate sites worldwide, a 100 percent increase from the year before. By March of 1999, that number had more than doubled again to 1,400 hate sites.[14]

It wasn't just right-wing groups taking their message to the internet. In 1998, fewer than half of what the US State Department classified as foreign terrorist organizations—primarily jihadist groups—had websites.

By the end of the following year, nearly all of them had an online presence.[15] This expanding footprint of online hate, combined with growing public use of the internet, finally sounded alarm bells in the media.

A study published in 2000 illustrated how the widely praised democratizing impact of the net also meant that a relatively tiny group of hate-mongers would gain "a voice disproportionate to the numbers."[16] In some cases, the sudden realization that vicious racist and anti-Semitic screeds were readily available online led to panic. Experts in the late 1990s claimed "the internet is the greatest thing to ever happen to hate."[17] After ten years of being mostly ignored, online hate sites' rapid emergence resulted in a "near continuous flow of stories" of articles about online hate.[18]

But even after the presence of hateful extremist material on the net was exposed for everyone to see, no one seemed to know quite what to do about it. A representative for AOL suggested that some software could be developed, but it would only impact the company's own customers, about half of America's internet users at the time.

What's more, though the mainstream publicity galvanized activism against the sites, it also advertised their existence. Some sites began to encourage media outrage. The neo-Nazi site World Church of the Creator, for example, built a kid's page with the intention of getting mainstream coverage about a site that was "targeting your children."[19]

David Goldman, perhaps the number one authority on the subject of online hate in the late 1990s, didn't buy into the handwringing. In 1995, the Harvard Law School librarian had begun monitoring the phenomenon on his site Guide to Hate Groups on the Internet. After cataloging hundreds of such sites over the next five years, he determined that, though the internet did provide advantages in cost and accessibility, it was not, as David Duke claimed, going to be the number-one tool for white revolution.[20]

By the turn of the millennium, the websites of both hate groups and mainstream businesses were plagued by the same problem: engagement. "It is difficult," said Goldman in 2001, "for any organization to get people to come back and to participate in its website."[21]

By then, many extremist groups had invested in flashy graphics and audio components for their sites, but even though the websites looked good, they functioned more like brochures for people who were already committed. Most Klan and neo-Nazi groups were unable to use their web presence to create communities or increase their user numbers. And, without offering the same kind of engagement or community found at Bill Riccio's WAR House or Richard Butler's Idaho compound, they remained relatively ineffective tools for radicalizing new members throughout the 1990s.

As with many other of the most infamous extremists of the 1990s, the early internet played practically no role in the radicalization process of Timothy McVeigh. Sources said that McVeigh was an ideal tenant,[22] so fastidious that he even fixed up the messes left by previous occupants of his various apartments and trailers. He was often the only one of his housemates who prepared food—and always the only one who cleaned up. McVeigh liked the order of neatly stacked dishes, which was likely one of the things he had enjoyed about the military. McVeigh was also very bright, winning a scholarship in high school. However, he never attended a university and dropped out of a local computer school. He was polite, although his classmates described him as unmemorable and quiet. He adored his sister but deeply resented his mom, who had left the family when McVeigh was a child. He once told a friend she was a "no-good whore."[23] His other biggest grievance was being quickly dropped from Special Forces training after serving in the First Gulf War.

Taken as a whole, McVeigh shared many broad similarities with Dylann Roof, Micah Johnson, and Muhammad Abdulazeez. He was intelligent but angry and a disillusioned army vet. He had a troubled family background, a loss of faith in religion, no future goals, and often no fixed address or job. But, unlike Dylann, Micah, and Muhammad, McVeigh's road to radicalization in the 1990s had virtually nothing to do with the then-emerging web. In fact, his external radicalizing factors looked an awful lot like they had for decades.

In 1989, for example, twenty-one-year-old McVeigh attended a KKK rally and bought a "White Power" shirt to protest the "Black Power" shirts of his fellow African American servicemen. In 1992, having served in the first Gulf War, McVeigh left the army and, once home, began writing letters to local newspapers citing federal taxes as preconditions for a bloody civil war.

After that, McVeigh spent two years marinating in extremist circles. He traveled through forty states, attending gun shows, and fraternized daily with other anti-government extremists, forming at least two close, personal relationships. He also sold copies of *The Turner Diaries*, a novel in which the lead character detonates explosives at the FBI's headquarters.

Like many right-wing extremists in the 1990s, McVeigh was deeply affected by the deadly encounter between federal law enforcement and the Weaver family in the mountains of northern Idaho. In August of 1992, federal agents surrounded the cabin of white supremacist Randy Weaver, who was wanted on a federal firearms charge. In a horrible series of events, Weaver's wife and son were killed, as well as a federal marshal.

An eleven-day standoff ensued. Because the Weaver cabin was only an hour from Richard Butler's Aryan Nations compound on Hayden Lake, neo-Nazis arrived to protest what they saw as federal government over-reach. Eventually, another well-known anti-Semite, decorated Vietnam Vet and militia leader Bo Gritz ventured up from Almost Heaven, his Idaho housing community, and negotiated an end to the standoff.

Widely covered by national media at the time, the event entered popular culture as a 1996 TV movie starting Randy Quaid, Laura Dern, and Kirsten Dunst. But most importantly, the showdown became one of the founding moments of the modern militia movement. After what became as "Ruby Ridge," McVeigh began passing out literature promoting the idea of killing Lon Horiuchi, the FBI sniper who had killed Vicky Weaver.

McVeigh's mobilization toward violence was also accelerated by the other seminal event of the 1990s for Patriot and militia groups: the siege of the Branch Davidian compound. On February 28, 1993, a botched weapons raid on the religious cult's buildings on a farm outside of Waco, Texas, resulted in the deaths of four federal agents and six Branch Davidians.

The FBI then set up a siege of the property, but negotiations went nowhere. The lack of progress in convincing the Branch Davidians to leave was somewhat predictable since they believed they were living in the End Times prophesied in the Bible. First, that meant they had stored a lot of food and water. Second, they thought the FBI and ATF were part of the Satanic End Times Antichrist system. As such, surrendering to the government didn't just mean risking jail time, but surrendering their everlasting souls to eternal damnation.

In mid-April, after fifty-one days, the FBI had decided to try and force the Davidians out by launching huge amounts of tear gas into the building where they were holed up. McVeigh traveled to the site in time to see its fiery end, watching as government law enforcement used the same Bradley tanks he had operated during the First Gulf War to launch chemical weapons at Americans. Tragically, the siege only ended after the main building caught fire, killing seventy-six members of the sect. The events at Waco triggered McVeigh to plan a horrific retaliatory attack against the Feds, the 1995 bombing of the Alfred P. Murrah Federal Building in Oklahoma City.

In short, the external forces that encouraged McVeigh's radicalization largely consisted of involvement and direct personal contact with extremists, their literature, and activities over a period of years. For the most part, they had nothing to do with the internet. The World Wide Web did exist in the mid-1990s, of course, but its relative importance is summed up by a 1995 *New York Times* article detailing how McVeigh's path to radicalization included access to a "radical new information network of videotapes, short wave radio, computer networks, newsletters."[24]

Even though McVeigh had shown early interest in computers, videotapes seemed to play a much bigger part in his radicalization than anything he might have found online. McVeigh repeatedly watched *Red Dawn*, the 1980s film about a group of high school students who fight back against a surprise Soviet invasion of the United States. He was also a fan of the dystopic film *Brazil*. McVeigh even used "Tuttle," the name of a heroic protagonist played by Robert De Niro, as an alias during the planning stages for his attack.

So while the broad process of McVeigh's radicalization has similarities to those of other extremists, future and past, the specifics of the external radicalizing forces that played a role in the process seem light years from the internet-mediated process experienced by Dylann, Micah, and Muhammad.

Future Olympics bomber Eric Rudolph kept a regular schedule when staying at his brother's house in Tennessee in the early 1990s: sleeping all day and staying up all night smoking pot, eating pizza, and watching movies by 1970s stoner-comedy act Cheech and Chong. His sister-in-law described the spectacle of the three Rudolph brothers hanging out in the living room as "like *Bill and Ted's Excellent Adventure*"—the 1980s movie about dim-witted, slacker teenagers.[25]

Much of Rudolph's life had not been so carefree. His father died of cancer when he was fifteen. Because his mother was only an occasional presence, Rudolph and his two brothers largely raised themselves in a remote area in the mountains of western North Carolina. He dropped out of school as a teenager, sometimes working as a carpenter. Though Rudolph later earned a GED, he only lasted a few semesters at Western Carolina University. He then enrolled in the army but was disappointed that he couldn't make it into the Special Forces and was subsequently discharged for smoking pot.

Rudolph had a familiar looking series of personal inhibitors and destabilizers—absent parents, limited social network, no career or future prospects, despite his intelligence—ones that left him adrift and vulnerable to radicalization.[26] But, although Rudolph's extremist attacks took place in the late 1990s, after McVeigh's Oklahoma City bombing, his radicalization still appears to have been exclusively offline.

Rudolph was exposed to extreme right-wing politics early on. In ninth grade, he wrote an essay explaining why the Holocaust never happened. Pressed for sources by his teachers, Rudolph produced an anti-Semitic pamphlet. His house was filled with similar materials, including *Thunderbolt*, a magazine produced by Georgia-based white supremacist minister Ed Fields.

Rudolph also had regular exposure to people with extremist beliefs, including Christian Identity minister Nord Davis, Jr.,[27] and a survivalist neighbor who lived in the mountains of North Carolina in a steel and cinderblock fortress stocked with guns, canned food, water, and gasoline. When Rudolph was eighteen, his mom briefly moved the family to a Christian Identity compound in Schell City, Missouri.[28]

After dropping out of college and then washing out of the army in eighteen months, Rudolph spent most of the next six years in an off-the-grid trailer in North Carolina's Appalachians, an unlikely spot for internet access. But, by 1996, with no known help from online materials, Rudolph was fully committed to violence directed by extremist ideologies.

He began his two-year campaign of violence with a bomb at the 1996 Summer Olympics in Atlanta that killed two and wounded over a hundred people. He would later bomb a gay nightclub outside Atlanta and two abortion clinics in Georgia and Alabama. Despite a growing amount of hate online, the most famous perpetrators of 1990s right-wing terrorism were slow-cooked and homegrown.

But if extremist websites were relatively unsuccessful at bringing new members into the fold, they did continue to grow in popularity among the already committed. In the 2000s, Don Black's Stormfront became the number one hate site on the web. It was modern, highly accessible, and indexed by search engines like Google.[29] Stormfront wasn't just popular compared to other hate sites. By 2005, it ranked in the top one percent of all sites by use.

This was a remarkable, and frightening, accomplishment. Virtually all of the other sites in that top tier provided services like shopping, early social networking, entertainment, or mainstream news. For a white supremacist website to have the reach of these massive corporations was shocking. Though Stormfront had nowhere near the same number of total unique visits as, say, ABC.com, the site was certainly leveraging the relative advantages of the internet as a medium for marginalized messages.

With Stormfront's success, the dream of pioneers like Louis Beam and Tom Metzger was partially realized. White supremacists—along with other extremists—were utilizing the web to communicate with each other across great distances anonymously and very cheaply. But, in the 2000s, as the internet continued to expand and more Americans spent an increased amount of time online, the problem that had dogged extremists throughout the 1990s remained. Online hate sites were invitations and gathering spaces for the already radicalized; during the first decade of the 2000s, they still weren't any more important to radicalization than they had been to Timothy McVeigh and Eric Rudolf in the 1990s.

Like countless mainstream businesses, extremists were still searching for some way to increase online engagement. Fortunately for them, the enormous amount of talent and money bouncing around Silicon Valley would soon offer hate groups an irresistible solution.

CHAPTER FOUR

THE SOCIAL NETWORK'S NEGATIVE MIRROR

By 2009, the internet was still disappointing as a force for radicalization, but its imprint on everyday life did at least begin showing up in the details around extremist attacks. For example, the two young American men who left the country to commit themselves to jihad, Daniel Maldonado and Omar Hammami, met in Egypt via an online forum before traveling on to Somalia to join Al Shabaab, a militant Islamic group. But the external forces of their radicalization still appeared to be non-web based.

After the 2009 Fort Hood shooting, in which army psychologist Nidal Hasan killed thirteen people, the radical Muslim cleric Anwar al-Awlaki claimed to have exchanged emails with Hasan. But it is far from clear whether this communication had any impact on Nidal's actions, or whether the contact occurred at all.

During the investigation following the 2010 Times Square car bombing, it came out that perpetrator Faisal Shahzad had bought the car he used for the bombing on Craigslist. He had also emailed his friends complaining about mujahideen being labeled "extremists." All of his training, however, had come while abroad in Pakistan.

By the end of the decade, extremists were using the internet in their daily lives just like everyone else, but they still weren't being radicalized by it in a meaningful way. How is it, then, that by 2015, the internet seemed to play such a large role in the radicalization of Muhammad Abdulazeez and Dylann Roof and, just a year later, in that of Micah Johnson?

In fact, according to one report, the internet suddenly became an important radicalizing force just a few years into the 2010s. A 2013 RAND corporation study of fifteen cases of terrorism and extremism underscored how central the internet is to the process of radicalization. "[T]he internet," the study found, "is clearly the running theme between most of the plots included in this dataset and it appears to be a very effective tool: it provides a locus in which they can obtain [radicalizing] material. . . . It provides them with direct access to a community of like-minded individuals around the world with whom they can connect and in some cases can provide them with further instigation and direction to carry out activities."[1]

But the study goes further: "There are a number of high-profile cases in which extremists have been radicalized through exposure to this content alone, without the presence of meaningful socialization with members of extreme groups."[2]

So, in just a few short years, the internet went from playing no role in the radicalization of the actors behind major extremist attacks to influencing every one of them. What transformed the internet into such an effective hate machine by 2013?

Jump back a decade earlier, the year when Google offered a Canadian tech entrepreneur named Jonathan Abrams $30 million for his year-old social networking company, Friendster. Social networking sites like Six-Degrees, Mixi, and Makeoutclub had been around since 1997, but were never able to gain the traction and reach of Friendster. Part of this was plain numbers. In 1995, just 14 percent of American adults said they used the internet.[3] By 2000, 46 percent did, and in 2005 that number was 66 percent. But this change in internet participation was starker than these numbers suggest: the experience of "going online" meant something radically different in 1995.

In the mid-1990s, most people used slower dial-up technology, and many had more limited access—only going online from work, say, or just once a week. By 2000, even as connection speeds and the proliferation of computers were expanding rapidly, 46 percent said they went online, but just 29 percent of respondents used the internet daily. However, in the first decade of the new millennium, the internet reached a kind of critical mass—more people online more regularly for longer amounts of time. This confluence made social networking more viable. Friendster was the right idea at the right time.

In 2003, Abrams knew he had hit on something huge. So, dreaming of even bigger fame and fortune, he turned down Google's offer. Soon thereafter, Friendster became a case study on how to ruin a good idea.

But the networking site's rapid demise was also a measure of how competitive the space had become. A 2006 *New York Times* article describing Friendster's collapse detailed how market leader Myspace had fifty times the number of monthly domestic visitors—but doesn't even mention Facebook among Friendster's competitors.[4] By early the following year, CEO Mark Zuckerberg was being offered millions to sell Facebook. An Associated Press article described the frenzy around Facebook as a manifestation of "the latest Internet craze, a communal concept of content-sharing that has been dubbed 'Web 2.0.'"[5] The rest of the story is well known: Facebook became a media behemoth and, to date, the only website whose origin story was adapted into an Academy Award-winning film.

At around the same time, growth in video sharing and other consumer-driven multimedia platforms like YouTube exploded. In 2006, only 32 percent of people were watching video clips online. By 2008, 83 percent were, making it "the quickest-growing platform in history."[6] With the right technology and platforms in place, mainstream America became familiar with the idea of using social networking not just to "stay in touch" but to create online communities. Both Facebook and YouTube would become critical for extremists to inject the poison of extremism into mainstream America.

This sense of community was exactly what would make Stormfront so successful. The site was a safe haven for an increasing number of neo-Nazis, white nationalists, and others, according to interviews conducted with eleven Stormfront members. Most of the interviewees said that they felt stigmatized and ostracized for their extremist beliefs in the offline world, be it by teachers, employers, or family.

In contrast, "*Stormfront* was like a second home to me,"[7] claimed one user. Another said that it was a place "where I have many comrades."[8] On one thread, members wished each other happy birthday, with beer mugs and other celebratory icons. Though many of the members never or only very occasionally met offline,[9] they had a place that offered them community. And one of the people who gathered there was Dylann Roof, who posted multiple times on the site before the 2015 shooting.

Compare these armchair racists with another scene from the 1993 documentary *Skinheads USA*. In this footage, Riccio's teenage skinheads, having been dispatched to downtown Birmingham, Alabama, to pass out white nationalist literature, are met with a range of negative responses.

Polite: "I don't want to be a skinhead," responds preppily dressed young white man. "Sorry y'all."

Dismissive: "Business investors do not like a climate like you are trying to create," says a middle-aged white man in response to their arguments about immigrants stealing jobs.

Insulting: "You're an asshole!" yells a young white kid after his friends argue with the skins.

What they don't get are positive responses. So while the flyering effort may be successful as a trial-by-fire bonding event, they've ultimately spent three hours without even getting a nibble on recruitment. A member of a different far-right group describes a similar scenario: canvassing, putting notices in mailboxes, "and having dogs chasing after you!"[10] In both instances, far-right extremists must face up to the reality that the vast majority of people they encounter either don't care about or actively dislike their ideology. Worse, they are confronted by people with a diversity of opinions and, frequently, better articulated arguments.

By 2008, in a country that was increasingly online and familiar with social networking, Stormfront offered a much more convenient and fun way to hang out with compatriots in the racist extreme right. So, even as he sat in a lousy motel room at the white supremacist convention in Memphis, the future still looked very bright for Don Black. He was working full time on his site, assisted by forty moderators.

If Don Black did have a problem, it was keeping up with demand. His servers had crashed the day after Obama's election as thousands of new members registered. Black was energized to use his network to fight back against the sort of globalizing multiculturalism that Obama represented. And in the coming years, as both the internet and right-wing extremism grew, Stormfront would expand from tens of thousands of members to 300,000 global members in 2016.

But, for all his success in the online world up to that point, Black couldn't have known exactly how the massive creative and economic resources poured into social media would change the way Americans communicated, related, and relaxed in the coming years. It's unlikely he realized how much the new platforms would advance David Duke's dream of the internet as the primary tool of white revolution. And Black certainly didn't see how, within a few years, these rapid transformations would leave Stormfront behind.

In 2009, the actor Ashton Kutcher went on Oprah Winfrey's show to introduce the masses to a new social media app called Twitter. On her show, Oprah sent out her first tweet: "HI TWITTERS. THANK YOU FOR A WARM WELCOME. FEELING REALLY 21st CENTURY."[11]

Kutcher had reached his own milestone, becoming the first user to collect a million followers. The race to a million had been promoted as a friendly contest between Kutcher and CNN's breaking news feed, with the winner promising to donate 10,000 mosquito bed nets to a charity dedicated to wiping out malaria in the third world. Kutcher won—by thirty minutes—but CNN donated 10,000 nets anyway, followed by Winfrey herself, who donated another 20,000.

The whole event gleamed positivity, good will, and an enormous faith in the power of social media. A CNN spokesperson said that, with Twitter, "the consumer is in the driver's seat." The CEO of Malaria No More, Scott Case, cited the contest as a way of "how we can leverage new technology to battle an ancient disease." Kutcher, he added, was "galvanizing his Twitter army to help end malaria deaths." A few days later, Kutcher claimed that Twitter wasn't about celebrity but "everyday people having a voice."

In 2010, this belief was reinforced by the role that social media, including Facebook, Flickr, YouTube, and Twitter,[12] played in the Arab Spring uprisings that began in Tunisia, Libya, Egypt, Syria, and other parts of the Arab world. A 2011 report found that almost 90 percent of

Egyptians and Tunisians surveyed in March of that year were using Facebook to organize or publicize protests.[13]

What's more, online advocacy and organizing was effective in driving events in the offline world, with all but one of the Facebook-initiated protests "coming to life on the streets." Largely because of the importance of Facebook in organizing offline events, the number of Facebook users jumped massively, 30 percent across the entire Arab world in the months between January and April. In some countries, usage more than doubled. In the United States and elsewhere, social media was viewed as playing an "idealized transformative role, bringing democracy and civil rights to the dark corners of the internet."[14]

American tech companies were also the most profitable sector of the economy, driving the stock market to record highs. Tech and social media CEOs like Steve Jobs, Mark Zuckerberg, and Jeff Bezos were the geniuses of the day. But just as with every advance made since the 1980s in dispersed, decentralized communications, the new technology had a negative mirror.

Bulletin Board Systems and, later, sites like Stormfront had long exploited the primary architecture of the internet—the "lower participation barriers and the ease of content management and creation."[15] But as basic human interaction and socialization "increasingly moved into the online space across the Western world,"[16] the capacities of extremism on the web also changed dramatically.

Previous advances had allowed extremists to digitize many of their radicalization and operational activities. After 2008, they were able to plug their whole agenda into some of the most powerful and wealthiest corporations on earth. In fact, the social media-driven expansion of the internet universe "facilitated a second explosion in radical-right internet use,"[17] which allowed groups to organize "and recruit on a scale previously unimaginable."[18] It was social media, with its promise of merging online and offline identities, which finally allowed extremists to radicalize individuals remotely, primarily through the internet.

ISIS leaders, who call for the return of a seventh-century legal system, speak dismissively of "moderns"[19] but, like the white supremacists before, they effectively hijacked the web to spread violent anti-western rhetoric.

From July 2014 to July 2016, ISIS's slickly produced online magazine, *Dabiq*, promised "photo reports, current events, and informative articles on matters related to the Islamic State." *Dabiq* was primarily available through the dark web, although, for two weeks in May and June of 2015, print versions of all nine editions could be ordered for $22 from Amazon and shipped within forty-eight hours.[20]

It was not *Dabiq*, however, but social media that allowed the radical Islamist group to gain adherents. The combination of social media's reach and video sharing proved a massively effective tool for radicalization. In a 2016 study tracking the behavior of 154,000 Twitter users in Europe, researchers discovered a strong link between recruitment efforts and the posting of graphic videos. The vast majority of pro-ISIS behavior, tweets or retweets, were activated "during the summer of 2014 when ISIS shared many beheading videos online."[21] By the summer of 2015, ISIS had 90,000 supporters on Twitter.

In fact, Twitter became such an effective recruiting platform for the group that the US State Department created an account called "Think Again, Turn Away"[22] to engage potential ISIS recruits. The account, which was often used to drag the US moderator into unwinnable debates about, say, American abuses of prisoners of war at Abu Ghraib, was a short-lived effort.

Another way in which online extremists were able to plug into the massive machine constructed around social networking was through very sophisticated user-tracking and behavior-tracking analytics. User information, not products, is what drives social media revenue. Originally, this information may have just been used to target ads, but these analytics are increasingly used to push targeted content—articles, videos, etc.—to users in order to increase clicks and page views. So, for example, if a user watches a Katy Perry video, YouTube will immediately suggest additional Katy Perry videos or related artists.

These analytics are one example of how social media is omnipresent, "even if you are not actively involved in social media. Today if you search for product, the results are dominated by user content and opinion—this shapes all online users' opinions."[23]

But this technology, while designed to increase user engagement, also meant that when Dallas cop killer Micah Johnson looked up police shootings of black males in his bedroom, he was automatically referred to similar stories or videos, much of which were more graphic, very emotional, or even essentially anti-cop propaganda. Likewise, the fundamental structure of social media would have guided Muhammad Abdulazeez and Dylann Roof to increasingly extreme material online. When certain people are repeatedly exposed to this material, their chances of becoming radicalized are elevated.

The analytics guiding a future extremist's online search are particularly dangerous because all people tend to consume content that confirms their particular viewpoint. This process of making sense of a nuanced, confusing world—one made even more complicated by the massive amount of information online—is known as "confirmation bias." The analytics employed by Facebook, YouTube, and other services have automated and weaponized this tendency. They took a human cognitive tendency and encouraged it to become a bionic mania.

More than anything else, perhaps, social media and other online content strive to make every online activity, including radicalization, more convenient, fun, and addictive. Someone with a passing interest in Black Nationalism can read online extremist propaganda for days. A white supremacist with a smartphone can go to a chat room and discover a whole new community. A shy fourteen-year-old kid can join a conversation on the InfoWars website about how the Parkland School shooting was faked. Sovereign Citizens can urge each other on and teach their tradecraft through the comment stream of mainstream online publications.

Even video games are used for recruitment: Islamic extremists have posted a video with overdubbed music and Arabic exhortations on video from the violent first person shooter game *Grand Theft Auto*. White nationalists are using video game chatrooms to recruit and radicalize youth into their white supremacy worldviews.

The capacity of this technology to radicalize people remotely and below the radar was, until recently, virtually impossible. A 2013 study, which interviewed convicted terrorists about the role of the internet in their radicalization, found that the process is increasingly covert, "where individuals are not attending mosques to discuss radical views, but are instead turning to the Internet to find information in line with extreme beliefs"—including, for example, sharing beheading videos.[24]

One of the biggest mysteries surrounding the crimes committed by the three young men at the beginning of this book was how their attacks appeared to come out of nowhere. By providing access to extremist ideology, charismatic leaders, and online communities, the internet essentially created sleeper cells. Johnson's mom referred to the material he consumed on the internet as "poison," but it was still hard for her, and many other people, to imagine that a communications device could play the same role in radicalization that living in a house full of skinheads used to. Nonetheless, social media functions as a kind of one-stop shop for radicalization, providing a sense of community and access to new ideological messages as well as "powerful video and imagery that appears to substantiate the extremists' political claims."[25]

The first high-profile evidence of social media's new capacity for radicalization came in April 2013 during the investigation of the Boston Marathon bombers, Dzhokhar and Tamerlan Tsarnaev. The two brothers were reportedly "motivated" by extremist Islamic beliefs but "not acting with known terrorist groups."[26] They were, however, well-versed in social media. In 2012, Tamerlan had created a YouTube channel promoting footage of Chechen jihadist leaders as well as a militant Islamic preacher.[27] Further, the brothers had reportedly learned to build "explosive devices from *Inspire*, the online English magazine of the Qaeda affiliate in Yemen."[28]

The bombing was probably the first successful domestic attack in which internet-based radicalization was a primary driver. It was a whole new threat, one that, according to the *New York Times*, "federal authorities have long feared: angry and alienated young men, apparently self-trained and unaffiliated with any particular terrorist group, able to use the Internet to learn their lethal craft."[29]

But some questions remained as to whether it was that neatly wrapped. In 2012, Tamerlan had reportedly been visiting a radical Islamic

Mosque while visiting his parents in Dagestan, Russia. A Boston-based man named "Misha" was reported to be another major offline catalyst.[30] Finally, the bombers' mother, along with Tamerlan, had been placed on a US watch list in 2011.[31]

Regardless of exactly what percentage of their radicalization and logistics were web based, the internet clearly played a huge role in the attack. But the foreign-born, Muslim brothers didn't represent the bigger threat to America. They had attracted at least some intelligence-community attention on their way to lasting infamy. Waiting in the wings were the much more dangerous native-born Americans who flew completely under the radar during their period of radicalization, right up until the moment of their attack. These were the pioneers of the extremist attacks carried out by Johnson, Abdulazeez, and Roof.

In December of 2013, Terry Lee Loewen was arrested for attempting to detonate a bomb at Wichita's Mid-Continent Airport. The fifty-eight-year-old, white Midwesterner, uniformly described by family and friends as "a good guy" and "normal,"[32] was believed to be primarily motivated by the website Revolution Muslim and videos of Anwar al-Maliki. He had also been active on Facebook, advocating for violent jihad.

This threat was born of the social media that had developed since 2008. The radicalization still followed the same broad diagnostic model developed decades earlier. On a personal level, it generally began with people who had frayed safety nets. But social media's capacity for remote radicalization made it much faster, deeper, and harder to detect. Three decades after Louis Beam hooked up his white supremacist Bulletin Board System, the internet had finally developed into a remarkable force multiplier.

"Open the door. It's the police. We're here to rescue you."

The group of people looked around the room where they had barricaded themselves. They had all fled the main hall during a concert in Paris on November 13, 2015, after ISIS-related extremists began firing into the crowd, eventually killing eighty-nine people. By show of hands, they decided not to open the door. The vote saved their lives. The man outside was one of the terrorists.[33]

What was remarkable aside from the attack's carnage, the worst in Paris since World War Two, was how well coordinated the attackers were. The assault began with an explosion at the Stade de France and continued south through multiple restaurants and cafes in the center of the city. By the end of night, 130 victims were dead and over 400 people were injured. Pro-ISIS groups began using the hashtag #Parisburns[34] on their tweets. And intelligence agencies were left wondering how the group of seven terrorists managed to plan and coordinate the attack without being discovered.

By 2015, they had plenty of options: Orbot, RedPhone, iMessage, and WhatsApp, all of which allowed users to communicate with anyone in the world essentially freely and anonymously using encryption. These apps were another gift from social media to extremists everywhere. In fact, social networking had become so important to product engagement that all sorts of non-telecommunications electronics had embedded communication capacities. The day *before* the Paris attacks, Belgium's minister of the interior Jan Jambon had suggested that "PlayStation 4 is even more difficult to keep track of than WhatsApp"—quickly turning media attention to a gaming system that has sold over thirty million units worldwide.[35]

PS4 did indeed allow gamers to communicate via encrypted text and voice chat as well as create their own private chat rooms. But some law enforcement officials suggested that communication via PS4 and other gaming systems could be hidden even without encryption, through techniques that sounded like a digital version of Cold War-era espionage.[36] For example, an operative could spell out an attack plan in *Super Mario Maker*'s coins and share it privately with a contact. Or two *Call of Duty* players could write messages to each other on a wall in a disappearing spray of bullets.

While it turned out that PS4 was not part of the November 2015 Paris attacks, the units were, in fact, being used to communicate with terror groups. Earlier in 2015, an Austrian teenager used a PS4 to contact ISIS. The console reportedly had information that included bomb-making instructions.[37]

The gaming systems had also been used to evade the attention of American law enforcement. In 2017, the FBI searched a PS4 as part of an investigation into a child pornography ring.[38] Later that year, the FBI compelled Sony to provide information from a PS4 user who was suspected of using the gaming console to communicate with a jihadist group.

In addition to radicalization and recruitment, social media offered a whole new range of tools to extremists preparing to take action. In August 1994, when Timothy McVeigh began collecting materials, he had to travel for hours, sometimes days, to buy explosives from gun collectors and fertilizer from farming co-ops. He borrowed a dictionary to look up the fuel "anhydrous hydrazine" before searching a telephone book for a company that would sell the volatile substance. He disguised himself as a motorcycle racer to buy the explosive fuel at a racetrack. He was turned down after asking an acquaintance for technical help on the bomb. In December 1994, he began on-site selection and surveillance on the Alfred P. Murrah building, four months before his eventual attack.

This was a tremendous amount of time-intensive work, all of which had to be accomplished without being detected. Access to Google Maps, YouTube, WhatsApp, and other modern social media would have completely changed McVeigh's timeframes.

The apotheosis of the internet's facilitation of remote radicalization and the wide availability of operational information are lone wolves: Johnson, Abdulazeez, Roof. Though McVeigh was the only one executed after the Oklahoma City bombing, he was not a true lone wolf. Three other people were arrested for their involvement in his plot: Terry Nichols, who was sentenced to life in prison; Michael Fortier, who received twelve years, and his wife, Lori, who was granted immunity in exchange for her testimony.

Since then, web-based resources have provided all sorts of valuable information about plots and, critically, for actors. None of this should come as a surprise, though. The internet doesn't just lower barriers to making a website or uploading a video or selling handmade knitwear; it reduces the logistical challenges of everything, including accessing terrorist tradecraft.

What's more, the internet is often heralded for encouraging and accelerating "online entrepreneurial activity."[39] This is exactly what we see in the negative mirror when we look at violent lone-wolf extremists. They are the ultimate self-starters, with a different focus. Instead of adding a credit card processing solution to their eCommerce site, they are using Google street view to create a complex targeting package. Thirty years after Louis Beam called for a "leaderless resistance" and a decade after Tom Metzger enjoined skinheads to "operate like a Nazi submarine," the internet had made it easier than either could have imagined.[40]

The social media driven revolution between 2006 and 2008 turned remote radicalization into a widespread phenomenon. Social media provides a one-stop shop to plug in an aggrieved, adrift young man. While not every detail of Micah, Muhammad, or Dylann's radicalizations and attacks were facilitated by these forces, it's hard to imagine them carrying out the same attacks ten years previously—or in any era without pervasive exposure to the resourceful and addictive network of computers, phones, and tablets.

The "success" of social media was very different, however, from what early pioneers of online hate had imagined. Its impact wasn't the result of lowering the financial cost and logistical issues of spreading extremist rhetoric and ideas, but lowering the social cost associated with these beliefs. In 1995, online extremist forums already provided anonymous, virtual meeting places for neo-Nazis who felt like outcasts among their neighbors, co-workers, and peers at school. But it wasn't until after 2008 that sites like Facebook normalized the idea of spending a huge chunk of your social time online, meeting new people, frequenting interest groups, and developing identities. By 2016, another form of web-based activity would change online social dynamics again in a bizarre and, in some ways, more profound way.

CHAPTER FIVE

4CHAN AND THE RISE OF ANTI-SOCIAL MEDIA

I n 2009, *Time* magazine named Federal Reserve Chairman Ben Bernanke its Person of the Year for his work tamping down the worst financial disaster in eight decades. That same year, someone named "moot" won the online poll for *Time*'s Most Influential Person of the Year with nearly seventeen million votes, a particularly impressive showing for a recluse whose age *Time* listed as "unknown."[1]

It turned out that moot was the pseudonym of Christopher Poole, a skinny twenty-one-year-old programmer who lived in his mom's apartment in a suburb of New York City. In February 2009, the *Washington Post* called him "the most influential and famous internet celebrity you've never heard of."[2] But though moot's accomplishment, founding 4chan, a website with roughly seven million users,[3] was impressive, his victory was a fraud.

According to tech blog *Music Machinery*, the scam began when users of 4chan realized that moot's name had, improbably, ended up on *Time*'s long list of candidates for Top 100 Most Influential People. Amused by the thought of their site's "overlord" winning the poll, several people designed autovoters, programs that essentially stuffed the online ballot box.

When the poll started, *Time* had lax online security, but after moot quickly went ahead by millions of votes, the magazine's tech staff reset moot's vote total and began requesting validation from voters. This crackdown merely enraged 4chan's technically adept users who retaliated by creating a special channel labeled #time_vote dedicated to dismantling *Time*'s anti-hacking defenses.[4]

It was not the first time the results of *Time*'s online poll had been suspect. The qualifications of the 1998 winner, wrestler Mark Foley AKA "Mankind," had also been questioned by staff. But, in 2009, 4chan users went further than fixing the top spot, they elegantly gamed the top twenty-one finishers. After moot, came Anwar Ibrahim, a Malaysian member of parliament recently accused of sodomy. Rick Warren, the evangelical pastor, came in third.

By the time this list of unlikely figures ran from one to twenty-one, the first letter of each winner's name spelled out "marblecake also the game"—a reference to obscene in-jokes that had developed on 4chan. The ambitious yet seemingly meaningless prank said a lot about the underground hacker culture that developed around sites like 4chan, 8chan, and reddit. After marinating for years underground, the culture would explode into the mainstream beginning around 2008, changing social media in a manner that would benefit extremist ideology in unexpected ways.

Poole had launched 4chan in 2003, after Friendster and Myspace were up, but before Facebook, Twitter, and YouTube. Like those sites, 4chan was quickly adopted by young people to message, post images, and create their own communities, but that was where its similarities with traditional social media ended.

First, 4chan relied on what Poole described as "decade-old code and decade-or-two-old paradigm."[5] It didn't have Friendster's cute branding, or attractive graphics, or even attempt to update its format. Instead, 4chan was a functional, bare-bones image board site. People selected a board with their interests—anime, pornography, cannabis, politics, or dozens of others—and used text and images to jump into the conversation along with millions of other users. In terms of layout, it had more in common with the pre-web bulletin board systems used by Louis Beam and Tom Metzger than Facebook.

In fact, 4chan succeeded precisely because it was a blank slate, a stark platform filled with an enormous variety of the alternately juvenile, surreal, hilarious, and obscene user-created content known as memes. In 2009, 4chan was best known for creating "lolcats"—cute pictures of cats with bits of humorous text, sometimes in broken English, which had become incredibly popular.[6] Lolcats were reportedly born on "Caturdays," weekends dedicated to posting pet pictures.

4chan was also known for pranks like "bait-and-switch" links that, when clicked on, sent the user to an unexpected location. The most famous of these pranks, called "rickrolling," eventually fooled over eighteen million people into clicking on phantom links which sent them to the awkward video for Rick Astley's 1987 number one hit "Never Gonna Give You Up."

Myspace's slogan was "A Place for Friends," but if 4chan had a credo, it was "Make fun of everyone." The site, populated at any minute by hundreds of thousands of, mainly, tech-savvy teenage and twenty-something males, was not nearly as cute and fuzzy as its mainstream manifestations suggested. For example, the punchline of the *Time* magazine hack, "marblecake also the game," included in-joke references to scatological humor and an obscene but ridiculous sex act. It was also a joke that very few people would understand.

To 4chan users, that was the point. Anyone could join the site, but users were extremely territorial. This defensiveness—even more fervent due to the ultimate impossibility of policing borders on a public website—was clear in their slang. A common insult on 4chan was "normie," meaning run-of-the-mill people. The term "basic bitch" was a derogatory term for consumerist mainstream women. "Chads and Stacys" were stereotypes of young men and women who were good-looking and athletic: one online graphic portrays them as a football player and cheerleader. 4chan users often considered themselves outsiders or nerds and were full of disdain, or resentment, for any form of mainstream "success."

So, while 4chan users were after lulz, or laughs, they didn't care who they offended, or who laughed with them. Some users created the loveable lolcats; others were invading a cat lovers' chat room with dead cat jokes. Users could also rally for more damaging large-scale lulzy action, like digital denial of service (DOS) attacks in which thousands of 4chaners blitzed a targeted site with so much traffic that its servers were overwhelmed and it crashed.

Another important difference between the evolving social media and 4chan was that while social media tended toward archiving a record of communication between users, 4chan boards had no retention and an absolute limit on the total number of posts. So, if a 4chan board was full at, say, one hundred posts, the next post would knock the last one into digital oblivion. On most boards, comments might last a few hours, but on 4chan's most popular board, known as "random" or /b/, posts might fall off within fifteen minutes.[7]

4chan's lack of memory was cost-saving, but it also changed the way people posted. On 4chan, said moot, if you post something and it's useless, "it's washed away."[8] The lolcats, rickrolling, and the other strange but infectious creations passed around the internet, known as memes, were born in this frantic environment. And because its best-known content came from /b/, "4chan" was often used as shorthand for its fastest moving board.

Absolute anonymity was also central to 4chan's appeal. Unlike social media, 4chan users didn't need to create accounts, pseudonyms or even log in. As a result, around 90 percent of them posted as "anonymous," a practice so central to the 4chan culture that users were known simply as "anons." According to Poole, eliminating the requirement of any kind of online identity provided anons with freedom. On the comment streams of most websites, he claimed, longtime users were often accorded the undeserved respect reserved for elders. Likewise, if a new user's first posts were considered unfunny, useless, or lame, their pseudonym would forever be associated with failure. Absolute anonymity unburdened 4chan-ers from the weight of identity while encouraging absolute freedom of speech. Poole figured that if 4chan was a place for cost-free failure, it would also be a place for limitless creativity. He seemed to be right. In 2008, *The Guardian* called 4chan "brilliant, ridiculous and alarming."[9]

What was absolutely certain was that 4chan—with its low-budget interface, self-identified outsider status, anonymity, and disdain for connecting with people offline—was the anti-Facebook. Social media was a platform where people willingly fused their offline and online identities; 4chan was a dark hole where anons joined a chaotic hive mind. In psychoanalytic terms, if social media's transparency made it the internet's superego, then the cloaked operations on 4chan were its id: A place for instinctive, repressed, and, often, antisocial desires.

The dark side of 4chan-style pranks was examined in an August 2008 *New York Times Magazine* piece about trolling. The term "troll" had been used since the late 1980s to describe a person who tried to get a rise out of someone else online. Trolls might, for example, make a stupid or offensive comment just to test the outcome from others online. And, as with prank phone calls, the best targets are people who take the caller seriously or get upset. Unlike phone calls, however, the incensed or floundering victim may quickly attract other online trolls in a feeding frenzy that finishes only when all the laughs have been gobbled up. Like in the fairytales, trolls can be very ugly.

In the expanding and anonymous space of the internet, trolling had already claimed at least one high-profile victim, a girl who committed suicide after being pranked and harassed via Myspace. The trolling had nothing to do with 4chan users; the girl's friend's mother orchestrated it. However, it prompted reporter Mattathias Schwartz to spend time with several established trolls. One young man, a Seattle-area based troll who shared his apartment with Schwartz for a few days, lived his days unexceptionally, going to work, Subway, coffee shops, and meeting his friends at a sushi restaurant. He would happily pass unnoticed on the street. Another, named weev, was more flamboyant, outwardly racist, and anti-Semitic.

Ultimately, though, Schwartz predicted that trolls would not be a real problem for the rapidly growing web. "It may not be a bad thing," he mused, "that the least-mature users have built remote ghettos of anonymity where the malice is usually intramural." He was right on one count. Over the next few years, trolling would not limit the internet's growth. But trolls and the 4chan culture they represented would soon bust out of their "ghetto" and run amuck in the real world.

In January 2008, a leaked video of actor and Scientologist Tom Cruise was briefly posted on YouTube. The interview, which was edited down from a three-hour Scientology-produced promotional video, shows Cruise speaking in delusional terms about the religion. His most famous quote describes how Scientologists were "the only ones who could help" people injured in car accidents. As they had for decades, the religion's lawyers aggressively leaped into action, quickly forcing YouTube to take down the video.

But this time, the internet fought back. The website Gawker obtained a copy of the video, reposted it, and, as news of Scientology's clumsy attempt at censorship spread, the Cruise interview went viral.

For many 4chan users, the opportunity to ridicule a Hollywood icon and push back on attempted censorship by a shadowy religion deserved special attention. Anons invented a mock religion called "Chanology" and created a separate board for planning retribution against the church.

In a video posted January 21, 2008, Operation Chanology announced itself in style. Images of grey clouds sped across an apocalyptic sky while a robotic voice intoned "Hello, Leaders of Scientology, we are Anonymous." After reciting a list of crimes, including "suppression of dissent," the voice declared: "Anonymous has therefore decided that your organization should be destroyed." The video ended with the over-the-top warning, "We are Anonymous. We are legion. We do not forgive. We do not forget. Expect us."

It was funny and compelling; everyone wanted to know what would come next. Anonymous had previous experience with various online pranks, so they began this much larger operation with similar techniques. They attacked Scientology websites, forcing them down repeatedly over several weeks. Secret church documents were stolen and distributed online. Local Scientology offices were overwhelmed by pages upon pages of black faxes, tying up phone lines, and drying up ink cartridges. A "Google bomb" gamed the search engine, making "Scientology" the first result for search terms "dangerous cult." Previously, critics of the church had effectively been silenced by Scientology's aggressive tactics, legal and otherwise. But the church's leadership found targeting anonymous enemies much more difficult.

Relatively quickly, however, Operation Chanology moved past the tried and true tactics of technically skilled anons. Instead of just getting a few chuckles by besieging the church online, organizers shifted to offline political action. On February 10, 2008, a group of what appeared to be a few hundred overaged trick or treaters marched through the well-manicured streets of Clearwater, Florida—the controversial religion's training base. In front of one of the buildings, the crowd broke into chants of "Xenu! Xenu! Xenu!"—a galactic dictator whose existence in Scientology's esoteric cosmology is widely denied by church leaders.

Anonymous's masks, ill-fitting suits, bandanas, and sunglasses gave the event a festival atmosphere, but they were also practical. The balconies of multiple Scientology-owned buildings were lined with people scanning the crowd with cameras. By remaining anonymous while offline, the protestors hoped to avoid legal or other forms of retribution.

The Clearwater march, combined with organized protests outside dozens of churches worldwide, gave some of the lulz-seekers a taste of social justice. It turned the 4chan-linked Anonymous group into the world's first high-profile hacktivists. Since then, Anonymous has gone to provide communication support for Iranians during the 2009 election protests and supplies to homeless around the world.

The secretive group has also often engaged in doxing, a term that developed from publicizing private "docs" or documents. Doxing victims would often see their phone numbers, emails, addresses, photos, and other information widely released on the internet, potentially as an invitation for harassment or worse. In one case, Anonymous hacked a Ku Klux Klan website and claimed to unmask one thousand alleged members. Doxing is a bit like frontier justice, though. It isn't always accurate and there is no court of appeal. Some people were erroneously accused of Klan membership but, once "convicted" online, there was no easy means to clear their names.

Doxing also wasn't new. The practice, if not the name, had been used by anti-abortion extremists two decades earlier. In these incidents, groups had used the internet to widely distribute abortion providers' phone numbers, addresses, photos, and so on. The web page, decorated with images of blood, was clearly a cyber hit list. When a provider was wounded, their name turned gray. If they were killed, their name was crossed out. These digital lists were terrifying, even if they focused on a relatively small number of people.

As Anonymous's activities grew, some charitable, some progressive, some viciously retaliatory, so did questions about their legality. But it was the group's commitment to social justice that offended some of their fellow 4chan-ers. Many anons were steadfast that the primary goal of online activity was to get lulz. But their preference was often for humor that was itself cynical and vicious.

South Park, a TV show that began appearing regularly on Comedy Central in 1997, was a cartoon animated in a particularly primitive cutout style, much like 4chan's almost premodern layout. The cartoon follows the adventures of four elementary school kids, but it is known for its profanity and dark humor. It was not intended for kids but relied on everything from relentless scatological references to endless racist slurs to an irreverent portrayal of the Muslim prophet Muhammad, and even mocked Scientology.

One of the main characters was also vehemently anti-Semitic, frequently attacking another main character, who was Jewish. Their relationship was played for laughs, albeit uncomfortable ones. And, though its creators have rejected all political labels, the show's relentless attacks on liberal shibboleths made it popular with "South Park conservatives," people who resented what they perceive as enforcement of "politically correct" speech and action.

Also first appearing in the late 1990s, *Vice* magazine prided itself for its profane attacks on hipster sensibilities, a dark, cruel humor premised on a perhaps ironic but very aggressive reaction to politically correct norms. Its "Dos and Don'ts" section mercilessly criticized the appearance and fashion of Manhattan pedestrians. The magazine was called infantile and "characterized by lewd masculinity"[10]—but was also incredibly popular, eventually becoming a media empire.

Around 2008, *Vice* magazine underwent an internal civil war between those who wanted to do more serious journalism and those who wanted to retain the magazine's original focus on brutal, sarcastic humor, much like 4chan's rift after Anonymous's drift into social justice. As a result of this split, Gavin McInnes, one of three co-editors and the one most dedicated to assaults on sensibilities, left the magazine—eventually reemerging as the head of the right-wing extremist Proud Boys.

On 4chan, the comedic legacy of *South Park* and *Vice* combined with an absolute commitment to free speech, The result, perhaps not surprisingly, was innumerable racist, anti-Semitic, and, especially, misogynist posts. In their efforts to push boundaries, anons often also fixated on Nazi imagery. 4chan users once swarmed an online children's game with swastikas.[11] On another occasion, anons hacked Google, positioning symbols depicting a swastika, planes crashing into the World Trade Center and the words "[f---] you google" on the search engine's trends list.[12] However, this hateful imagery was almost always wrapped in impenetrable self-referential humor and a slippery irony.

4chan wasn't given a free pass by the media. It was called both a "meme factory" and, later, the "Internet Hate Machine," but it still remained extremely hard to tell truth from fiction from prank. Despite all the jokey hate on the site, and Anonymous's occasional hacktivism, in 2009, 4chan still seemed too chaotic, gross, and insular a place to support any widespread sustained politics. Over the next seven years, though, 4chan's trollish culture shifted politically rightward and became a locus for a uniquely dangerous new kind of extremism.

The first, terrifying glimpse at 4chan-style politics began in 2013. In February, a developer working under the name Zoë Quinn released a video game called *Depression Quest*. It was not heroic journey, single-shooter, or any of the usual gaming genres. Quinn, who had long suffered from depression, wanted to create an educational, immersive experience that helped people realize and talk about their mental health. Along with the game's sobering subject, it had a unique format. Players were regularly confronted by passages that added up to a book-length amount of text. All gameplay decisions were made in a despondent haze.

Quinn's game received some good reviews, but also scathing criticism from gamers furious that she had departed from skill and violence-based entertainment. There was a shared ethos and membership between the 4chan and gamer communities: both were defensive of their territory and,

all too often, virulently misogynist. Gamers were outraged that Quinn—
an avid gamer herself—had, as they saw it, invaded the boys' club and
asked them to talk about their feelings.

While the initial response to *Depression Quest* was ugly, the episode
soon ignited into a much more vicious melodrama. In a blog written
months after *Depression Quest*'s release, Quinn's former boyfriend attacked
her, implying that she had only received a favorable review because of a
sexual relationship with a writer at the gaming website Kotaku. The
reviewer in question quickly responded by pointing out that he had never
reviewed the game. Quinn's boyfriend later corrected his post.

By this time, however, the reputed scandal had made it to 4chan,
where it prompted outrage, acrimony, and a fresh wave of attacks on
Quinn. Her social media accounts were hacked, and she was doxed, with
her phone number, home address, and personal information widely published on the internet. Her family members' details were also published,
and a caller told Quinn's father she was a "whore." Several nude photos
of her were circulated online. In August of 2014, after multiple death
threats, Quinn fled her house to stay with friends.

Quinn was not the only victim. Multiple people came to Quinn's
defense, including video game developers Phil Fish and Brianna Wu,
and feminist critic Anita Sarkeesian. All were mocked as overly earnest
SJWs (Social Justice Warriors), doxed, and, in some cases, were victims of
attempted "swatting"—fake calls to emergency services designed to get
a SWAT team to respond to victim's address. Fish ended up selling his
company, while Wu also fled her home for a while.

The actor Adam Baldwin contributed the snappy hashtag #gamer-
gate to refer to the supposed evidence that the gaming industry was non-
transparent and had a left-wing bias. The hashtag successfully spread the
outrage on social media, although its logic was suspect. If the outcry was
intended to force gaming reviewers into more transparency, the attacks
should have been leveled at writers and online gaming publications.
Instead, the vast majority of the abuse was targeted at Quinn and her supporters, particularly women.

While the Arab Spring and, for many, the protests against Scientology showed the liberating potential of huge, networked groups of anonymous individuals organizing against despots and speaking truth to power, Gamergate very clearly exposed the dangers.

For one, Gamergate was impossible without anonymity. One of the victims of the attacks, developer Brianna Wu, fled her house after having her personal information revealed and receiving thousands of threats. But Wu then turned the tables. She posted an $11,000 bounty for personal information about her doxers so they could be prosecuted. In effect, she threatened to dox the doxers. For her attackers, even the mere threat of losing their anonymity and facing some sort of consequences was too much. Wu claimed that as soon as the bounty was announced, the "rape and death threats instantly stopped."[13]

The immediate cessation of attacks also suggested something else: the rabid attacks weren't based on an ideological commitment to "transparency in the gaming industry," but more like an exercise in abusing the boundaries of anonymity. Compare, for example, the reaction of the countless suddenly silent Gamergate trolls with the original doxers: anti-abortion extremists and their provider hit list.

The FBI eventually discovered the existence of the hit list and identity of some of its contributors. As a result, the extremists viewing and contributing to the list knew that their identities were vulnerable. But the threat to doctors did not stop. Anonymity was preferable for these extremists but, for the most deeply radicalized, it was not essential to continuing their participation. Many were firmly and violently committed to ending abortion in America.

Anonymity had also made hate sites like Stormfront popular with white supremacists. Unless they chose otherwise, all the site's users were cyphers, even harder to identify than a hooded Klansman. Without worrying about any consequences, they were free to discuss things that they perceived as prohibited in the offline world. As one neo-Nazi said, "The Internet provides a core feeling of freedom . . . to live out one's own ideology . . . without the danger of facing social resistance or exclusion."[14]

However, the perception of existing in a space where there are no boundaries or consequences encourages some people to go beyond simply expressing themselves. On 4chan, anons would try to get laughs from an unlimited number of people by creating offensive images that they might even not show to their best friends offline. Likewise, some neo-Nazis reported that approaching the world from behind a screen didn't just make some of their comrades comfortable, it made them outright aggressive. As one interviewee explained, "Some are very shy or introverted in real life but online they are pure agitators." As a result, they "run riot, placing swastikas wherever they can."[15]

A University of Queensland psychological study added another wrinkle to Gamergate phenomenon. While anonymity can enhance abusive behavior, the study found, the abuse is actually rooted in group dynamics. In 2008, *New York Times* reporter Mattathias Schwartz imagined a ghetto in which the trolls were safely contained. By 2015, 4chan had 20 million unique visitors a month, making it one of the most trafficked websites ever.[16] The ghetto was spilling into the streets, their trollish behavior was spreading, and their huge numbers exacerbated the abusive group dynamics.

As social media researcher Jamie Bartlett explained, once one person found a home address, another tried to get to the next level by, say, finding her dad's phone number or pictures of her friends. "The herd mentality kicks in," said Bartlett, "and the victim becomes nothing but an object of strange competitive urges."[17]

In other words, the escalating tussle set anonymous attackers against a victim they only imagined. Quinn's attackers may have seen pictures of her, even nude ones, and they felt intensely enough to post abusive comments, dox her, threaten her, etc. But she never existed as a person, as someone who might be scared of the violent abuse heaped on her by strangers. Like in a video game, she was just an avatar they attacked, each trying to get a higher score.

This dynamic, becoming more common as a trollish 4chan ethos expanded across an increasingly crowded, anonymous web, also describes virtually every offline extremist attack. Extremism isn't about hating an individual person, but hating a person's generalized religion, race, profession, political opinions, and so on. It's even less personal for terrorists who, by definition, don't attack their ultimate targets. Terrorists set off bombs or shoot people so they can terrify a group of living people, be they Muslims, Communists, law enforcement, research scientists, etc.

In 2009, Ashton Kutcher was lauded for using his army of followers to fight malaria. Anonymous had deployed doxing and a massive digital army of trolls against the KKK. Now these same tools were being used to discharge hate on a massive scale. And, instead aiming their ire at institutions or members of hate groups, Gamergate advocates were terrorizing private individuals on the basis of false information for the alleged crime of creating a video game whose politics they disliked. Easy to launch and hard to police, Gamergate was a massive digital nightmare that demonstrated how trolling could be utilized for explicitly political purposes: resistance to the reputed "culture war" being waged by feminists and other advocates of left-wing "politically correct" ideology.

Christopher Poole, or moot, 4chan's founder, shared some of the same personality profiles as eventual extremists—including divorced parents and social insularity. He was also constantly immersed in an online universe filled with extremist rhetoric. That he never went down the path of radicalization shows how predicting future extremist activity based on superficial evidence is somewhere between useless and dangerous. In fact, though moot had founded 4chan and championed anonymity and free speech, he did enforce some basic rules on his board. Once it was clear that 4chan was a hub for planning Gamergate attacks, for example, he banned all related discussions on the site. But, despite his legendary status, moot was not immune to attacks from 4chan-ers who called him a "soulless informant."[18]

This was not the first time moot had received death threats from angry anons. Wary of being doxed himself, he refused to provide his current location, countries he recently visited, or the name of the university he attended for a few terms.[19] He had been worn down by dealing with controversies linked to the site. Gamergate was the final straw. Poole walked away from the site in 2015 and started a job at Google the following year.

The culture that had grown up around message boards like 4chan was now a beast he didn't want to, or couldn't, control. And its cynical, outrageous ethos was infecting the mainstream media.

CHAPTER SIX

ATTENTION HIJACKING

On January 15, 2009, a Latvian investor named Janis Krums tweeted: "There's a plane in the Hudson. I'm on the ferry going to pick up the people. Crazy."[1] His tweet and photo went out to 170 followers, making Krums the first to report what was quickly dubbed "The Miracle on the Hudson"—the safe ditching of United Airlines Flight 1549. By beating the national media to the scene, Krums even became part of the news; he was interviewed live on MSNBC half an hour after his tweet.[2] The day was also a defining moment for Twitter, its emergence as a crowd-sourced news provider with millions of reporters globally.

Krums's tweet showed that social media could be faster than mainstream media, but it didn't completely transform the dynamic between traditional and crowd-sourced news. Within a few minutes, organizations like CNN and the *New York Times* took over with more in-depth and substantive reporting. The old-guard mainstream media was still able to assert itself as the authority. But over the next few years, as social media became many people's primary news source, mainstream media began to cover the online ecosystem as news itself. Online trends became newsworthy simply because the sheer number of people talking about something made it news. The status of social media had metamorphosed again—this time more profoundly. Crowd-sourced reporting went from being traditional media's speedy little sibling to actually creating news.

In 2014, for example, *Time* ran an end-of-year piece called "Top 10 Things that Broke the Internet"—a list that included "Kim Kardashian's butt," a viral video of "The Apparently Kid," and surveillance camera footage of "Solange and Jay-Z's Elevator Fight."[3] Entertainment and human-interest stories have always been popular, but these items became news solely because of the popular reaction to them on the internet.

Mainstream media's difficult new role in breaking news was crystalized in another item on the list, "The Celebrity Nude Photo Leak,"[4] that resulted from hackers publishing private, naked photos of three female celebrities to sites including 4chan. Journalists faced a paradox: the photos were clearly illegal invasions of privacy, but even critical coverage would advertise their existence, effectively encouraging millions of people to search for them online.

When the traditional media covered stories about what "broke the internet," it was, in a sense, being radically democratic. But, by chasing online trends simply because they were trends, it also abdicated its role as a gatekeeper for what was newsworthy. The mainstream media began increasingly offering itself to internet mobs as a megaphone for rumors, fads, and hoaxes.

On July 20, 2012, James Eagan Holmes entered a movie theater in Aurora, Colorado, during a midnight screening of a Batman movie. After tossing tear gas canisters into the aisles, he began firing multiple firearms, killing twelve people and wounding over a hundred.

Holmes's attack resulted in the most casualties in any mass shooting in modern American history, although that number has since been surpassed multiple times. In the rush to cover it, the media seized upon an online group of self-professed Holmes supporters who called themselves "Holmies." Because of the inherent difficulties of confirming details on the anonymous web, accurately covering online activity is difficult. In the case of the Holmies, however, reportage went far beyond minor errors. Some stories suggested the group could have tens of thousands of members. In the end, it turned out that the "Holmies" were fewer than a dozen trolls.[5]

Here was the catch: The reporting was massively flawed, but it was not a failure—at least not in economic terms. The story—sensationalist, hyperbolic and exploitative—was popular with readers. In the developing online media ecosystem, the economic imperative was to drive page views.

Trolls, especially the well-organized, tech-savvy kind on 4chan, could be a huge nuisance for journalists. Nonetheless, the "Holmies" ruse handed the media bankable content on a silver platter. By widely broadcasting the Holmies story, reporters inadvertently paid the trolls back with huge publicity. "In short," wrote Whitney Philips in her book *This is Why We Can't Have Nice Things*, "trolling works for trolls and works for mainstream media because it turns into page views and page views into advertising."[6] The mainstream media was effectively encouraging the trolls to come out of their ghetto. In the second decade of the new millennium, 4chan's antisocial ethos began informing more and more interactions on the internet—including social media.

Part of this was due to the rush of people joining social media networks. Between 2010 and 2015, the number of active Twitter users in the United States exploded, from ten million to sixty-six million. Tens of millions rushed to leverage the app to network, promote their personal brand, and add value to their social media platform.

In the face of what amounted to growing competition for wavelength, Twitter users developed various solutions, many of which bore strong resemblances to the well-worn techniques of 4chan anons from earlier in the 2000s. One was obsessiveness, relying on near constant posting or retweeting to expand a network. On 4chan this activity was known as "meme-forcing"—constantly reposting a meme in the hopes that it will catch on.

Twitter's format, a constantly updating feed and a 140-character limit, also encouraged users toward hot takes and snappy hashtags. Just like 4chan's architecture that forever deleted posts, sometimes in fifteen minutes, users were steered away from thoughtful, nuanced messaging. Tweets needed to be easily digestible bits on a fast-moving feed.

Other Twitter users relied on creating controversy and acrimony as an easy way to drive up retweets, a trollish skill perfected by 4chan-ers who baited their online victims with offensive comments.

The changes to the social and political environment brought about by Twitter, Facebook, comment streams, and other social media beginning around 2008 were enormous. They were too numerous and multifaceted to be defined in one particular way, but perhaps their biggest impact was creating an addictive medium that expanded by injecting overheated and divisive political and social issues into the rhythm of everyday life. It birthed what was descriptively called "outrage culture."

The result was that, although 4chan was still the potty-mouthed teenager in the room, many reputedly "mature" social media interactions were becoming increasingly antisocial. And, as ripe as 4chan culture was for ugly eruptions like Gamergate, it was hardly corrupting an otherwise innocent internet. To be heard above the internet's background noise, more and more users of mainstream social media joined an often funny, frequently angry, but always frantic race to the bottom—or the zenith— of offensive hostility.

Since 2010, as mainstream media increasingly relinquished its gate-keeper role and rewarded trollish behavior while acrimonious interactions on Twitter and other social media became commonplace, an unholy alliance of the exploding 4chan culture and social media's massive reach created new opportunities for enterprising extremists.

One of the earliest journalists to cover Gamergate was a British-born technology writer named Milo Yiannopoulos. By the age of twenty-nine, Yiannopoulos had dropped out of his grammar school and two universities, started an unsuccessful European technology journal, and created a soon defunct ranking system for tech startups. But, in the year following Gamergate, his career began to take off.

On September 1, 2014, a month after violent threats led developer Zoë Quinn to flee her house, he posted an article on right-wing news site Breitbart titled "Feminist Bullies tearing the Video Game Industry Apart." Yiannopoulos claimed Gamergate was a culture war, one which he used to leapfrog into issues far beyond technology. Yiannopoulos became a well-known, outspoken, and sometimes outrageous critic of Islam, feminism, and political correctness, among other right-wing bugbears. By March 2015, he had established enough credibility as a social critic that he was invited to talk about feminism and discrimination against men on an episode of the BBC's daytime "issues" television show *The Big Questions*.

His employer, Breitbart News Network, also had big plans for Yiannopoulos. Breitbart had started in 2005 as a right-leaning online news aggregator. Over the next few years, founder Andrew Breitbart became more extreme in his attacks on liberalism as well as some traditional conservative positions and publications, what he referred to as the "old guard." Following Breitbart's 2012 death, executive chairman Steve Bannon continued reshaping the organization. In October 2015, Bannon named Yiannopoulos editor of the new Breitbart tech section, but his plans for the young writer—who was at home in an internet culture defined by controversy, trolling, and semi-ironic attacks on politically correct ideas—were much bigger.

On December 8, 2015, Yiannopoulos published an anti-feminist screed with the typically outrageous clickbait headline "Birth Control Makes Women Unattractive and Crazy." That afternoon, in emails later released by BuzzFeed, Bannon contacted Yiannopoulos to berate him for merely writing silly articles and not focusing on the larger agenda of the far right.

"Dude," wrote Bannon "—we r in a global existentialist war where our enemy EXISTS in social media and u r jerking yourself off w/ marginalia!!!! U should be OWNING this conversation because u r everything they hate!!! Drop your toys, pick up your tools and go help save western civilization."[7]

Yiannopoulos wasn't a great writer or reporter—much of his work for Breitbart was ghostwritten[8]—but Bannon wasn't looking for superlative prose. In Yiannopoulos, he saw someone who could spread the gospel of what was becoming known as the alt-right by tapping into the convergence of 4chan culture and social media's power to dictate news.

Throughout 2016, with Bannon's support, Yiannopoulos's star rose as he fomented angry social media encounters that were reminiscent of Gamergate. He created inflammatory public appearances, like a May 2016 speech at DePaul University in which he equated feminism with cancer. These appearances led to angry protests on campus that were videoed and uploaded to YouTube, gaining so many views that they were covered by mainstream publication while they were endlessly debated in angry social media encounters.

By simply enraging huge swaths of the left, Yiannopoulos became a headline-grabbing celebrity. The media, in turn, rewarded him for his trollish stunts with profiles in mainstream magazines. To his fans, he was the "poster child for offensive speech" and a champion of first amendment rights. He was a 4chan troll who had emerged from the online sewer with a sharp suit, dyed hair, and a specific political agenda.

Yiannopoulos was well aware of his unique value to Breitbart and other elements of the alt-right. Traditional conservatism, by its nature resistant to social change, was associated with stodgy, old, white men. By contrast, Yiannopoulos was an immigrant, gay, and had a long-term African American boyfriend. He happily weaponized his "fabulous catty gay male behavior"[9] for the alt-right, peppering his anti-feminist speeches with obscenities and references to gay sex. At the same time he authored articles with homophobic headlines like "Gay Rights Have Made Us Dumber, It's Time to Get Back into the Closet" and claimed on television he would probably choose not to be gay if possible—even though it would be "career suicide."[10] To his fans, Yiannopoulos's form of free-wheeling transgression made hate seem fresh and fun. He shamelessly directed bile at women and Muslims before claiming it was all a big joke and that Social Justice Warriors should loosen up.

Like any good troll, Yiannopoulos also tried to flip the tables on some of his left-wing critics, especially campus protesters. Quick to be outraged by his stunts, Yiannopoulos cast the often successful attempts to shut down his speeches as moralizing and restrictive.

"I have said in the past," Yiannopoulos wrote to BuzzFeed, "that I find humor in breaking taboos and laughing at things that people tell me are forbidden to joke about. But everyone who knows me also knows I'm not a racist."[11] Yiannopoulos and 4chan shared the same two rules: nothing is prohibited and make fun of everything. But Yiannopoulos's flippant denials that his most offensive behavior actually meant anything were, at best, dubious.

In April of 2016, Yiannopoulos was videoed in a Dallas karaoke bar singing "God Bless America" to a crowd, including a well-known thirty-

eight-year-old white nationalist named Richard Spencer, who were uni-
formed in preppy pastels and crew cuts and raising their arms in Nazi
salutes. After realizing what was happening, the bartender at One Nos-
talgia Tavern kicked out the obnoxious group.

Though he entered the bar with well-known racists, Yiannopoulos
lamely claimed not to have seen the Nazi salutes due to his "severe
myopia."[12] Likewise, while Yiannopoulos may never have "really believed"
in fascist ideologies, he certainly knew his value to the far right in vili-
fying Islam, feminists, left-wing "political correctness," and other frequent targets.

Another young man who would eventually wrangle 4chan and social
media for his right-wing extremist purposes, grew up in suburban
Columbus, Ohio, during the early 2000s. Andrew Anglin would spend
hours online in his parents' basement, trollishly encouraging people to
send anonymous death threats to the violently homophobic Westboro
Baptist Church or mocking the KKK. During his freshman year at an
alternative public high school, he had shoulder-length hair and dated the
only other vegan in his class.

Over the next few years, however, Anglin's personality and politics
changed. Friends describe him as becoming angry and violent, once slam-
ming his head repeatedly on a sidewalk outside a party. At around the
same time, he moved away from his left-of-center political pranks. An
avid 4chan anon, the emotionally unstable Anglin claims to have first
discovered neo-Nazi ideology on the site. After a personal journey that
included travels in Southeast Asia and several failed websites, he launched
the neo-Nazi news site Daily Stormer on July 4, 2013.[13]

Daily Stormer took its name from the rabidly anti-Semitic weekly
German tabloid *Der Stürmer*, which published from 1923 until the end
of WWII. Unlike the official Nazi party newspaper, *Der Stürmer* made
no pretense of respectability, running profane cartoons and calling for
the extermination of Jews in the early 1930s.

Anglin imitated this bombastic ethos while borrowing the authority
of mainstream sources and leveraging the trollish techniques perfected

on 4chan. Daily Stormer's outdated logo, for example, was a nod to 1980s kitsch, while Anglin's over-the-top writing was less *Mein Kampf* than the sort of biting parody and sarcastic wit popularized in the 1990s by *Vice* and *South Park*.

Like 4chan trolls—or, for that matter, millions of Twitter users—Anglin was also less interested in being taken seriously than in getting media attention, even if it was overwhelmingly negative. In one campaign, Anglin encouraged his "Troll Army" to create fake "White Student Union" Facebook pages at elite universities and then forward the links to local media. As with the "Holmies" ruse a few years earlier, the "media took the bait, and reports of racist student groups appeared in several places."[14]

Anglin also used the media to amplify troll attacks. He insisted that Daily Stormer articles about some "enemy Jew/feminist" always include links to the subject's social media—implicitly inviting attacks. "We've gotten press attention before when I didn't even call for someone to be trolled," said Anglin, "but just linked to them and people went and did it."

Like Breitbart's Milo Yiannopoulos, Daily Stormer's bread and butter was outrageous headlines that drove curiosity and, thus, page views. But, unlike its 1930s fascist namesake, Daily Stormer always hedged its fascism with a hint of irony. One of the most infamous headlines—"All Intelligent People in History Disliked Jews"—was so overblown that it might have been a parody of anti-Semitism.

Anglin's entertaining approach to hate, pseudo-ironic bluster mixed with *Sturm und Drang*, brought in a large collection of younger and more ideologically diverse readers than traditional hate sites. Daily Stormer was so successful at drawing traffic that, in just three years, it surpassed Don Black's long-time leader Stormfront to become the most visited hate site on the web.

Daily Stormer also operated as a kind of convergence point for the strange journey of 4chan from a chaotic, creative, ridiculous, and obscene virtual clubhouse for nerdy millennials to a neo-Nazi website and troll command center. For example, weev, the hacker interviewed in the 2008 *New York Times Magazine* article, has served as the Daily Stormer's webmaster for several years, following his release from prison. The site was intentionally modeled after successful liberal blogs like BuzzFeed and Gawker,[15] the site that hosted the Tom Cruise video that set off Anonymous's crusade against Scientology. A more far-reaching indictment came from the leaked version of the Daily Stormer's style guide, a document that explicitly spelled out the game plan of Anglin's 4chan-inspired fascism.

Some of the seventeen pages address traditional style concerns—insisting, for example, that links not "stretch into the spacing between words"—but the guide also discusses hijacking the mainstream media. To integrate its neo-Nazi propaganda with more familiar authority, the guide encourages using large block quotes from mainstream sources.[16]

In fact, aspiring writers are encouraged to make mainstream sources a critical component in every story with a three-part format: commentary, quote from mainstream source, more commentary. Just as the troll armies hijacked the media to spread fake stories and encourage trolling attacks, the Daily Stormer is designed to "co-opt the perceived authority of the mainstream media."[17]

While Anglin cites *Mein Kampf* as required reading, his approach to spoon feeding fascism to readers is pure 4chan. Writers are advised to "always hijack existing cultural memes in any way possible. Don't worry if the meme was originally Jewish."

Similarly, the guide insists on retaining some sort of humor while attacking Jews or feminists. The claim that "dehumanization is extremely important, but it must be done within the confines of lulz" is also reminiscent of 4chan's credo to do everything for the laughs. Anglin was determined not to make the same mistakes as Anonymous, after its foray into earnest, offline politics left it open to attacks that it was excessively serious.

But the guide also exposes the darkness behind this insistence on abrasive sarcasm. Anglin describes his half-ironic approach to extremist tropes as "I am a racist making fun of stereotypes of racists, because I don't take myself super-seriously." Then, the truth behind all this obfuscation: "This is obviously a ploy and I actually do want to gas kikes."[18]

Visitors to the Daily Stormer are thus bombarded by articles cloaked in the authority of mainstream media mixed with familiar memes and seemingly facetious humor. The goal is to confuse readers, especially those whose first reaction is resistance to fascism. "The unindoctrinated [sic]," the guide notes, "should not be able to tell if we are joking or not."[19]

The then-emerging "alt-right" movement associated with Breitbart and 4chan had been jokingly called "Nazis who like memes." And though Breitbart had tried to position itself both as a rallying point for the "alt-right" without being explicitly racist, Anglin draws a direct line between the two publications. Breitbart's content, he said, is "basically stuff that you would read on the Daily Stormer."[20] Likewise, the slippery, dangerous irony of the Daily Stormer is, in fact, essentially the same game plan advanced by flamboyant, over-the-top Breitbart provocateur Milo Yiannopoulos.

In both cases, the desired result is an innovative form of radicalization. Both websites used amusing clickbait headlines to draw in readers, both quoted mainstream sources in an attempt to co-opt their authority, and the articles were often little more than topics to start angry discussions on the voluminous comments thread. There were a few, minor differences. Anglin's prose, blunter and more offensive, was targeted at millennials, while Breitbart's slightly more coy style was easily digestible for less hip, older readers. Unlike Daily Stormer, Breitbart never explicitly endorsed anti-Semitism. In fact, Andrew Breitbart, who was Jewish, founded the site to be ferocious defender of Israel. Nonetheless, coded references like the echo symbol around the names of Jews—e.g., (((Andrew Breitbart)))—were rampant on Breitbart's comment sections.

The similarities were more important, though. Readers of both Daily Stormer and Yiannopoulos may have clicked on the article for a chuckle. But these memes and humor were just like the "cherry flavor"[21] in children's medicine. It didn't really matter why readers visited the Daily Stormer, as long as a whole new crop of potential extremists were being exposed to white supremacist memes and arguments.

By bringing readers in through "curiosity or naughty humor,"[22] Anglin solved one of the longstanding problems of extremist websites: they had tended to attract people who were already converts to the cause. Both Yiannopoulos and the Daily Stormer made far-right and even neo-Nazi politics part of a larger conversation. And they packaged it in cynical hipster humor, making it easily digestible for a whole new crop of potential extremists with nothing more than a cell phone.

Among the millions of people attracted to the Daily Stormer was someone with the username "AryanBlood1488." The number "14" is a reference to a white nationalist credo, while 88 is an alphanumeric code for "Heil Hitler," since *H* is the eighth letter of the alphabet. The numbers have significance for white supremacists and neo-Nazis either separately or together. Daily Stormer cheekily paid their writers $14.88 per story.

After Dylann Roof's murderous outburst, it came to light that passages in his manifesto exactly matched posts by "AryanBlood1488." Roof had cited other sources for his inspirational material, movies, websites, in his manifesto. Why he didn't attribute these quotes?

Roof, it turned out, was "AryanBlood1488." In fact, after shooting nine churchgoers in Charleston, Dylann became a hero to many of the site's readers. Anglin referred to him as DyRo, like a celebrity's shortened name. Roof even received the ultimate 4chan tribute: his own meme, an image representing the bowl cut he always wore.

The role Anglin and weev's website played in Roof's radicalization versus, say, Stormfront is unknown. Completely obvious, though, is how Daily Stormer was designed to appeal to a "normal" twenty-something with no initial interest in neo-Nazi ideology. More importantly, the new media ecosystem in which the Daily Stormer flourished—frantic tweeting, overheated rhetoric, attention hacking of mainstream media, and slippery, mocking hostility—was just as critical to the spread of extremism between 2008 and 2016 as the sharp economic downturn. There was, however, one less recognized factor that contributed greatly to that extremism-friendly media ecosystem.

CHAPTER SEVEN

~~~~~~~~~~

DEADLY FICTIONS

One early October evening around 1871, two scholarly young men met at a spot overlooking the Vltava River in central Prague. After a brief discussion, they continued to the nearby old Jewish Cemetery, where they concealed themselves behind tombstones. About an hour later, a key clicked in the lock. After a long silence, the gate creaked open, and the hidden men glimpsed a slow procession of long-coated white figures entering the cemetery.

The first knelt before a tombstone, touched the stone three times with its forehead, and whispered a prayer. Twelve more figures followed, walking up to the tombstone and repeating the ritual before kneeling down on the ground. At the stroke of midnight, a sharp metallic sound rang out from the grave and blue flame appeared, illuminating the thirteen kneeling shapes.

A dull voice spoke: "I greet you, Roshe beth Aboth of the twelve tribes of Israel."[1]

"We greet you, son of the accursed," responded the leaders of the tribes of Israel.[2]

"A hundred years has passed," continued the voice. "Where do the princes of the tribes come from?"[3]

Starting with the Prince of Judah, the tribes reported in from cities in every part of Europe—including Amsterdam, Toledo, Krakow, Constantinople, and London. Then the voice called the prince of the Tribe of Aaron to conduct the meeting. He came forward and asked each representative how they could fulfill their plan, which, it quickly became clear, was to enslave Christians and dominate the world.

The Tribe of Reuben said, "All the moveable capital must go over to the hands of the Jews."[4] The representative of Judah demanded: "Transforming the artisans into our factory workers, [so that] we will be in a position to direct the masses for our political purposes."[5] The Tribe of Levi suggested seeding "free-thinking, skepticism, and conflicts"[6] with regard to church and schools "under guise of progress and equal rights for all religions." The leader of the Tribe of Zebulun stated that "support[ing] every kind of dissatisfaction, every revolution, increases our capital and brings us nearer to our goal."[7]

Other representatives suggested controlling the press, the financial markets, abolishing usury laws, destroying the Christian conception of family, placing the weakened military class under the power of money, controlling every business based on speculation and profit, intermarrying with Christians, and taking over positions in government as well as becoming scientists, doctors, artists, actors, and philosophers. The Tribe of Simeon advocated controlling the ownership of land and rent collection, but the harsh sarcasm his comments drew suggested that his advice was a little obvious.

Finally, the meeting was adjourned for another hundred years. After the cemetery emptied, the two scholars agreed to sound the alarm about this dire threat to society.

These events as depicted in Sir John Retcliffe's *The Jewish Cemetery in Prague and The Council of Representatives of the Twelve Tribes of Israel* are, of course, fictional. The ghostly meeting in a cemetery, the secret rituals, even the presence of Satan were all pieced together by what the publisher described as Retcliffe's "fantastic imagination."[8] Unfortunately, the stories would quickly transmogrify into truth for millions of Europeans.

As Herman Bernstein explains in *The History of a Lie*, Retcliffe's novelette—his name was actually Hermann Goedsche—was updated by members of the Russian tsarist secret police and republished in 1905 as *Protocols of the Elders of Zion*, supposedly penned by Sergius Nilus, a mysterious Russian mystic. The *Protocols* purports to be the minutes of a meeting passed on to Nilus by a prominent, but unnamed, Russian conservative who had in turn received it from an unknown woman who had stolen it from an influential Jewish Freemason in France.

In this version, powerful Jewish leaders gathered in the late nineteenth century to discuss their goals of global hegemony through, among other things, controlling the press and financial markets, as well as subverting the morals of gentiles. It sounds familiar, because it is. According to Bernstein, "Every substantive statement contained in the *Protocols* originates with [the] Goedsche-Retcliffe novelette."[9]

As it turns out, the tsarist police had published the work in hopes of diverting attention from the unrest that was rife in Russia at the time, spurred in part by a humiliating 1905 military defeat at the hands of the Japanese and a series of subsequent revolutions. That effort ultimately failed—the 1917 revolution ended with the murder of the imperial Romanov family—but the *Protocols* lived on, carried by the exiled Russian elites across Europe.

Far from condemning the fanciful tale to the dustbin of history, its vague details—dates, places, sources—made the narrative more adaptable. The framework in the *Protocols* was leaned on to explain the Jewish influence behind both Communist revolt and capitalist usury. The evil cabal was reportedly masterminding the perceived decline in Christian morality while the actions of Jewish bankers and Kaiser Wilhelm II, reputedly a Jewish agent, explained the German defeat in World War I.

Indeed, the *Protocols* was so successful in promoting numerous conspiracy theories over such a short time frame that, in 1921, the *Times* of London published an exposé debunking the work's veracity. Bernstein's book painstakingly traced the direct path from a fictional novelette to a reputedly real document that appeared that same year, but facts alone could not put a stake in the heart of this preposterous story.

The following decade, a version of the *Protocols* was assigned as factual by some German schoolteachers. Far from disappearing, the ideas promoted by the *Protocols*—that Jews are responsible for the evils that befall white Europeans—were very much present during the extermination of two-thirds of Europe's Jewish population.

After the horrors of the Holocaust, Nazi emblems, literature, and symbols were banned outright in Germany and restricted or stigmatized in much of the rest of Europe. But the idea of a secretive, international group pulling the strings behind every major event in the world lived on, shape-shifting as needed to accommodate extremists on the right, left, and beyond.

On the far right, anti-Semitism tends to express itself crudely, even flamboyantly, in swastikas, Stormtrooper apparel, and Nazi-era salutes. Sometimes, the debt to the *Protocols* can be obvious on other points of the extremist spectrum. Consider, for example, Louis Farrakhan's Saviours' Day Address in Chicago on February 25, 2018. "The Jews were responsible for all of this filth and degenerate behavior that Hollywood is putting out turning men into women and women into men," the Nation of Islam leader told his audience, then added, "Farrakhan, by God's grace, has pulled the cover off of that Satanic Jew and I'm here to say your time is up, your world is through."[10]

More often, far-left groups avoid explicit anti-Semitism, while still employing code words and phrases that have developed as acceptable euphemisms for the secret Jewish interests "exposed" by the *Protocols'* various authors. Thus "financial elite," "international bankers," "banksters," and the "Israel lobby" all became part of the common vernacular of the anti-globalization movement of the late 1990s.[11] Not surprisingly, the *Protocols* also enjoy popularity among Islamic extremists. In 2006, Osama bin Laden described the US-led invasions of Afghanistan and Iraq as the "Zionist-crusaders war on Islam."[12]

But the *Protocols* also hold a more mainstream appeal in parts of the Muslim world. In 2002, an Egyptian television series called *Horse without a Horseman* showed one episode each night during the holy month of Ramadan. In the early twentieth century, the heroic Egyptian character fighting British occupiers comes across the *Protocols*. He has it translated and discovers that many of the things described in the book are happening. Mohamed Sobhi, the well-known actor who played the main character and co-wrote the script, said that the issue of whether or not the *Protocols* story was authentic didn't matter. "Zionism exists," he said, "and it has controlled the world since the dawn of history."[13]

Conspiracy theories cut across the political spectrum because, ultimately, they are the oxygen that extremism breathes. Such theories combat facts with emotion. They explain the world dualistically, as good versus evil, and often provide easy scapegoats for complex societal problems. By discrediting the mainstream media and actual experts of all kinds, conspiracy theories create a fertile seedbed for radicalization, and in so doing, they set the stage for violent extremism.

Renowned domestic terrorist David Lane is a case in point.

At one level, David Lane was just another hard-luck kid. He was born in Iowa in 1938 to an alcoholic father who beat him, his siblings, and their mother. The father even sometimes pimped out his wife to friends for booze money. Lane later described him as a "drunk, a scoundrel and low-life of the worst kind."[14] His father died when Lane was only four, although not before he had beaten Lane's brother so harshly that he was permanently deaf. Afterward, Lane's mother had trouble making ends meet and was soon arrested for stealing food scraps out of a garbage bin. All her children were put in an orphanage, and Lane was soon adopted by a Lutheran minister and his wife.

As a child, Lane grew to strongly dislike church and Christianity. He was close with his adoptive mother, but described his new father as having "a personality which practically no one could bear."[15] The family moved to new parishes constantly. At every new school, Lane said he had to fight to prove himself, making him tough, but a "bit of a loner" and resentful of richer classmates.[16]

Lane eventually graduated from high school in Aurora, Colorado, and went to work for the power company as a troubleshooter. He married his high school sweetheart, but their relationship soon fell apart. He left the power company and became a real estate agent but lost that job for refusing to sell houses in white neighborhoods to African Americans.[17]

Still in his early twenties, Lane was clearly adrift. He'd found some work but nothing like a career. He actively disliked religion and appeared to have had a weak social network. In addition to the absence of inhibitors, Lane was rife with destabilizers: a divorce, shifting jobs, long-term grievances against his richer classmates, and so on. In such a rudderless state, conspiracy theories gave him narratives that explained his life: none of this was his fault because hidden malevolent forces were controlling his life.

Lane claims his first inkling of these conspiracies was a result of the reputed cover-ups in the assassination of John F. Kennedy in 1963.[18] Soon thereafter, he joined the John Birch Society, a vehemently anti-Communist group that provided an excellent introduction into conspiratorial thinking for many future right-wing extremists.

As Michael Barkun writes in *Culture of Conspiracy*, all conspiracists tend to converge around three points: 1) Nothing happens by accident; 2) Nothing is as it seems; 3) Everything is connected.[19] The John Birch Society, a group which may have had up to a hundred thousand members in the 1960s, followed these tenets, but saw everything through paranoid Cold War visions of hidden Communist agents everywhere. For example, clergy-led civil rights groups marching for the right to vote were reputedly Moscow-controlled agents who wanted to create a "Soviet Negro Republic." Dire threats emanated from the liberal media and the New York "Eastern establishment."[20] The group was so unhinged that its leader even accused President Dwight Eisenhower of Communism.[21]

As much as Lane appreciated the group's insistence that "powerful, evil, deep, forces control human destinies," he eventually came to believe that the Birchers were focusing on the wrong enemy. After doing his own research, Lane decided: "The Western nations were ruled by a Zionist conspiracy."[22]

Now well down the path of right-wing extremism, Lane tried to recruit others to his cause. He began arriving to work early to print out hundreds of copies of his free pamphlets. His goal was to distribute the racist, conspiracy-laced literature around the entire Denver area. Although Lane never specifically referenced the *Protocols*, their direct influence is clear. In "The Death of the White Race," for example, Lane wrote "The JEWS, who have sworn to destroy our Race and who now own all three TV networks, the major movie companies, and nearly all newspapers and publishing companies, make it front page headlines, if they can find a nonintegrated school or neighborhood anywhere."[23] Lane also repeatedly refers to the "JEWSMEDIA."

His "White Genocide Manifesto" expanded this *Protocols*-inspired conspiracy: "Zionist control of the media, as well as of all essential power points of industry, finance, law and politics in the once White nations is simply fact."[24]

By the mid-1970s, Lane was fully on the path of radicalization. He had dived even deeper into the Denver-area far right, first becoming an organizer for the local KKK before joining the Aryan Nations, a group steeped in "Christian Identity," the pseudo religion that teaches that Jews are the literal descendants of Satan. He also became involved with neo-Nazi groups in northern Idaho. Eventually, though, he tired of the lack of action among other white supremacists.

Then, in September 1983, he joined a new, secretive subgroup of the Aryan Nations in northern Idaho. The creation of this new band of white supremacist brothers was based on a violent, conspiratorial piece of fiction published a few years earlier.

The Turner Diaries, written by the neo-Nazi National Alliance's William Pierce, but published under the pseudonym Andrew McDonald, was a violent call to action against a global conspiracy. A kind of dystopic science fiction, the book tells the story of Earl Turner through two years of his diary entries.

In brief, Turner has joined a violent white supremacy group called The Organization in its violent struggle against The System, an anti-white, anti-gun US government that keeps restricting people's liberties. The System is, of course, run by the Jews and their willing dupes on the left, but Turner also has extreme contempt for conservatives and "ordinary" white people who would rather remain comfortable than face up to the horrifying reality of their enslavement.

After launching a series of mortar attacks on Washington, DC, Turner is recruited into The Order, the elite, secretive survivalist group at the center of The Organization. Throughout the novel, Turner prepares for, and participates in, violence, such as blowing up federal buildings, stockpiling biological weapons, going on racist shooting sprees, graphically cutting the throat of a Jew, and assembling pipe bombs for Jewish and black targets. In the final entry, toward the end of 1999, Turner is about to fly a crop duster with a strapped-on warhead into the Pentagon, The System's last stronghold. Although his diary ends there, we find out that The System crumbled after Turner's suicidal attack, creating a white supremacist paradise.

The group that Lane joined in 1983 was originally called the *Brüder Schweigen* (German for "Silent Brotherhood") but soon became known, in homage to Pierce's novel, as The Order. Their goal was also taken directly from the book: kick-start a race-based revolution that would ultimately lead to an all-white nation. The goal of this fictional conspiratorial organization also marked a sharp departure from the traditional mindset of groups like the KKK, which has long wanted to restore the racial order that existed decades or centuries previous. The Order didn't want to return to the Jim Crow South or even slavery; they wanted to erase blacks, Jews, and any other people they considered nonwhite from the country. What's more, the death of white Americans was an acceptable cost. As the Southern Poverty Law Center (SPLC)'s former editor-in-chief, Mark Potok, puts it, The Order marked "one of the opening shots of a truly revolutionary radical right, perfectly willing to countenance the mass murder of American civilians for their cause."[25]

The Order relocated just across the Idaho border to Metaline Falls, Washington. Timber was a big industry there and was going to fund the group, but according to former member Gary Yarbrough, logging didn't work out because "the men were a bit lazy."[26] They also failed at counterfeiting—a member was arrested for trying to pass off fake money—and robbing pimps, because they didn't know how to find them. Eventually they settled on robbing armed cars, including a $3.8-million haul in northern California, which was organized by an ideologically sympathetic employee of Brinks security.[27]

With their finances secure, The Order entered the next stage of their plan, drawing up a hit list. Number two on the list was Alan Berg. A left-wing Jewish attorney, Berg hosted a popular Denver-area radio talk show notable for its confrontational interviews and strident criticism of the far right. On the evening of June 18, 1984, Berg returned home from dinner with his ex-wife, with whom he was attempting to reconcile. He parked in his driveway and stepped out of his black Volkswagen. Automatic gunfire rang out, striking Berg twelve times. He collapsed next to his car and died almost immediately.

The following March, Lane was arrested in Winston-Salem, North Carolina, charged with driving the getaway car after Berg's shooting and was eventually convicted as an accomplice to the murder. He served twenty-two years before dying in a federal prison in Indiana in 2007.

Lane, though, did not go quietly into the night. From his prison cell, he became a prodigious writer. He was "the Renaissance man of late 20th-century white nationalism," as the SPLC once described him.[28] It was Lane, for example, who composed the famous "14 Words" for white supremacists— "We Must Secure the Existence of our People and a Future for White Children"—that turned the number "14" into a credo and coded reference for white nationalists and supremacists, including Dylann Roof. True to his conspiracy roots, he wrote that the military is controlled by Jewish bankers and that all the silver and gold is in the hands of Jews.[29] There is, however, one substantive difference between Lane's influential prison writing and the *Protocols*. In the second half of the twentieth century, the Zionists weren't *planning* to dominate the world, they had already succeeded.

William Pierce, who was reportedly surprised by the popularity of *The Turner Diaries*, once commented that he thought novels could be effective because "if the protagonist comes to believe in something . . . the reader tends to do the same thing."[30] Despite holding a doctorate degree in physics and being a former assistant professor at Oregon State University, Pierce deliberately wrote *The Turner Diaries* using very simplistic words and phrases, so anyone with a middle school level of education could read and understand it.

Certainly, that's part of his book's lasting success, but the *Diaries* tap deeply into some of the deepest and oldest narratives in Western history. In Judaism, Christianity, and Islam, a messiah leads a chosen people from a polluted earth to a golden age. End-times conspiracy theories are also a natural fit with right-wing evangelicals, survivalists, and doomsday preppers. It's no coincidence that Turner's attack takes place in 1999—the narratives of those groups often rely heavily on cycles of a thousand years.

The Turner Diaries also shares quite a bit in common with the 1999 film *The Matrix*. Early on, the protagonist, Neo, is given the option to choose between two pills: a blue one will return him to his false but comfortable life, while the red one will show him the world for what it is, a terrifying conspiracy. Neo chooses the red pill and wakes up to find out that people's conception of reality is manufactured by machines, which are actually harvesting humans for biochemical energy. He then fights back against the evil system, eventually sacrificing himself to defeat the machines. Because the movie's plot tracks perfectly with a conspiratorial mindset, the term "red-pilled" has become slang for suddenly becoming aware of a reality hidden from the mainstream.

By tapping into conspiracy theories and sweeping narratives, Pierce's "powerful teaching tool" was an incredibly effective piece of radicalizing propaganda. The FBI has called *The Turner Diaries* the "Bible of the racist right." The fantasy of being a suicidal freedom fighter against an evil conspiracy has radicalized innumerable violent extremists for years following the book's publication.

Timothy McVeigh sold the book for several years before trying to make it a reality. His choice to blow up a federal building in 1995 was directly inspired by *The Turner Diaries*, pages of which were found in his car as he fled the scene.

Three years later, in 1998, a white supremacist in Texas named John King reportedly announced, "We're starting *The Turner Diaries* early," before he and two other men dragged a black man, James Byrd, Jr., behind their pick-up truck for three miles.

In 2002, Michael Edward Smith was spotted pointing an AR-15 assault rifle at a synagogue in Nashville, Tennessee. After police apprehended him, he led them to a large cache of weapons including a shoulder-fired anti-tank weapon, armor piercing ammo, dynamite fuses, and a copy of *The Turner Diaries*.

The success of books like the *Protocols* and *The Turner Diaries* is similar to that of the Harry Potter series: both have nearly timeless fantasies. But, as frightening and, in a sense, impressive as these narratives have been for over a hundred years, social media's capacity to multiply and spread conspiracy theories has increased exponentially since 2008.

CHAPTER EIGHT

FALSE FLAGS AND THE END OF FACTS

In 2002, a figure wearing a bulletproof vest, a rubber skeleton mask, and blue fatigues with "Phantom Patriot" spelled out in red across his chest entered a two-thousand-acre redwood grove near the Russian River in California. Richard McCaslin was equipped with a specially modified double-barreled shotgun assault rifle hybrid, a .45 caliber pistol, a crossbow, knife, homemade bomb launcher, and two-foot long sword.

After making his way into the grove of old-growth redwoods, his flashlight ran out of batteries. The Phantom Patriot stumbled around in near complete darkness—the high, dense canopy didn't let in any natural light from the moon or stars. Eventually he happened upon a large bunkhouse, broke inside, and slept the night in a bed.[1]

At daylight, he continued his mission. He soon located his primary target, a giant owl statue on the edge of a small lake. McCaslin believed this was the site where an elite group of politicians and businessmen assembled annually for a ceremony in which a casket was rowed across the lake on a boat by hooded figures. Once they reached the other side, the casket was cremated at the foot of the idol while music played and fireworks went off. The Phantom Patriot also suspected child abuse and human sacrifice might be taking place.

McCaslin attempted to burn down the hollow owl statue, but it turned out to be concrete over steel supports. Instead, he placed a verse from Leviticus at the foot of the owl and set fire to a nearby mess hall. This part of his plan was also foiled by the sprinkler system. Soon thereafter he was discovered by the maintenance man and caretaker. He later surrendered peacefully to local law enforcement.

McCaslin wasn't completely delusional; all the greatest lies have a kernel of truth. He had broken into the Bohemian Grove, which does indeed host a sort of all-male elite summer camp for two weeks in July. (Participants over the years, both as members and guests, have included—just to scratch the surface—both Presidents Bush, Ronald Reagan, Richard Nixon, Colin Powell, David and Nelson Rockefeller, Teddy Roosevelt, Karl Rove, and Henry Kissinger.) There is also a bizarre "Cremation of Care" ceremony involving the owl, fires, costumes, and sound effects. But there is no reliable evidence of sexual abuse or human sacrifice.

Paroled in 2008, McCaslin came out unrepentant. Three years later, he was protesting outside an Alcoa plant in Davenport, Iowa, during President Obama's 2011 visit. The Phantom Patriot was now wearing a superhero prison outfit: a black shirt with an angry emoji face on it, black-and-white-striped pants, and a matching hat that read "THOUGHT CRIME." His sign featured a picture of the president with yellow reptilian eyes, a long red tongue, and a satanic star on his forehead. The sign read "Reptoid Royalty No Blue Bloods in the White House."[2] His protest wasn't just aimed at the current president.

"Every American president has British peerage, and royalty has always said they have the right to rule by their bloodline," McCaslin explained to a fourteen-year-old girl waiting for the motorcade. "Their ancestors weren't human; they were aliens, probably of the reptilian type."[3]

McCaslin was the sole protestor, but he was hardly alone in his beliefs. The source for his impromptu tutorial on presidents, royal bloodlines, and Satanic alien influences source was conspiracy propagandist extraordinaire Alex Jones, whose radio show has two million listeners. His website, InfoWars, has around ten million monthly visits, more than the sites for *Newsweek* or the *Economist*.[4]

By his own account, the man who would become the world's leading purveyor of conspiracy theories had a normal childhood in the suburbs of Austin, Texas. Jones's dad was a dentist, his mom a homemaker. As a teenager, he read a 1972 book titled *None Dare Call It Conspiracy* by Gary Allen, a John Birch representative. The book, which owed an obvious debt to the *Protocols*, described the actions of an international banking cartel that financed the Russian Communist revolution and is now working to enslave global populations through centralized monetary policies, income taxes, and social welfare programs, among other nefarious schemes.

Jones graduated from high school the same year as the standoff at Ruby Ridge, which left two Weavers and a federal agent dead. The following year, 1993, the federal siege of the Branch Davidian compound ended in a conflagration that killed seventy-six church members. That event, which played out in nearby Waco, Texas, prompted Jones to quit community college and begin a public-access TV program.

For the next few years, Jones honed his bombastic style while claiming that, among other things, the 1995 Oklahoma City bombing was engineered by federal agents for whom Timothy McVeigh was a patsy. In what would become a common theme following violent attacks, Jones claimed the attack was a "false flag" designed to create support for increased federal crackdown on Americans. It was, Jones said, "just like the Reichstag!"[5]

In 1996, Jones moved to Austin's KJFK-FM to host a show called *The Final Edition*. Two years later, he led an effort to rebuild the Branch Davidian church as a memorial. He also publicly assailed then Texas governor George W. Bush in person, suggesting that the Federal Reserve be dismantled.[6] Although Jones's show proved popular and he tied for the *Austin Chronicle*'s "Best Austin Talk Show Host," in 1999, he was dropped from the station for refusing to make his show more commercially accessible by engaging a wider range of topics.

For Jones, this temporary setback ultimately paved the way to great riches. He began broadcasting his radio show online. As the medium rapidly expanded, Jones built up a massive base that stuck with him even after station managers dropped him for claiming that 9/11 was an inside-government job.

"Those were controlled demolitions," Jones told his audience. "You just watched the government blow up the World Trade Center."[7]

A few years later, Jones began posting on YouTube, the massive video-sharing platform that would essentially become his promoter. Like other online formats, video sharing provided an end run around mainstream media that considered his claims ludicrous. What's more, as the site developed algorithms to encourage people to spend as much time as possible on YouTube, it also, inadvertently, began pushing Jones's videos.

Guillaume Chaslot, a software engineer in artificial intelligence who worked on the site's recommendation engine, remembers noticing between 2010 and 2011 that YouTube's algorithms began steering people toward conspiracy videos. As NBC News reported, Chaslot found that "the best way to get people to spend more time on YouTube was to show them videos light on facts but rife with wild speculation."[8] At about the same time as extremists of various stripes began making use of Facebook, Twitter, encrypted communications, and other technologies to promote their marginalized ideas and plan attacks, Jones was getting a huge boost from YouTube.

Aside from having the world's largest video platform on his side, Jones also enjoyed huge exposure to mainstream conservatives post-2008, thanks to Matt Drudge. The Drudge Report, one of the most popular websites on the right, had gained adherents in the late 1990s by breaking news like the Monica Lewinsky scandal. In the two years beginning April 2011, Drudge linked to 244 different articles on Jones's websites InfoWars and PrisonPlanet.[9]

The mainstream right was thus exposed to man whose career was built on an almost limitless number of unsupported and far-fetched claims including, but not nearly limited to: NASA's footage of the moon landing was faked, the Federal Emergency Management Agency is setting up concentration camps for American citizens, and the US government is deploying chemically laced juice boxes to encourage homosexuality so people won't have children.

Jones also popularized the idea that the government used weather weapons to geo-engineer, for example, Hurricane Irma and the 2013 Oklahoma tornado outbreak. Further, Bill Gates is a eugenicist, Lady Gaga's 2017 Super Bowl halftime show was a satanic ritual, and right-wing Fox News commentator Glenn Beck is a CIA plant.[10]

Jones dependably claims just about every mass shooting is a "false flag" event, including the Sandy Hook Elementary School massacre in 2012. Similarly, according to Jones, James Holmes's 2012 attack in an Aurora,

Colorado, movie theater—which spawned the fake, media-trolling "Holmies" fan club—may have been the result of CIA mind control.

Jones also smelled something fishy when Andrew Breitbart, the founder of Breitbart News Network and Matt Drudge's first staffer, died—Jones suggested that he may have been poisoned. Every time The Drudge Report linked to Jones's material, the possibility that these conspiracy theories weren't crazy got incrementally higher.

But the recent spread of conspiracy theories also owes a debt to the self-destructing mainstream media.

In late August 1968, Gore Vidal, then one of the most famous authors in America, called William F. Buckley, Jr., the leading man of the academic right, a "crypto-fascist" on live television. Suddenly enraged on the drab soundstage, Buckley shot back: "Now listen, you queer, stop calling me a crypto-Nazi or I'll sock you in the goddamn face and you'll stay plastered."[11]

The two men, political opposites who deeply loathed one another, had been paired off by ABC News to debate the Republican and Democratic conventions. It was an experiment created out of desperation. ABC News lagged far behind NBC and CBS in ratings and couldn't afford the traditional full-time coverage of the conventions. Instead they presented daily debates between the two men, which resulted in verbal fireworks and, in this climax, a slur and threat of violence.

The debates were unlike anything anyone had seen before on television, an "intrusion of full-contact punditry into the staid pastures of the evening news."[12] ABC gained a ratings boom with the debate model and the lesson for television executives was clear. As screenwriter Aaron Sorkin put it: "Incivility rates."[13]

When Cable News Network (CNN) first went on air twelve years after the 1968 debates, its main focus was providing a constant stream of news—differentiating itself from the networks that had news only at certain times of the day. In 1996, a competitor, Fox News, began eating into CNN's market share with reporting and opinion shows slanted right.

That same year, MSNBC was also introduced to the cable-news market but languished in the rankings for almost a dozen years until networks executives began introducing more opinionated and openly left-leaning coverage. The strategy worked: Between 2008 and 2016, MSNBC began overtaking CNN in key audience metrics. By 2012, the *New York Times* was referring to the network as the "Anti-Fox."[14] The new lesson for news executives: "Partisanship rates."

Those two elements—Vidal-Buckley-style shout fests, mixed with intense partisanship and large doses of opinion—have increasingly become the way Americans learn about the world. By 2016, 57 percent of Americans were getting their news from television, but—unlike in 1968—virtually equal numbers of people were watching cable TV versus the previously dominant network news.[15]

While the ratings formula may work, the disappearance of actual reporting from cable news is marked. According to a 2013 Pew research poll, CNN is the only of the three leading networks to broadcast more reporting than opinion and commentary. Right-leaning Fox's programming was 55 percent opinion while left-leaning MSNBC's broadcast content was 85 percent opinion-based.[16]

Additionally, as cable news networks created visions of the world that were not just different from each other but in stark opposition, they fed off of and fomented the same angry dynamic as the political parties for which they increasingly acted as appendages. In January 2016, a poll by NBC and *Esquire* found that the news made 67 percent of Democrats and 77 percent of Republicans angry at least once a day.[17]

In the 1990s, Fox News created a broadcast model premised on, as author David Neiwert puts it, coaching "half of America to hate the other half."[18] By 2008, that dynamic had accelerated two-fold. MSNBC realized it could stake out a place in the massive American market simply by positioning itself as the opposite of Fox. For the rest of President Obama's term, over two-thirds of the cable news ecosystem was controlled by two channels belittling or contradicting the opinions of the other. During the Obama administration, according to a biography of Fox News CEO Roger Ailes, "the right-wing media and the Republican Party started to fuse into this single entity."[19]

The roughly 38 percent of Americans primarily getting their news online were subject to an even more partisan and fact-free zone. Both left-leaning websites like Daily Kos, BuzzFeed, and Huffington Post, and right-tilting sites like The Drudge Report, Daily Caller, and The Blaze tended toward skewed partisan bias or even lies.[20]

All this bickering and transparent partisanship led the sources of news for the majority of Americans to suffer the same fate as the nation's political parties. Following 2008, the public's trust in television news—as well as other forms of mass media—plummeted. In 1976, following the Watergate exposé, Americans' confidence in the media hit 72 percent. Throughout the late 1990s and early 2000s, it was lower, but still stayed above 50 percent. By 2009, fewer than half of Americans expressed a great deal or fair amount of trust in the media. By 2016, that level of faith had plummeted to 32 percent.

Extremists and conspiracists have always attacked the media, established arbiters of truth, because it casts doubt on their own. David Lane lambasted the "JEWSMEDIA," while Atlanta Olympics bomber Eric Rudolph and The Order founder Robert Jay Mathews called television "the Electronic Jew." From 2008 onward, mainstream media's hostile and oppositional environment was creating confusion, anger, and historically low levels of trust. This dynamic was both a self-inflicted wound and a huge gift to conspiracists like Alex Jones.

One other unlikely stream fed into the decay of mainstream authority. At least since the 1960s, academics have been opening up, dismantling, and deconstructing meaning and narratives. Over the past several decades, the establishment of "identity politics, post-modernism, hollowness of meaning, polyphony of narratives, safe spaces et al became dominant."[21] Ironically, these efforts—long associated with the left and repeatedly lambasted by conservatives—have recently been most effectively employed by right-wing extremists. 4chan trolls and conspiracy theorists have taken quite happily to "undermining media agendas" and promoting "alternative narratives."

Likewise, the literary criticism that became widespread in American universities in the 1980s argued that a text was open to multiple interpretations, there was no baseline truth. Again, conspiracy theorists ran with these ideas, but the result was not multiple truths in some sort of rigorous academic context. For better or worse, this academic critique was generally aimed at complicating or "problematizing" the truth.

Conspiracy theories do the opposite. They argue that mainstream reality is fake, flawed, or only one possibility, but then replace it with incredibly simplistic—if convoluted—explanation for the nature of reality. Alex Jones, for example, promotes theories that are both wild and incredibly predictable. Essentially, any major event, political figure or institution isn't what it seems, and it all links back to secret cabals running the world, trying to take away the docile, unaware masses' liberties.

Despite all of Jones's success in claiming the mantle of the world's best-known conspiracy theorist, it's clear that he isn't always in control of the fantasy universe he's played such a large role in creating. In 2015, Jones challenged David Duke to a debate after Duke said Jones's claims about FEMA concentration camps were delusional. However, Jones was forced to delete the video of the interview after Duke received overwhelming support from not just his white supremacist base, but from Jones's own fan base.

The problem for Jones was that his ideas are so similar in form to the anti-Jewish *Protocols* that he attracts people who then attack him for not being explicitly anti-Semitic enough. In fact, Jones, whose ex-wife is Jewish, has been labeled an Israeli agent and plagued on Twitter by the hashtag #jewwife.

Although he tries to avoid the most obvious anti-Semitism, Jones has made clear that "true patriots" need to violently resist encroachments on their freedoms. Unfortunately, several people who have listened or watched his shows and "documentaries" have adopted a *Turner Diaries* style of activism.

In 2010, Byron Williams engaged in a twelve-minute firefight with police in Oakland, California, after a traffic stop. Inspired in part by Jones, Williams was on his way to kill people at the American Civil Liberties Union (ACLU) and left-leaning Tides Foundation in San Francisco and start a right-wing revolution.

In 2011, an Idaho man, Oscar Ortega, traveled across country to assassinate President Obama. His inspiration: the Jones-written and produced *The Obama Deception: The Mask Comes Off*, which describes how the president worked with the New World Order by turning the US into Nazi Germany and imprisoning Americans in FEMA camps.

That same year, Jared Loughner killed six people including a nine-year-old girl at an event in Tucson, Arizona, in which US representative Gabby Giffords was speaking. (Giffords was nearly killed as well.) Loughner was a fan of the Jones-produced *Loose Change*, as well as the *Zeitgeist* trio of conspiracy films about the international monetary system that heavily borrowed ideas and examples from Jones.

In 2013, a family member of Boston Marathon bomber Tamerlan Tsarnaev revealed that, in addition to jihadi sites, Tsarnaev took an interest in InfoWars. True to form, Jones claimed that the incident, which killed three runners and two police officers and injured 260 people, was an FBI plot.[22]

It would be incredibly simplistic and irresponsible to claim that conspiracy theories resulted in this violence. In most, if not all, of these cases, the perpetrators suffered from weakened inhibitors and strong destabilizers like anger or grievance. But the combination of psychological factors and angry, extremist ideas certainly played a significant role in creating the potential for violence directed at certain groups.

In the fall of 2016, Alex Jones—along with 4chan anons, certain reddit communities, and even future national security advisor Michael Flynn propagated the "Pizzagate" conspiracy theory. Based on supposedly close readings of the emails of Hillary Clinton's campaign manager, the theory claimed that high-ranking Democratic Party officials, including presidential candidate Hillary Clinton, were operating a sex ring involving minors. The theory, which became connected to a Washington, DC, pizza restaurant called Comet Ping Pong, was a weird mix of trolling, pseudo-ironic humor, and hardcore conspiracy theory.

Nonetheless, Comet Ping Pong employees were harassed via social media and phones, even receiving death threats. Then, in December of 2016, Edgar Welch, a registered Republican from the small town of Salisbury, North Carolina, drove up to Washington, DC, to "self-investigate" these myths. Welch, who had no previous history of violence, entered the crowded restaurant with an AR-15 assault rifle and a .38 caliber handgun. After people fled through the back door, Welch fired three shots in the restaurant and began searching for the tunnels through which children were reportedly being smuggled.

Though Welch found no one and surrendered peacefully, this fantastic and violent intrusion into the real world wasn't over. Welch still refused to accept that the story wasn't true. More disturbingly, a poll taken two days *after* the shooting showed that nearly one in ten registered voters thought Pizzagate's claims were true—and one in five weren't sure.[23]

In other words, slightly fewer than fifty million registered US voters were either convinced or open to the idea that former first lady, senator, and secretary of state Hillary Clinton was involved in a child-sex ring based out of pizza restaurant in Washington, DC. This incident revealed a nation that had gone beyond even the hyper-partisanship long practiced by both parties. Believing such a serious accusation without a shred of evidence is more akin to mass hallucination.

But it was also the result of a very specific combination of factors, all of them related to social media. Over the course of 2008–2016, this new media ecosystem overrun with conspiracy theories provided the unstable platform for the reemergence of some nearly forgotten extremist movements with long histories of violence.

PART III

RETURN OF THE REPRESSED

CHAPTER NINE

PANTHERS, PATRIOTS, POLICE, AND SOVEREIGNS

Eighteen-year-old Aaron Dixon sat in the front row of his high-school auditorium while Stokely Carmichael, chairman of the Student Non-Violent Coordinating Committee, delivered a fiery speech. Dixon, who had bought Ray-Ban Wayfarer sunglasses just for the event, hung on Carmichael's every word. The well-known civil rights leader pushed past the mainstream rhetoric of the 1950s and early 60s. It was 1967: "We Shall Overcome" was out; "Black Power!" was in.

In his memoir *My People Are Rising*, Dixon remembers, "A slow current of anger began to brew inside me, and to my mind whites were now the cause of all the problems that Black people faced."[1]

Dixon had grown up in a solid family in a segregated neighborhood in Seattle. His parents, who had relocated their family from Chicago to get away from the city's endemic crime, preached the importance of school and hard work. By 1967, Dixon was already politically and socially active. A few years earlier, he had marched with Martin Luther King, Jr., to end housing segregation in Seattle. More recently, he had volunteered to be on the frontlines of integration, busing to the mostly white high school where Carmichael gave his speech.

As he sat in the auditorium amidst repeated shouts of "Black Power!," Dixon was relatively well grounded, but new destabilizers, including anger, rebellion, and grievance, were strengthening. Like every other radicalization process, Dixon's would weave together personal traits and external forces. But, unlike many other examples in this book, his process would be driven by a pervasive, stifling sense that injustice was being visited upon African Americans.

The steady stream of violence on the television news over the past four years—the beatings of King and his nonviolent marchers, the assassinations of civil rights leader Medgar Evers and Malcolm X, John F. Kennedy's murder, and devastating nightly reports from Vietnam—had been steadily eroding Dixon's faith in nonviolent approaches to changing the political establishment. Encountering Stokely Carmichael brought him face-to-face with an electric, charismatic force.

"I walked out of the auditorium transformed," Dixon later wrote. "I was not the same person who had entered. From that day forward, I looked at the world and everyone around me with anger and rage."[2]

A year later, the other shoe dropped. On April 4, 1968, King was assassinated, deadly riots erupted in over a hundred cities across the country, and Carmichael called for black people to get guns to defend themselves. A few weeks later, Aaron Dixon formed the Seattle branch of the Black Panther Party (BPP).

The BPP had begun two years earlier in Oakland, California, to monitor police harassment of people in black neighborhoods. Armed citizen patrols trailed police through majority African American parts of the city with their guns in full view. When confronted by police, they claimed they had broken no laws and were merely exercising their rights under California's open-carry provisions.

The following year, the group exploded into the nation's consciousness after more than a dozen armed members entered the California State Assembly during debate over the Mulford Act, which would make open-carry illegal. The images of young black men with sunglasses, berets, leather jackets, and shotguns occupying the stately building was either terrifying or energizing, depending on who you were. It was also an amazing publicity coup.

The Panthers had expanded their local recruitment through social programs, like free breakfasts for kids and a community medical and legal aid center, but guns were central to their identity. Along with an ideology influenced by worldwide revolutionary Communist struggle—they bought some of their first firearms with money earned from selling copies of Communist leader Mao Zedong's *Little Red Book*—guns were the single biggest difference between the rising black militancy of the late 1960s and early 1970s and the previous, emphatically nonviolent civil rights movement.

The BPP was also defined by its complex and violent relationship with law enforcement. When Dixon set up his Seattle branch in 1968, he emulated the Oakland Black Panthers' modus operandi by providing what was normally law-enforcement and social-service functions in African American neighborhoods. Seattle Panthers provided a food pantry, resolved landlord and domestic disputes, engaged drug dealers to limit violence, and aggressively monitored Seattle's virtually all-white police force.

As in other cities, Seattle's Black Panthers soon migrated from watching law enforcement to replacing the police and government. Party members marched freely with weapons through the majority-black Madrona Hill. On the few occasions that the Seattle police came to the neighborhood, they never left their cars.[3]

The flip side of relatively peacefully replacing police was out-and-out warfare between the two groups. In 1968, two days after MLK was gunned down in Memphis, the Black Panther Party's Minister of Information, Eldridge Cleaver, led two other party members in an armed ambush of Oakland police officers that resulted in two officers being injured. Cleaver himself was wounded and another Panther killed.

In November of 1969, a shootout between Black Panthers and Chicago police left two police officers and one party member dead. The next month, the Chicago police and the FBI raided the apartment of Illinois BPP leader Fred Hampton in the early morning, killing Hampton and member Mark Clark. The well-orchestrated attack on Hampton's apartment was alleged to be an orchestrated assassination by the Afro-American Patrolmen's League and the white mayor of nearby Maywood, Illinois.[4] For the Panthers and police, though, the bad times were just beginning.

In 1965, the Watts riots in Los Angeles, initiated by alleged police brutality after officers pulled over an African American motorist, had totally overwhelmed the Los Angeles Police Department. To restore order, thousands of National Guardsmen were deployed. Even then, the riots lasted five days and resulted in thirty-four fatalities.

Afterward, police in Los Angeles began looking for solutions to extraordinary circumstances like urban unrest, mass shooters, and armed extremist groups like the Black Panthers. A new select group of volunteer officers was put under command of Inspector Daryl Gates to receive additional training in Special Weapons and Tactics (SWAT). In 1968, the new police unit was granted extraordinary powers by the California legislature, but it wasn't until December 9, 1969—two days after Fred Hampton's shooting—that the new SWAT teams saw their first significant deployment.

Forewarned by the Chicago attack, the LA branch of the BPP was well-prepared for a police raid on its own headquarters. They turned their house into a fortified bunker with sandbags against walls and a supply of tear gas masks, as well as a well-stocked arsenal. Party members had even spotted the initial police approach on their house and shot and wounded three cops, who were dragged away by their fellow officers. But no one could have expected what happened next.

The raid turned into a long-running shootout in a crowded urban neighborhood. Streets were shut down. Gates eventually called the Pentagon to get approval to use a grenade launcher. To cordoned-off bystanders, it looked like Vietnam had come home. As a tank was preparing for a final assault on their house, the Black Panthers surrendered.

Party members were acquitted of the most serious charges brought against them, including attempted murder of police officers; the jury found they had acted in self-defense. Nonetheless, the high-profile use of SWAT units, who replaced standard-issue six-shot revolvers with submachine guns, tanks, and grenade launchers, provided a militarized policing model the rest of the nation soon followed.

In 1969, FBI Director J. Edgar Hoover declared that the Black Panther Party was "the greatest threat to the internal security of the country."[5] Over the next few years, the bureau launched an extensive, and sometimes illegal, effort to infiltrate the group, harass and publicly humiliate members, and incite violence between the Black Panthers and other black militant groups and street gangs.

After only a few years of the program, known as COINTELPRO, many BPP leaders were either dead, imprisoned, or in exile, and the party itself was splintered by power struggles and paranoia stoked by FBI informants and forged letters. Black militant extremist activity dropped off sharply after the early 1970s. However, the use of militarized police tactics had only just begun.

Beginning in the 1970s, the use of SWAT teams rapidly grew as part of President Richard Nixon's war on drugs. In 1972, police launched a few hundred SWAT-led paramilitary raids across the United States. By the early 1980s, there were three thousand such raids annually.

The 1981 Military Cooperation with Law Enforcement Act furthered the link between policing and the military by providing military intelligence and weapons to local law enforcement. As Michelle Alexander wrote in *The New Jim Crow*, that legislation made official the ongoing transformation of police operations by carving "a huge exception to the Posse Comitatus Act, the Civil War-era law prohibiting the use of the military for community policing."[6]

In preparation for the 1984 Los Angeles Olympics, Mayor Tom Bradley authorized Daryl Gates, by then chief of the LAPD, to round up all known and suspected gang members and hold them until the conclusion of the games. Despite the measure's likely intrusion on habeas corpus rights—most of the detainees were never charged—those types of sweeps continued to be used by the LAPD. Both the militarization of police and the holding of people on suspicion of crime troubled some civil liberties advocates but, largely because the tactics were deployed against poor and mostly African American and other minority groups, there was not a huge public backlash.

Nonetheless, African Americans' widespread sense of being under siege by an unjust use of law enforcement continued to stoke a kind of righteous anger similar to what Aaron Dixon felt when he joined the Black Panther Party. In some cases, such as the rioting following the acquittal of police officers filmed beating black motorist Rodney King, this hostility toward law enforcement expressed itself as destructive rage.

But in other cases, the combination of poverty, lack of future prospects, anger, and grievance created fertile ground for new cases of radical-ization. In 1997, for example, the shooting of a mentally unstable African American man in Watts energized the creation of the Black Riders Lib-eration Party, a Black Nationalist and anti-capitalist group. Two other extremist groups, the New Black Panther Party and Huey P. Newton Gun Club, emerged in the public outrage that followed police shootings of black men. By 2015, these groups' hate-filled extremism was available to everyone online. Among others, Micah Johnson visited their website prior to killing five Dallas police officers. The websites alone didn't cause his violence, but they certainly played a role in his choice of targets.

The continued use of the aggressive, militarized law enforcement tech-niques first tested on the left-wing Black Panthers in the 1960s had a less likely impact nearly thirty years later: inspiring a massive wave of mostly white and right-wing paramilitary militias.

The aggressive response to a weapons charge at Ruby Ridge was based on tactics first used against the Black Panther Party and largely African American rioters in the 1960s. In the form of drug raids, the same tactics had been disproportionately used against people of color throughout the 1970s and 80s. But after those tactics resulted in the death of two white survivalists, outrage spread among a certain subsection of right-wing extremists. John Trochmann, a forty-eight-year-old veteran of the white supremacist movement centered in Noxon, Montana, in the 1980s, called for "private citizen armies" to defend local communities from out-of-con-trol law enforcement. Trochmann's reaction to perceived police harass-ment was essentially the Black Panther model relocated from the inner city to small town America.

The aggressive law enforcement efforts at the Branch Davidian complex in Waco, Texas—which also had their genesis in the militarized assault on the LA-based BPP's compound—further ratcheted up right-wing extremist paranoia and hostility. Like inner-city African Americans, many rural whites felt like they were under attack by an unjust govern-ment that was always on the verge of suspending habeas corpus and imprisoning Americans without due process. The resulting atmosphere, full of anger, paranoia, grievance, and a desire for revenge created the sort of external forces that encouraged the radicalization and the emergence of the 1990s Patriot and militia movements—as well as the Black Riders Liberation Party and Huey P. Newton Gun Club.

The paranoia of right-wing militias and Patriot groups in the early 1990s was also heightened by the successful passage of two gun control measures, the so-called Brady Bill, which created a five-day waiting period on purchases, the other a ban on certain assault rifles. For people already expecting the federal government to strip constitutional protections, this confirmed their worst fears.

What's more, the high-powered weapons now available to militarized law enforcement convinced militias and Patriot groups that not only did they need guns to stave off the encroaching feds, they couldn't protect their freedoms with anything less than an AR-15.

In a 1994 feature for *Guns & Ammo* magazine titled "Freedom's Last Stand—Are You Willing to Fight for Your Guns?," the author declared, "We cannot hope to prevail against a tyrannical government armed with fully automatic weapons when we are reduced to bolt actions or worse."[7] Militias were spurred into an arms race with increasingly militarized law enforcement.

Radicalization across the political spectrum starts with a combination of psychological factors and external radicalizing factors like ideologies, activities, and leaders. So, ultimately, it's not really that surprising that some ideologically opposed extremist groups overlapped at places. In this case, both the Communist, black militant Black Panther Party of the 1960s and 70s and the right-wing extremist militias of the 1990s shared an angry and violent distrust of law enforcement and intelligence agencies. A perception of injustice and persecution fueled their respective movements. There were, however, groups that even more steadfastly opposed not just law enforcement, but the legitimacy of government at all.

Posse Comitatus is a case in point. An anti-Semitic, white supremacist ideology born in California but formalized in Portland, Oregon, Posse Comitatus's adherents claimed that no citizen has to submit to any authority higher than a county sheriff, vehicle registration is illegal, and paying taxes is sinful.

The movement spread slowly across the country during the 1970s, then took off by recruiting victims of the 1980s farm crisis. People devastated by the loss of their farms were particularly susceptible to false claims that the catastrophe was the result of hidden forces such as leaving the gold standard, Jewish bankers, or the Jewish-controlled Federal Reserve.

After an early 1980s explosion in membership and violence, many of the leaders of Posse Comitatus groups were arrested, imprisoned, or killed in shootouts with law enforcement by the end of the decade. However, the movement's anti-government message and embrace of violent resistance didn't fade with the eclipse of Posse Comitatus itself.

In mid-afternoon on August 19, 1997, New Hampshire state trooper Scott Phillips pulled over a pickup truck at an IGA supermarket in the tiny town of Colebrook. Phillips knew the driver, sixty-two-year-old Carl Drega, was a bit of a nutcase. He was sure Drega wouldn't be happy to be informed his vehicle was too rusty for the road. But, still, Officer Phillips didn't expect Drega to pull out an AR-15.

Phillips escaped to a nearby field and fired back, but Drega—who had the more powerful weapon—followed and killed him. Drega then shot and killed another state trooper, Leslie Lord, who had followed the men into the field.

Drega walked back to Phillip's cruiser and drove over to the offices of the Colebrook *News and Sentinel*. Vickie Bunnell, a lawyer and judge who shared offices with the newspaper, had been terrified of Drega for years. When she saw Drega coming toward the building this time, Bunnell jumped up and yelled: "It's Carl! He's got a gun! Get out!"[8]

Bunnell fled out the back door, but Drega still managed to kill her, shooting from about thirty feet away. He also killed a newspaper editor who tried to tackle him.

Drega hopped back in the cruiser and drove to his house, which he burned to the ground. He then put on Phillips's hat and drove across the nearby Connecticut River into Vermont. Fish and conservation officer Wayne Saunders recognized Phillips's car and thought it had been dumped in the woods after some kids took it for a joy ride. But as Saunders approached, Drega began firing. One of his rounds struck Saunders's badge, fragmenting into shrapnel that went into his shoulder and arm.

Drega fled back into New Hampshire, where he waited to ambush the other officers in pursuit. He wounded two more state troopers and a border patrol agent before being shot dead.

On one hand, this was the bloody saga of a loner who cracked. But there was a telling backstory to Drega's rampage. Twenty-five years earlier, in 1972, Drega's wife had died from cancer on the same day he was scheduled to appear before the local council, the Columbia Board of Selectmen, to discuss permitting for a barn he was building on his riverfront property. Some in the community thought he blamed the selectmen for her death. Whatever the case, that incident presaged a long history of paranoia and animosity toward any kind of legal authority.[9]

After being told the soil he'd dumped on the shoreline in front of his house was changing the river's course, Drega took a fish and conservation officer to court. Years later, when a tax accessor visited his property, Drega came out armed, ordered him to leave, and impounded his car. When Selectman Bunnell arrived to deal with the situation, Drega fired shots over both their heads. Paranoid, Drega always carried a rifle to get his mail. After his death, a search of the burnt remains of his property found a large stash of ammunition and explosives. And while Drega had no known association with extremist groups, he had signed correspondence as a "Sovereign Citizen."

Speaking about the shooting twenty years later, fish and game officer Kevin Jordan remembered, "We all thought he was a joke."[10] And, although Sovereign Citizens are well known to harass, and sometimes attack, lawyers, law enforcement, tax collectors, and other public officials, their bizarre ideology sounds comical at first.

A loosely organized group of individuals, Sovereign Citizens believe that all forms of state and federal government are illegitimate. The endless and convoluted pseudo-legalese that supports these beliefs is a combination of unconventional theories cobbled together from the Magna Carta,

Bible, English common law, various nineteenth-century state constitutions, and the US Constitution, among other sources.

Take their claims that the traditional responsibilities of citizenship don't apply to them, which stretch credulity to the breaking point. For example, the Fourteenth Amendment, which granted slaves full citizenship rights, reputedly also created a separate "corporate" United States, with jurisdiction restricted to Washington, DC, Guam, Puerto Rico, and other federal enclaves like military bases and Native American reservations. The people born in those areas are called "Fourteenth Amendment citizens" and have to follow federal laws. Everyone born outside of federal authority is a "freeman" or "natural-born person" and not subject to US, or state, laws.

Sovereign Citizens also argue that the only true form of government is "de jure," or one comprised of the American people and inspired by God. What are generally considered the legitimate US and state governments are regarded as "de facto," fraudulent, man-made institutions and codes that don't apply to freemen. In short, as a Sovereign Citizen, Drega would have believed that permits, building codes, vehicle inspections, conservation officers, judges, lawyers, selectmen, and police officers were all harassing manifestations of an illegitimate government bent on enslaving him. Note that all Drega's targets—save the newspaper editor who tried to tackle him—were representatives of the legal system and law enforcement whose authority he refused to recognize.

Drega, it needs to be noted, was something of an outlier among Sovereign Citizens. Rather than violent insurrection, most adherents were involved in white-collar scams, like offering reputedly legal ways of escaping taxes, zoning ordinances, or other claims against them.

They might, for example, explain to clients that signing their name on any legal documents—contracts, social security cards, driver's licenses—meant accepting enslavement to federal laws. If they do sign such documents, Sovereign Citizens often insert inappropriate grammatical marks, like "Doe; John"—and then claim that, legally, this person is not the "John Doe" created by the government. Sovereign Citizens may also offer "asseveration" documents to liberate clients from federal and state laws and claims, returning them to their natural state.

In court, Sovereigns also often play with the formal elements of language as part of their defense. "Sovereigns believe," notes the SPLC, "that if they can find just the right combination of words, punctuation, paper, ink color and timing, they can have anything they want—freedom from taxes, unlimited wealth, and life without licenses, fees or laws, are all just a few strangely worded documents away."[11]

In one criminal case heard in US district court, for example, judges noted that the defendant and other Sovereign Citizens were "fascinated by capitalization. They appear to believe that capitalizing names have some sort of legal effect." The court added that the defendant "appears to believe that by capitalizing 'United States,' he is referring to a different entity than the federal government. For better or for worse, it's the same country."[12]

But no matter how invalid their arguments are, courts often puzzle over exactly how to deal with the nonsense. In that case, the court "feels some measure of responsibility to inform Defendant that all the fancy legal-sounding things he has read on the internet are make-believe."[13]

Sovereign Citizen gurus have also organized seminars, charging up to $1,000 or more per person, to demonstrate how to file a phony Corporation Sole. Participants are manipulated into believing that their counterfeit Corporation Sole provides a "legal" way to avoid paying income taxes, child support, and other personal debts by hiding their assets in a tax-exempt entity.

Like their ideological forebears in the Posse Comitatus, many Sovereign Citizens are white supremacists and anti-Semitic. More than a few have resorted to violence. But at the core of Sovereign Citizens' beliefs is a deep disparagement of any kind of legal entity or law enforcement. And this turned out to be a quality that made Sovereign Citizen ideology attractive to a wider circle of people, including African Americans.

In the early twentieth century, African Americans began to move in large numbers from the South to escape oppressive racism and get better paying jobs. The migration created a higher standard of living for many, but moving away from family in the rural South to factory jobs in the Northeast and Midwest left many African Americans stressed, frustrated, and confused about who they were.

In 1913, one of these Southern transplants, calling himself Noble Drew Ali, founded the Moorish Science Temple of America in the booming industrial town of Newark, New Jersey. Drew's religion was based on a wide-ranging syncretism, including a reputedly lost section of the Koran and a description of Jesus's travels in India, Egypt, and Palestine during the years not accounted for in the Bible. Drew also claimed that African Americans are descendants of the biblical Moabites and should be called "Moors" as opposed to Black, Colored, or Negro. His mysticism and Moorish pride appealed to many of the immigrants lost in a strange industrial environment.

Soon, Moorish churches sprang up in every city with large African American populations—New York, Detroit, and Washington, DC, among them. By the 1930s, Drew had gained thousands of adherents, but his religion's greatest influence was on two other African American groups.

The first, and most direct, began when a Moorish leader named Wallace Fard Muhammad left the Moorish Temple in Chicago and began preaching his own syncretic brand of Islam in Detroit. His organization, also aimed at newly arrived African American migrants, became known as the Nation of Islam.

The second, and much less predictable, reemergence of Moorish thinking began in the 1990s when some of the religion's terms and ideas combined with Sovereign Citizens' philosophy. From Moorish Science came the idea that African Americans are of Moorish ancestry, primarily from an enlarged Moroccan Empire. (Moorish adherents often use "Bey" or "El" in their names to represent rejection of their slave names.)

From Sovereign Citizens came other pseudo-legal justifications that African Americans constituted an elite class within American society and are beyond federal and state authority.[14] In addition to traditional claims concerning a repudiation of the illegitimate "de facto" federal and state government—as well as their laws, taxes, ordinances, permits, licensing, and so on—Moorish Sovereigns claim they were given special rights because of a 1778 treaty between the United States and Morocco.

While embracing descent from African "Moors," Moorish groups also sometimes claim to be indigenous to the Americas. In fact, one of the earliest groups to merge Moorish Science and Sovereign Citizen ideas was the "Washitaw Nation," whose Empress Verdiacee Turner Goston asserted that Moors are the rightful owners of all lands ceded to the United States in the Louisiana Purchase.[15] She also claimed that the Washitaw Nation occupies the fictitious United Nations Indigenous People's Seat 215.

Beyond the grand claims to land and titles, much of the day-to-day work of Moorish Sovereigns closely resembled that of their white counterparts. They offered training seminars that taught legal financial scams and methods to avoid paying taxes. They sold a wide variety of bogus legal documents and permits such as fake license plates and counterfeit passports.[16] Some particularly bold members occupied expensive, empty houses, presenting fake ownership deeds when questioned. On occasion, they have also been involved in violent encounters with law enforcement.

Moorish Sovereigns occupy a unique space in the extremist universe. They find common ground with black nationalists in their promotion of African American heritage and identity. Some Moors claim the middle third of the country, while black separatists often claim a large part of the southern United States as a homeland. On the other hand, they've never formed a mass movement with specific demands, and their bizarre legalese is directly descended from white supremacists.

By 2007, the Patriot movement was still a shadow of its former self, and black nationalists hadn't been a major threat for over thirty years. But this silence wouldn't last much longer. The deep inventory of fear, paranoia, and hate directed at the government, particularly its law enforcement and legal system, was about to erupt again. First the militias and Sovereign Citizens and, later, black militant groups—extremists whose heydays had been separated by decades—all saw historic increases in activity. Between 2008 and 2016, it was as if the preceding four decades of anti-police extremism had been condensed into a much smaller time and space.

But not only were all these extremist actors in play at once, these groups were also re-emerging into a country where politics, media, and even intrapersonal relationships were now processed through a web-enabled, hyper-partisan, outrage-fueled, troll-driven, click-hungry, conspiracy-laced, all-immersive media culture. This time, any actions—even peaceful ones—ricocheted rapidly around the media ecosystem, creating a uniquely American conflagration.

CHAPTER TEN

OATH KEEPERS, THREE PERCENTERS, AND STRANGE BEDFELLOWS

April 19, 2009: A Yale-educated lawyer in his thirties looked out from a small wooden podium on the village green in the center of Lexington, Massachusetts. There were under a few hundred people in attendance, but forty-three-year-old Elmer Stewart Rhodes could see a movement afoot. On the 234th anniversary of the first battles of the American Revolution—and the 14th anniversary of the Oklahoma City bombing—Rhodes had come to speak about the existential threats facing the country today. Under a cloudless sky, Rhodes warned the crowd that their freedoms existed on a knife's edge.

"You need to be alert and aware," he warned, "to the reality of how close we are to having our constitutional republic destroyed."[1]

Rhodes was a gun-rights columnist for *SWAT* magazine, a libertarian who had been a volunteer coordinator for Congressman Ron Paul. He was also a former army paratrooper injured during a night jump, a lawyer with a strong constitutionalist bent, and a devout Christian. Over the past year, he'd begun blogging about his concerns that the government was already eroding and, ultimately, dead set on extinguishing Americans' constitutional rights.

His political message, spiced up with a few Bill Clinton jokes, resonated with many of the history buffs in attendance. Rhodes's politics could also be divined by some of the other notables in the crowd that day. One was former sheriff Richard Mack, whose refusal to enforce the Brady Bill waiting period for gun purchases made him a hero of Rhodes.

Another familiar face in the crowd was that of Mike Vanderboegh, a fifty-seven-year-old veteran of the 1990s militia movement. Following the 1993 Waco standoff, Vanderboegh had authored an article called "Strategy and Tactics for a Militia Civil War" in which he lauded snipers who could take out "enemy forces" such as law enforcement and the intelligence groups tracking the militia movement.

Schisms let loose by the Oklahoma City bombing had weakened the militia movement, and George W. Bush's presidency had sent it into steep decline, but by 2009, the militia movement was back, and so was Vanderboegh. He founded a group called the Three Percenters (also styled 3%ers, III%ers or 3pers) who had vowed to resist gun laws—violently, if necessary.

His group was based on the idea that, over two centuries earlier, only three percent of colonials had taken up arms against the British.[2] But that small, dedicated group was able to force out the most powerful military in the world. Vanderboegh stood on the hallowed ground where Americans began their resistance against a mighty empire, ready to do so again—except this time the American government was the oppressor.

On stage, Rhodes was lambasting the most recent threat to liberty: intelligence analysts at the Department of Homeland Security (DHS). Their just-released 2009 report had warned that a confluence of events, including an African American Democratic president, a weak economy, and the current high employment rate, could lead to a surge in right-wing extremism.

Like *Washington Times* columnist Michelle Malkin and multiple Republican politicians, Rhodes blasted the report as an attack on conservatives everywhere. "The No. 1 focus of DHS is not Islamic terrorists—it is me and you," said Rhodes. "They will unleash the government against you, silence you and suppress you!"[3]

Rhodes's speech that day mostly stayed out of raging extremist territory. But the blog he'd posted when building his movement the previous year was riddled with conspiratorial thinking. Rhodes asked readers to imagine a scenario in which Hillary Clinton, whom he called "Herr Hitlery," was elected in 2009. Soon thereafter, he predicted, a domestic terrorism incident would provide cover for her to push through a United Nations ban on firearms.[4]

Following that, "Hitlery declares that [militia members] are subject to secret military detention without jury trial, 'enhanced' interrogation techniques, and trial before a military tribunal hand-picked by the dominatrix-in-chief herself. Hitlery then orders police, National Guard troops and active military to go house-to-house to disarm the American people and 'black-bag' those on a list of 'known terrorists,' with orders to shoot all resisters."[5] Rhodes's apocalyptic "imagination" spat out essentially the same scenario envisioned by militias and other extremists for decades, at least as far back as *The Turner Diaries*.

By the time of his Lexington speech, Rhodes didn't have to worry about another President Clinton, but he didn't seem that convinced that an Obama presidency would be much better. On July 4, 2009, Rhodes publicly repeated his dire warning and laid out his action plan. The military veteran had long been intrigued by the notion that Hitler would have been stopped in his tracks if the German army and security forces had refused to cooperate. With what seemed to him the near inevitability of totalitarian intrusions on Americans' constitutional rights, Rhodes presented a list of ten things his group of current and ex-military and law enforcement should swear to never do—even if commanded to do so by superiors. This promise became the *raison d'etre* for his group and inspired their name: the Oath Keepers.

Rhodes's orders to resist were largely based on conspiracy theories about fantastic federal overreach. For example, Oath Keepers vowed not to take part in unconstitutional activities such as forcing Americans into concentration camps, confiscating their guns, blockading cities, imposing martial law, or cooperating with foreign troops occupying the US.[6]

This list of ten "thou shalt not do" activities had a distinctly biblical tone to it, as well as echoing the number of Amendments in the Bill of Rights. It also struck a chord with many Americans. Within a few years, membership in the Oath Keepers was estimated at around thirty thousand.[7]

Other Patriot and militia groups saw dramatic rises in numbers at the same time, rivaling the original boom in militia activity in the 1990s. But the Oath Keepers was no 90s revival. Rhodes's new group weren't off-the-grid survivalists who flouted laws and ran drills in the woods to take on the military and ATF. The Oath Keepers *were* the military and law enforcement, or at least former members of. Though embedded in organizations based on rigid chain of command, they followed a higher order. Starting in 2008, tens of thousands Oath Keepers—mostly retired or current law enforcement and military—had sworn allegiance to the organization, not to the government they were employed by. They were essentially making a promise to commit treason, if necessary.

Rhodes directed a particular degree of ire at DHS intelligence analysts' suggestion that "disgruntled" veterans were potential future extremists.[8] This wasn't a surprising stance for a veteran starting a group based around recruiting members of the military, although it failed to acknowledge that veterans returning from the frontlines had unleashed a disproportionate amount of extremist violence. But Rhodes was correct that, like the reaction to aggressive policing in the 1990s, the ongoing War on Terror was creating intense blowback.

While the lawyer was making his address in Lexington, Massachusetts, detainee 001 in the United States' War on Terror was sitting in a cell in a federal penitentiary in Terre Haute, Indiana. John Walker Lindh, popularly known as the "American Taliban," was a US-born convert to Islam who, in April 2001, volunteered to fight in Afghanistan for the Taliban against the Russian-backed Northern Alliance. A few months later, after the 9/11 terror attacks, the United States allied itself with the Northern Alliance and declared war on the Taliban.

In December 2001, Lindh was captured by the US military. His treatment was not exemplary, or even legal. He was held at a US Marine base in southern Afghanistan, where he was stripped, bound to a stretcher with duct tape, blindfolded, and left in a frigid shipping container. On other occasions, the FBI interrogated him without the presence of a lawyer, ignoring the Justice Department's ethics office recommendations.

As a result, the government, which had been determined to prosecute Lindh as a great victory for the legal system over terrorism, had to settle for a plea bargain. The Pentagon and White House did not want evidence of Lindh's torture to be presented as evidence in a courtroom. Instead, Lindh admitted that he had served as a soldier in Afghanistan, violated an economic sanction imposed by President Clinton, and that he had possessed rifles and grenades. He was also required to relinquish his claims of torture.

In 2003, another American citizen, José Padilla, was detained as an enemy combatant for three years in a military brig—a period of time that Padilla claimed included torture and that many experts claimed violated his constitutional rights against unreasonable search and seizure. In 2007, Padilla was finally convicted of conspiracy to commit murder and fund terrorism.

One might expect that there would be little sympathy on the extreme right for either man, both Muslim coverts. But for conspiracy theorists who already believed that 9/11 was a false flag that would be used to justify the imprisonment of innocent US citizens, the Lindh and Padilla stories were cautionary tales. As Americans deprived of due rights in the War on Terror and then given stiff sentences despite never having actually attacked any American targets, they gave some factual heft to rampant conspiracy theories.

The 2001 Patriot Act, which approved increased surveillance on American citizens by federal intelligence agencies, played into right-wing extremists' fears and obsessions as well. The law was frequently seen as a harbinger of future limitless expansions of government power.

Meanwhile, revelations of the widespread use of torture on prisoners captured during the occupations of Iraq and Afghanistan became valuable recruitment propaganda for both ISIS and al-Qaeda. The long-term US occupation of Iraq also created the overcrowded prisons where the local leadership of ISIS first met. The rapidly expanding jihadist use of the social media, which was pioneered by American companies, further inspired numerous lone-wolf domestic extremists in the United States. Muhammad Abdulazeez's attack on military targets was also the result of deadly US intervention in the Arab world that had dragged out for fourteen years at that point, more than half of his lifetime.

These attacks, in turn, convinced right-wing militias, and many mainstream Americans, that they needed weapons to keep themselves safe from an encroaching threat. After Abdulazeez's attack, for example, Oath Keepers urged members to serve as armed guards outside recruiting stations around the nation.

In short, the ongoing restrictions of civil liberties and jihadist domestic violence related to the War on Terror fueled right-wing paranoia toward both Islamic extremists and the US government, helping to ignite the explosion of violence that came to characterize the Obama years.

In Pinellas County, Florida, a dog license costs $20. If you are dedicated Sovereign Citizen, though, the amount doesn't matter. In 2010, Donna Lee Wray fought a protracted legal battle against a county prosecutor, filing ten Sovereign documents over two months to avoid paying for both the license and the $25 fee for not buying the license. This type of practice, sometimes referred to a "paper terrorism," can be very effective. Finally, the prosecutor decided it wasn't worth the county's time and dropped the case.

For Sovereign Citizens, small victories like this only encourage them to protest other fees, fines, infractions, taxes, and even criminal proceedings. Sovereign Citizens have won multiple cases using Wray's method: swamping the legal system with a huge volume of legal nonsense.

As with other elements of extremism that emerged between 2008 and 2016, the internet and social media played a large part in the expansion of recent Sovereign Citizen activity. Today, thousands of websites and videos purport to offer fixes for everything from criminal charges to child support. But this pitch also found a large audience as a result of the prolonged recession following the 2008 financial crisis. The majority of new recruits were looking for a quick fix out of debt or foreclosures,[9] and this appeal easily crossed racial lines. Despite the white-supremacist roots of the Sovereign movement, it spread rapidly through the African American Moorish community. Indeed, in multiple cities with large black populations—including Chicago, Detroit, and Philadelphia—African Americans comprise the majority of Sovereigns by 2016.[10]

Like white Sovereigns, the Moorish Sovereign ideology spread through Facebook and YouTube, but it also moved virally through a more traditional venue for criminal education: prisons across the country.

In one such case, a man named William Mitchell and his three co-defendants each stood up in a federal courthouse in Baltimore during a preliminary hearing and repeated, "I am not a defendant, I do not have attorneys."[11] They explained that the court "lacks territorial jurisdiction over me"[12] before wandering into the same speech about the Federal Reserve and gold standard.

Though the men refused to listen to their court-appointed lawyers, the stakes were incredibly high. The prosecution had a very strong case that could convict them of, among other crimes, weapons possession, drug dealing, and five counts of first-degree murder. A guilty verdict would likely lead to their execution.

Stymied by the men's reckless refusal to mount a real defense, the judge researched the case until he found the same language online linked to Sovereign Citizens. It turned out that Mitchell had learned Sovereign Citizen techniques from another prisoner, Michael Burpee, who had been transferred up from Ocala, Florida, on drug distribution charges. Burpee, also facing serious time, had picked up on the pseudo-legal scams from yet another prisoner in Florida. In Baltimore, Burpee taught other inmates the strategies, and the court was soon dealing with an influx of bizarre, amateur legal filings.

The amazing thing about the endless and nonsensical motions filed by Mitchell and his co-defendants is that the often unintelligible paper-work probably saved their lives. In cases where prosecutors are pushing for execution, even arguments that are ridiculous on their face need to be given weight because convictions risk being overturned upon appeal. When functioning properly, the justice system meets exacting standards and process. It's not designed to deal with a barrage of inex-plicable garbage.

In a way, the court's dilemma applied to the wider rise of extremism between 2008 and 2016. Established systems, including media and other mainstream arbiters of truth, were simply not designed to deal with the massive amounts of untethered conspiracies, potentially ironic memes, and other indecipherable material that began shooting out of both sub-terranean message boards and mainstream social media.

These bizarre scams are also sometimes just a few degrees removed from violent extremism. The woman who argued the dog-licensing fee, Donna Lee Wray, had recently become the "common-law wife" of Jerry Kane, who traveled the country with his sixteen-year-old son, Joe, putting on seminars on how to avoid foreclosure.

In May of 2010, the father and son were pulled over in Arkansas for their unusual Ohio license plate on their aging Plymouth Voyager. After arguing with a police officer on the shoulder of the road, Jerry shoved him into a roadside ditch. The younger Kane—who was home schooled, able to recite the Bill of Rights from memory, and, from the time he could walk, always carried a realistic-looking toy gun—emerged from the minivan and shot the officer in the chest with an AK-47. He then turned the gun on a second officer, who took shelter behind his SUV. The officer fired several shots but was outgunned.

Joe Kane chased him down and put a bullet in the back of his head. The Kanes then fled, with Joe continuing to fire out the window at the dying officers. A couple of hours later, they were spotted at a nearby Walmart, where they wounded two more officers before being shot dead.

Like so many extremists before him, Jerry Kane's life was almost a textbook example of progressive destabilization. He grew up in the blue-collar town of Springfield, Ohio. After graduating from high school, he made the first of several unsuccessful attempts to be elected City Commissioner. He later began work as a trucker and married a nurse named Hope. In 1993, Joe was born.

There is no record of any extremist behavior on Jerry's part up until this moment. Then, in 1995, his daughter died of what was diagnosed as Sudden Infant Death Syndrome. The grieving father was outraged after being told by his lawyer that he had to allow an autopsy be carried out on his daughter. According to his lawyer, that's when Jerry Kane "started asking questions."[13]

Beginning in the early 2000s, Kane experienced other stressful events.

In 2002, his property was foreclosed on. In 2003, he tried to buy a different property at a sheriff's auction with an IOU. The next year, his property was foreclosed on again. That same year he shot at a passing teenager with a BB gun and then complained to the sheriff about being sentenced to community service. In 2007, his wife died.

With millions of Americans losing their houses in the mortgage collapse, Kane took his son Joe on the road to help with running foreclosure-scam seminars. Sovereign con artists also hosted mortgage and debt elimination seminars,[14] during which attendees would pay a fee to gain insider knowledge about how to stall the foreclosure process, not pay interest on credit cards, or evade paying income and property taxes.

Despite the collapsing economy, Kane was not as successful as other Sovereign Citizens running similar scams. In the days leading up to the shooting, Kane had only six attendees, combined, at his last two events. He had also become enraged by a traffic stop in New Mexico, which he called a "Nazi Checkpoint" on his internet radio show while promising revenge on the arresting officer. "I found out where he lives, his address, his wife's name."[15]

A couple of days later, the Ohio police officers had the misfortune of pulling over the angry man and his son. Kane's safety net had begun fraying long before. He'd long been exposed to extremist literature that portrayed law enforcement and the legal system as illegitimate and hostile entities. He'd gone through multiple stressful events and life-changing setbacks, including a failing business venture. He was carrying semi-automatic weapons. It was a perfect storm to push an extremist to violence.

The spike in gun-related violence committed by extremists like Jerry Kane was, at least partially, enabled by the gun control environment that existed between 2008 and 2016. The early 1990s gun control measures that inflamed conspiratorial militia groups were the result of multiple, horrific mass shootings in the late 1980s and early 90s.

On January 17, 1989, Patrick Purdy shot and killed five children and wounded thirty-two others on a school playground in Stockton, California. A year and a half later, George Hennard drove his Ford Ranger pickup truck through the front window of a Luby's Cafeteria in Killeen, Texas, and began hunting down customers with two 9mm pistols, killing twenty-three people and wounding another twenty-seven. In July of 1993, Gian Luigi Ferri exited an elevator into a law office in San Francisco and opened fire, eventually killing eight people and wounding six.

The wave of high-profile mass shootings quickly galvanized action in Washington, DC. Four months after the shooting in San Francisco, the long-stalled Brady Bill, which required a five-day waiting period for gun purchases, became law. The following year's get-tough crime bill included an assault weapons provision that banned nineteen types of semi-automatics. Although the bill passed with significantly less support from Republicans than Democrats, two former Republican presidents, Ronald Reagan and Gerald Ford, both publicly supported a ban on semi-automatic weapons. The bills also had the support of most Americans.

Though the National Rifle Association (NRA) opposed both laws, Timothy McVeigh resigned from the group because he felt they weren't militant enough. McVeigh, who didn't need a single gun to blow up the federal building in Oklahoma City, may have been pleased when, a week after the bombings, NRA executive vice president Wayne LaPierre refused to disavow an earlier fundraising letter describing government officials as "armed terrorists dressed in Ninja black . . . jack-booted thugs armed to the teeth who break down doors, open fire with automatic weapons and kill law-abiding citizens."[16] But LaPierre's theatrics also met strong bipartisan criticism, including former president George H. W. Bush resigning from his life membership to the NRA.

As the wave of gun control tightened up requirements for sales, Attorney General Janet Reno said, "This is an expression not only that people want these guns off the streets, but that the whole attitude toward guns, that America's love affair with guns, is coming to an end."[17] She was wrong. The anti-gun control forces had lost the battle of the early 1990s; by 2016, they were clearly winning the war.

Two years after the assault weapons ban went into effect, a 1996 Gallup poll showed that 57 percent of Americans said they supported laws that would make it "illegal to manufacture, sell or possess semi-automatic weapons known as assault rifles." But, beginning in 2000, support for these measures went into free fall. In 2004, when the provisions of the assault-weapons ban expired, there was little political will to renew them. By 2007, more people opposed than supported a ban on assault rifles. By 2016, 61 percent opposed such legislation while only 36 percent supported it, a 21 percent drop in support over twenty years.

This massive turnaround reflected several things. First, the attacks of 9/11 and subsequent terror episodes made Americans more paranoid about their personal safety. Second, the NRA had been very successful in fighting tooth and nail against any new federal gun control measures as well as loosening a number of states' laws regarding open and/or concealed carrying of weapons in public places. A longer-term trend was the broader change in the relationship between Americans and how they used guns. For most of the twentieth century, guns were most linked to hunting and sport shooting. But since the 1970s, the number of hunters in America has gone into steep decline. In 1977, 32 percent of Americans lived in a house with at least one hunter. By 2015, that number was more than halved.[18] Nonetheless, guns kept selling at a rapid rate. This was largely because people no longer thought of guns as hunting or sport-shooting weapons: 67 percent now say their major reason for owning a gun is protection.[19]

Perhaps strangely, by 2015, the number of people with at least one gun in their house was at an all-time low as well. Gun sales have kept pace only because those fewer Americans who bought guns, mostly white males, owned far more guns per person. They weren't hunters so much as hoarders. This change in market dynamics created an economic imperative for companies and lobbying groups to make people feel vulnerable to attack, either by criminals, terrorists, or even a tyrannical government bent on destroying the Second Amendment. The sales pitch for weapons was paranoia, a tactic that fit neatly into the hyperactive media environment. And, despite these low numbers of gun ownership, most Americans agreed that assault weapons should be legal as a defensive option.

This new relationship between Americans and gun control was painfully apparent in the different response to the huge numbers of high-profile mass shootings between 2008 and 2016. In 2009 alone, eleven people were shot and killed in Geneva County, Georgia, and fourteen each in Fort Hood, Texas, and Binghamton, New York. In 2012, ten people were killed in Aurora, Colorado, while twenty-eight, mostly elementary school children, were slaughtered in Sandy Hook, Connecticut.

In the early 1990s, three shootings with lower body counts had played a critical role in convincing politicians to pass significant gun control. Americans supported this legislation, because they thought fewer guns would make them safer. By 2012, the logic had been reversed. A significant number of people now thought that more guns would make them safer. As a result, shootings did not lead to gun control, but they were very effective at making people buy more guns.

After the failure of any significant gun control legislation—even measures with broad public support—to be passed in the wake of the shooting at Sandy Hook Elementary, a kind of fatalism set in among many supporters of gun control. Thus, between 2013 and 2016, as a total of eighty-nine people died in just four mass shootings spread around the country—a military facility in Washington, DC, a community college in Oregon, an office party in San Bernardino, California, and a nightclub in Orlando, Florida—not only did no gun control legislation not get passed, but large amounts of weapons and ammo were sold.

Another result of this shift in public perception was the social normalization of semi-automatics. Micah Johnson and Muhammad Abdulazeez, non-hunters who lived in relatively safe, middle class suburban neighborhoods, had no obvious need for military-grade weapons. In another time or place, they would have been more likely to face social resistance or scrutiny for owning the weapons—their parents may even have refused to allow the guns in their house. But, by 2015, semi-automatics were just another toy for adults.

Another marker of the acceptance of paramilitary culture came in 2012, when the prepper movement got, not one, but two TV shows. National Geographic premiered *Doomsday Preppers*, while the Discovery Channel launched *Doomsday Bunkers*. The premise of *Preppers* was simple: the show follows various people as they explain why and how they are preparing for an apocalypse.

In *Doomsday Preppers*, which ran for two seasons, the proud preppers show off their solar panels, the "bug-out" vehicles in which they will escape, secret stashes of food, and huge arsenals of weapons and ammo. The stars of the show generally explain that they are spending so much money and free time teaching their kids to shoot semi-automatics and prepare sea cucumbers as a post-apocalyptic protein source for one reason: to protect their families. But there is also a sense that prepping is really Dad's—they are mostly men—obsessive, paranoid hobby. Eventually prepping, the fear of apocalypse, leads to not just a conviction but a perverse desire for their worst predictions to come true. Preppers need to abbreviate Shit Hits The Fan (SHTF) because they discuss it both constantly and with a sense of knowing inevitability.

As a review in the *New York Times* said, these obsessive hobbies can be interesting at first, but the amusement gives way "to annoyance at how offensively anti-life these shows are, full of contempt for humankind."[20] Many preppers are also convinced that, when the SHTF, they will have to kill untold numbers of unprepared, starving hordes.

The movement also had high-profile sponsorship in the form of Fox News host Glenn Beck who, beginning in 2010, pitched "gourmet-quality" freeze-dried Food Insurance survivalist kits. In the ad copy, Beck echoes the paranoid tone of preppers: "[P]repare yourself for what we all hope won't happen, but probably will, if you're not prepared."[21]

The prepper movement runs across the ideological spectrum, but they are all motivated by fear of a cataclysmic event that will destroy, or at least massively disrupt, civilization. The event could be environmental devastation, the failure of the electric grid, or a crackdown on dissent by a United Nations-sanctioned one-world government. Preppers share much in common with the live-off-the-earth survivalist movement that emerged in 1970s, while often combining religious fervor and a wide variety of conspiracy theories.

While the show doesn't broadcast racist or anti-Semitic conspiracy theories, one episode featured a man named Tyler Smith who aggressively promised that, when the SHTF, he would assault all his neighbors and steal their supplies. "We are the marauders," he said. "We are your worst nightmare. And we are coming."[22] It turned out that Smith, a felon, was not allowed to own his weapons and was arrested by local police after the show was filmed.

Although the episode with Smith was mothballed after his arrest, *Doomsday Preppers* makes no judgment about the extremist paranoia extolled passionately by its subjects. Instead, the production values, breathless narration, and ominous music are designed to maximize Americans' paranoia. The show also gives preppers a regular mainstream platform to spread an ideology—living off-the-grid with enough weapons to keep everyone else away—that neatly overlaps with violent Sovereign Citizens and anti-government militias.

The growing public acceptance of paramilitary weapons effectively lowered the social cost of owning, or even stockpiling, assault rifles. But these mainstream shows, along with Fox News celebrities' plugs for prepping, drove a dramatic normalization of paranoid paramilitary culture that was unimaginable in the rest of the developed world. The media attention further encouraged the Patriot and militia groups, which had been training in the woods for a chance to confront "enemies, foreign or domestic," to move in from the fringes of society.

CHAPTER ELEVEN

THE TRAYVON EFFECT

On February 26, 2012, a twenty-nine-year-old Neighborhood Watch volunteer named George Zimmerman called the police in Sanford, Florida, to report a suspicious person walking through the Retreat at the Twin Lakes neighborhood.

When police arrived minutes later, Trayvon Martin—a seventeen-year-old African American—was lying face down in the grass, having been shot in the chest by Zimmerman. Martin had died almost immediately. Zimmerman, bleeding from his nose and head, was handcuffed and taken to the police station where he was questioned. Five hours later, the police determined that there was no evidence to refute Zimmerman's claim that he had acted in self-defense and released him.

Two days later, Martin's father, a resident of the neighborhood where his son was shot, identified photographs of Trayvon after filing a missing person report. He retained an attorney, but either unsatisfied with, or simply not trusting, the Sanford police department to handle the case appropriately, Martin's father also hired a publicist on March 5. Two days later, the shooting received its first national coverage via Reuters. By March 8, the story was exploding into the hyperactive and politicized media ecosystem that had emerged over the past few years.

Left-leaning outlets like the Young Turks and Huffington Post were among the first high-profile broadcasters of the events, questioning why Zimmerman had gone free. The next day, mainstream media followed as *ABC World News* featured the story. Hashtags related to the shooting began trending on Twitter, with many people angrily demanding that Zimmerman be prosecuted. As it grew, through both social and traditional media, the shooting became the first story of 2012 to eclipse the ongoing presidential race.

Under the pressure of intense media coverage, Zimmerman was eventually charged with second-degree murder. During an April 27, 2013, interview, Zimmerman's lawyer, Mark O'Mara, said, "I think if I could do away with all media, including all social media, I would not have an involvement in a criminal case."[1] The Martin family lawyer, Benjamin Crump, marveled at the impact of social media in bringing the case to court: "We didn't engage social media," he said. "It's almost as if social media engaged us."[2]

The prosecution of George Zimmerman is just one example of the chain reactions set off by reports of a teenager killed in disputed circumstances after a scuffle, a story that likely would have never punctured the nation's consciousness a decade earlier. Instead, the Trayvon Martin case became a near perfect example of how the hyperactive, outrage-culture that had begun to typify social media could set off chain reactions throughout social media and into the offline world.

For example, the event inspired #blacklivesmatter, a hashtag that became a mainly leaderless national movement. In the years following the Martin shooting, Black Lives Matter (BLM) had continued to use social media to organize high-profile public protests against police shootings of African Americans.

By 2014, Black Lives Matter had faced some criticism for its tactics and claims about racially charged police killings. But, after two on-duty police officers were killed in New York City, a flood of right-wing outrage was unleashed. The perpetrator had apparently killed the officers in retaliation for the deaths of unarmed black men at the hands of police. For some, BLM was somehow complicit in the killing. The rejoinder hashtag #bluelivesmatter began trending.

The Trayvon effect was not done yet. In fact, it was the online debate following the Trayvon Martin shooting that had prompted Dylann Roof to search Google for "Black on white crime." That search landed him at the website of the white supremacist Council of Concerned Citizens, a moment he said changed his life forever—and presumably played a critical role as an external factor of radicalization.

After his 2015 shooting of nine African American parishioners, online pictures of Roof posing with the Confederate flag were widely circulated. The seemingly unavoidable conclusion that the Confederate flag had some symbolic meaning to Roof led the South Carolina legislature to remove the flag flying above the state capitol. This action in turn jumpstarted the removal of other Confederate statues and symbols across the South. In response, groups including white supremacists began protesting the removal of historical artifacts, sometimes violently.

Another backlash kicked off following Micah Johnson's deadly 2016 attack on Dallas police officers. Later that year, BLM and President Obama were sued by an African American police sergeant from Dallas named Demetrick Pennie, accusing them of inciting "their supporters and others to engage in threats of and attacks to cause serious bodily injury or death upon police officers and other law enforcement persons."[3]

The claim was a stretch, at best, as the courts eventually would determine, but it did ask the bigger question about relationship between this cycle of protests and counter-protests, extremism, and violence. Black Lives Matter, #bluelivesmatter, and the media ecosystem in which these groups were situated were certainly *related* to the extremism and even violence that developed around issues they publicized. They just weren't, by themselves, responsible for any one person's radicalization. The same can be said of another world-changing communications technology that developed around 2008.

The violence following the 1992 Rodney King verdict was, in a sense, the result of technology: a man named George Holliday filmed the beating of King from his nearby balcony, sent the footage to a local television station, and it was eventually broadcast around the world. Because Holliday happened to have a video camera on hand, millions of Americans were already convinced of the officers' guilt even before the trial began. When the officers were found not guilty, the sense of disbelief and anger was magnified a thousand fold by the seemingly incontrovertible video evidence.

Fifteen years later, in 2007, Apple introduced the first iPhone, completely changing the cell phone market. Within a few years, most phones were touchscreens, had full-capacity web browsers, and were powered by an expanding number of apps. They also featured increasingly powerful cameras, and as smartphones became ubiquitous, people began reflexively reaching for their phones to photograph their kids' recital, funny cat antics, and concerts. Sovereign Citizens were early adapters at using cell phones to monitor police activity, recording events like traffic stops as early as 2008. But after Trayvon Martin's killing kicked off #blacklivesmatter, filming police activity became a nearly reflexive impulse for millions of Americans.

Not only did smartphones guarantee that everyone had a camera, they also allowed people to immediately upload the footage to Facebook or YouTube. In the 1960s, the Black Panthers had monitored local police by following them with guns. More recently, the militant Black Riders Liberation Party's website updated that approach, promoting using phones instead of guns for its "Watch A Pig" program.

The result of this new technology was that, from at least 2014 onward, a steady stream of video was injected into the racially charged, partisan, and overheated media ecosystem. Over just ten months of 2014 and 2015, cell phone footage showed at least six fatal police shootings, all them widely shared across media platforms.

Combined with footage from police dashboard cameras and the relatively new body cams that some officers were required to wear, public confidence in the police tied a low, with just 52 percent of Americans saying they had "a great deal" or "quite a lot" of confidence in law enforcement. Over the previous twenty-two years, that level was matched only in 1993, the year of the Waco standoff and one year after Ruby Ridge.

This widely broadcast narrative of racially motivated police shootings combined with readily available footage certainly seems to have played a role in Micah Johnson's radicalization. At a vulnerable moment following his disgraced return from Afghanistan, an enormous amount of media attention was being focused on the issue of police violence primarily against young black men. Johnson also viewed incitement to violence on the Facebook page of the African American Defense League, whose leader called for the murder of police officers around the country as payback for the shooting deaths of African Americans.

But social media wasn't just about flooding inboxes and Twitter threads with the latest events. It was also an incendiary archive. Leading up to the 1992 acquittal of the police officers involved, the beating of Rodney King had been shown on television news multiple times. For years after the riots, it only sporadically appeared in documentaries. But by 2014, YouTube hosted a video of the beating, which Micah reportedly watched incessantly in the months leading up to his shooting rampage.

Micah's extremist actions were part of a broader movement. In 2014, the Southern Poverty Law Center (SPLC) reported that there were 113 Black Separatist groups. A year later, that number had shot up to 180, the highest in decades.[4] Again, it's hard to imagine that extremist black groups, which had not represented such a threat since the late 1970s, would have achieved such rapid growth without the cell footage of police shootings of African Americans bouncing around the internet. Not coincidentally, the 2015 spike came following a year of protests in a suburb of St. Louis, Missouri.

On August 9, 2014, Michael Brown, an eighteen-year-old African American, was involved in a scuffle with Darren Wilson, a white police officer sitting in his SUV. Wilson fired a shot. Brown ran down the street. Wilson jumped out in pursuit and shot Brown multiple times, killing him.

People, many of them African American, quickly gathered on the street where Brown's body lay. It was a hot summer day in soon-to-be-famous Ferguson, an area with a history of deep hostilities between the black community and police force. It was also two years after the Trayvon Martin shooting had launched #blacklivesmatter and ignited an online debate and offline protests of police killings of African Americans. Street action was nearly inevitable, but few people could have anticipated how extraordinary it would be.

The following night was set aside for peaceful marches and a candlelight vigil for mourners and protestors of Brown's death, but 150 St. Louis County police officers showed up nonetheless, with riot gear and militarized vehicles. Later on, looters broke into stores and burned down buildings.

The next day, August 11, a few protestors threw rocks at police. The police fired back at protestors with tear gas and nonlethal bean bag rounds. The following evening saw SWAT teams, smoke bombs, flash grenades, rubber bullets and tear gas deployed. These three events, peaceful protests, destructive looting, and a heavy-handed police response, would remain constants for months.

Over the next few days, national media also began covering the story, turning it into another hotly contested discussion on race and policing. A CNN cameraman filmed an officer yelling, "Bring it, you fucking animals. Bring it." On the night of August 13, reporters for the *Washington Post* and Huffington Post were roughly arrested in a McDonald's. An *Al-Jazeera America* journalist was tear gassed and shot with rubber bullets, and had his camera taken apart by a SWAT team. Protestors threw Molotov cocktails; police fired more tear gas and smoke bombs.

On August 14, after criticism over the militarized police tactics by Missouri senator Claire McCaskill and governor Jay Nixon, the chief of St. Louis County police handed over leadership duties to the head of the Missouri State Highway Police, who was African American. Relationships between police and protestors seemed to improve initially, but the unrest continued for months with curfews, occasional protests, counter-protests, looting, and arrests.

Once again, the new media ecosystem played a central role in fanning the flames of unrest. When riots broke out after the 1968 King assassination, there were relatively few news sources. As a result, the vast majority of Americans saw the same footage on network television and read the same articles from wire services or national newspapers. By contrast, the Ferguson protests played out around the country on 4chan forums, YouTube channels, Facebook pages, the Twitterverse, and cable news talk shows. What's more, in 2014, audiences could pick the coverage of events that best reflected their politics and existing biases.

For example, a story about a neighboring Glendale police officer who had posted to Facebook, "These protesters should have been put down like a rabid dog the first night," and "Where is a Muslim with a backpack when you need them"[5] was pushed by left-leaning news organizations like the *New York Daily News* and *Russia Today*.

Likewise, coverage of Ray Albers, an officer who pointed his assault rifle at Ferguson protestors while they were livestreaming, said "I will fucking kill you," and then, in response to requests to identify himself, responded, "Go fuck yourself," was most evident on liberal sites Gawker and *New York* magazine. The internet's insatiable appetite for polarizing and offensive humor churned out a popular meme called "officergofuckyourself."

On the other side of the spectrum, an FBI sting operation near Ferguson that captured two members of the New Black Panther Party planning to set off bombs to kill law enforcement officials was peddled most effectively by Breitbart and WorldNetDaily,[6] both of which count far-right extremists among their readership. Depending on their appetite, Americans could choose to have the Ferguson protests portrayed as rife with police abuse or a locus for violent Black Nationalism. But the most alarming extremist story to come out of Ferguson was not African American militants but an overwhelmingly white and heavily armed group.

CHAPTER TWELVE

"A FREE-FOR-ALL ARMAGEDDON"

On the night of November 25, 2014, website designer Greg Hildebrand stepped out of his shower and noticed a man standing on the next rooftop over. He quickly reached for a towel before pushing up the window.

"Hey, can I help you?" Hildebrand asked.[1]

The man, who was wearing military gear and armed with an assault rifle, told Hildebrand that he was "security." The previous night, a grand jury had decided not to indict Officer Darren Wilson in the shooting death of Michael Brown. Rioting had ensued, and several businesses on Hildebrand's street had been broken into and vandalized.[2]

What the armed man on the roof didn't announce was that he was one of the Oath Keepers. Following the previous night's looting, the group had put out a nationwide call for members to converge on Ferguson to help protect businesses and keep the peace.

A few days later, after concerns raised by local officials, media, and protestors, the police ordered the Oath Keepers to stand down on the basis of an ordinance regulating paid security guards. After arguing, the Oath Keepers complied but then—fully armed—joined the protest criticizing the St. Louis County police chief. A few days later, the group's leaders decided that the ordinance didn't apply to them.

"Once we read the statute, we laughed at it," said Sam Andrews, a local leader of the Oath Keepers. "Then, the next night, we were there."[3] Although unhappy with the militia's decision, the police capitulated, and the Oath Keepers stayed on the roofs.

In interviews, the group claimed to be apolitical and not to tolerate racism. But a 2012 speech given by St. Louis County cop Dan Brown to local Oath Keepers suggests politics that weren't conducive to even-handed security work. In a YouTube video of the speech, Brown said that he retired early from the military because he wouldn't take orders from an "undocumented president," that the government will put kids in indoctrination camps, and that, as soon as Muslims "exceed you in numbers," they will kill you. The video, in which Brown also boasted of his blood thirst, led to the officer's suspension.[4] It was hard to say if his speech was a greater indictment of the police force or the Oath Keepers.

Many protestors also felt that the presence of white men in combat gear with multiple high-powered weapons in the midst of a largely African American protesters raised tensions. But, for other residents, the Oath Keepers' bid to take on the role of police force was welcome.

Even before the protests, the local police's credibility among many African American residents was low. The police had already made military gear commonplace on the streets of Ferguson. Even worse, their heavy-handed response had been widely seen as ineffective. According to a *St. Louis Post-Dispatch* story, many people who lived and worked near the businesses where Oath Keepers stood watch, both African American and white, were glad the militia members were there.[5]

In the 1990s, plenty of white, rural Americans might have trusted a local militia more than federal authority. In 2014, a militia replacing the police in an overwhelmingly African American, urban environment were tolerated by authorities and welcomed by at least some residents. The relatively successful venture in new territory would only encourage the conspiratorial, anti-government militia to continue mainstreaming its practices of supplementing or replacing police functions.

After their successes in Ferguson, the Oath Keepers were quick to provide armed resistance for what they saw as infringements on Americans' constitutional rights around the country. In April, they joined other militias at Cliven Bundy's ranch near Bunkerville, Nevada. Bundy had been grazing his cattle on six hundred thousand acres of federal land for decades without paying associated fees. After a prolonged legal battle, a federal judge issued an order for Bureau of Land Management (BLM) to seize Bundy's cattle until he paid the fees, which had grown to over a million dollars.

Bundy was a "Mormon Constitutionalist," a right-wing extremist belief system that combines prophecies of Christ's return, America's divine founding, and God's role in inspiring both the Founding Fathers and the US Constitution. As for the fees the government demanded, Bundy believed that Mormon pioneers had worked the land before the BLM existed and that, ultimately, God had created the federal land in question. Additionally, he thought the federal government was unable to exercise enforcement powers in the state of Nevada. As a result, Bundy thought, the government had no basis to charges fees for land use.

This unyielding ideological disconnect—not dissimilar to the one that backgrounded the events in Waco, Texas, over twenty years earlier—was the backdrop for the events of April 5, 2014. A combination of roughly two hundred armed Bureau of Land Management and National Park Service officers began rounding up Bundy's cattle, estimated at five hundred to nine hundred head. The federal officials were quickly met with resistance by the Bundy family and some supporters, many of whom were also armed.

The tussle between armed militias and the "gathers" looking for cattle across a rocky red desert was full of drama, like a scene from some particularly chaotic Western. But as was usual by now, the scene was chopped up and condensed into singularly divisive talking points through the distorted media coverage, which tended toward the right. The showdown was soon covered regularly on Fox. By April 9, Cliven Bundy was being interviewed for Sean Hannity's program.

A cell phone video of one of Bundy's sons being shot with a Taser after kicking a federal agent's dog went viral on YouTube, provoking outrage and rallying supporters to the Bundy ranch. On April 8, Nevada governor Brian Sandoval claimed that the operation was trampling constitutional rights. Nevada senator Dean Heller echoed his concerns, and both men's comments were hyped up in a right-wing media discourse.

The following Saturday, April 12, saw a bizarre test of the Sovereign Citizen claim that the county sheriff is the highest law officer in the land.

Cliven Bundy ordered Clark County Sheriff Doug Gillespie to disarm federal agents near his ranch. Gillespie, who had been quietly trying to defuse the situation, stared straight ahead without responding.

But while beliefs in alternative legal systems had no impact, the hundreds of militia supporters, including Oath Keepers and 3%ers, who had rallied for Bundy did. Nearly all were heavily armed. Some had taken up strategic positions, such as a nearby highway overpass, their rifles out and aimed at federal agents. Seeing the possibility of an even worse Waco-style bloodbath, the federal agents backed down, returned the cattle, and abandoned their efforts to collect Bundy's long overdue grazing fees.

For a brief minute, Bundy, a man who avoided paying over twenty years of grazing fees to the government through the threat of violence, was a folk hero to right-wing figures like Texas congressman Ron Paul. Fox's Sean Hannity celebrated while also pedaling dissident Arizona Sheriff Richard Mack's baseless conspiracy theory that the weekend defeat was a false flag and the federal government was still planning to raid Bundy's ranch.

When Harry Reid, Nevada's senior senator and the ranking Democrat in Congress, called Cliven Bundy a "domestic terrorist," Senator Heller shot back that he regarded them as "patriots." Bundy supporters wore "domestic terrorist" name tags to a party honoring their victory.[6] The whole event, including partisan political coverage and an embrace of illegal and anti-government rhetoric by elected officials, was becoming distressingly normal.

Bundy hero-worship died off soon thereafter when he made comments about how African Americans might have been better off under slavery. His militias also angered some local residents of Bunkerville after setting up checkpoints with armed men regulating who was allowed in and out of the town. But the complete victory over the federal government further emboldened the Oath Keepers and other militias.

In early September of 2015, a viral video showed a gay couple being refused marriage licenses by Kim Davis, a Rowan County clerk in Kentucky. That story quickly exploded from social media to mainstream nightly news broadcasts.[7] Davis, who claimed "God's law" prevented her from following a Supreme Court decision legalizing same sex marriage, was briefly arrested by federal marshals.

Soon thereafter, Stewart Rhodes jumped into the debate, saying that the Oath Keepers would travel to Kentucky with their guns to protect Davis. Rhodes even threatened the judge who ordered Davis arrested, saying he "needs to be put on notice that his behavior is not going to be accepted."[8] Soon thereafter, though, Rhodes's offer to form an Oath Keeper security guard for Davis was declined by her legal team.

The next major militia action, the occupation of the Malheur National Wildlife Refuge in western Oregon, did not have the official blessing of the Oath Keepers or 3%ers. It was, however, 100 percent inspired by them. The events during the standoff were widely reported, but its beginning and ending provide the best insight into the growing entitlement felt by these groups.

In November 2015, Cliven Bundy's sons, Ammon and Ryan Bundy, began using social media to publicize the plight of two ranchers in western Oregon who were facing jail time for burning federal land. Heartened by their success at staring down the BLM and Forest Service the previous year, the Bundy brothers put out a call for "patriots" to rally around the Oregon ranchers, Dwight and Steve Hammond. During the fall of 2015, anti-government militia members began moving into Harney County, Oregon, with Ammon Bundy arriving in December. Although the occupiers' initial idea was to rally local support for their cause, it didn't go as expected.

After several negotiations with the Hammonds, their lawyer declined the Bundys' offers of assistance. Ammon Bundy and his supporters then requested that the county sheriff, whom they regarded the supreme law of the land, protect the Hammonds from federal officials. Sheriff David Ward refused.

The group also tried to establish a local "Committee of Safety," modeled after the colonial-era shadow governments that were designed to usurp power from British officials. In their minds, of course, they were now the oppressed colonials fighting the British, represented by the current American government. These committees didn't get much traction with locals, either.

The group continued to make attempts to rally the public to their side, but at least some militia members began taking a different tack all together. In December 2015, police and residents of Burns reported multiple episodes of harassment, including being followed by SUVs and trucks with out-of-town license plates. These people included likely targets of militia ire such as a pastor who had been a vocal opponent of their tactics, the wife of a BLM employee, the teenage son of a policeman, and the parents of Sheriff Ward.

Ward's wife also set up cameras at the end of their driveway to record the unfamiliar trucks that regularly pulled in and sat there for from ten to forty minutes. Ward himself said he received death threats after refusing the Bundys' request to protect the Hammonds from federal officials.

After this harassment was reported, a conspiratorial counter-narrative began on the internet, positing that the intimidation tactics were carried out not by militia members but by FBI agents posing as them in a classic false flag operation to discredit the militias.[9]

One other ominous sign that preceded the occupation was a book recently self-published on Amazon by LaVoy Finicum, a fifty-four-year-old rancher and foster parent from Arizona, who became the primary spokesman for the occupiers. His novel, *Only by Blood and Suffering: Regaining Lost Freedom*, which was part *Turner Diaries* and part *Doomsday Preppers*, followed the Bonham family after a nuclear attack destroys civilization. In the midst of murder, rape, and cannibalism, the well-prepared Bonhams use their extensively described arsenal of guns to fight off their starving neighbors, as well as government officials intent on taking their weapons and forcing them to share their stockpiled food with the larger community.

On December 30, with tensions building, employees at the wildlife refuge were dismissed early and told not to come back until instructed. Multiple people, including at least one Bureau of Land Management employee, left town. On December 31, militia member Jon Ritzheimer took to YouTube to claim he was "100 percent willing to lay down my life to fight against tyranny in this country."[10] The militia members moved into the refuge on January 2, 2016, but the town had felt occupied for weeks, and a violent, apocalyptic ethos was pervasive.

Over the next few weeks, various local, state, and federal law enforcement officers took up positions around the refuge but allowed occupiers free passage in and out. Finicum and others basked in the international media attention but did not gain any more local support. The 3%ers of Idaho arrived to set up a "security perimeter" but were asked to leave by Ammon Bundy. A Sovereign Citizen-style "grand jury" was created to charge government officials with crimes, while both the Harney County judge and Sheriff Ward asked the occupiers to leave. Photographs show occupiers toting assault rifles and other weapons.

On January 15, 2016, Rhodes weighed in on the situation via the Oath Keepers' website. Although he had distanced his group from the occupation from the beginning, he still urged military and law enforcement not to take part in any Waco-style aggressive action.

"Your brothers in heaven are watching," he wrote. "Do the right thing. Stand down, and refuse to obey evil, ghoulish sociopaths who salivate at the prospect of watching Americans die on camera." Failure to do so, he warned, could lead to "a conflagration so great, it cannot be stopped, leading to a bloody, brutal civil war."[11]

On January 26, law enforcement took the opportunity to arrest all the leadership, including both Bundy sons, while they were traveling to meet with a sympathetic sheriff in a neighboring county. LaVoy Finicum was shot and killed during the operation.

By February 10, just four out of the dozens of occupiers remained. As part of their prolonged series of negotiations with the FBI, the group requested to speak with a supportive Nevada assemblywoman named Michele Fiore. The legislator flew into Portland and, during the four hour drive to the refuge, talked with the occupiers on an open YouTube livestream while up to sixty thousand members of the public listened in.

In a show of delusional chutzpah, Cliven Bundy flew into Portland that same night to support the remaining occupiers. He was promptly arrested at the airport for events related to the 2014 Bundy standoff.

That same night, a YouTube video was posted by two of the remaining occupiers, Sandy and Sean Anderson, as they sat in their tent. They were calm but also displayed a remarkable sense of entitlement and disregard for the law. The Andersons, who had traveled from out of state to join a heavily armed occupation of federal territory and refused to leave after being served notice by both the sheriff and county judge, complained about their "false imprisonment" at what they had named "Camp Finicum."[12] They were also upset that, during negotiations, the FBI wouldn't agree to drop all charges against them.

That same day, Sean Anderson also posted a disorienting video in which he was outside, holding an assault rifle, glancing around and quickly yelling down at his phone.

"Media's been ordered to leave! That means they're coming to kill us!" he said. After glancing around, Anderson added, "There are no laws in the United States now. This is a free-for-all Armageddon."

A few seconds later, he repeated the Oath Keepers' claim that law enforcement officers that don't abide by oath are "the enemy." He signed off by yelling, "If they stop you from getting here, kill them."[13]

CHAPTER THIRTEEN

WHITE LOVE

Thomas Robb's route to the upper echelons of white supremacy initially followed a well-worn playbook. His parents' politics leaned far right, and he had followed suit. Robb read the anti-Semitic newspaper *Common Sense* as a teenager and joined the conspiratorial and maniacally anti-Communist John Birch Society in high school. He later graduated from a theological institute based on Christian Identity, the racist religious philosophy that believes whites are the true Hebrews and Jews are the spawn of Satan.

In 1979, Robb joined the Knights of the Ku Klux Klan (KKK) and settled in Arkansas to raise his family. He climbed rapidly through the ranks and was named grand wizard in the early 1980s. At one point in the 1990s, his group's trial membership included Oklahoma City bomber Timothy McVeigh.[1]

But as the US economy boomed in the second half of the 1990s, membership across the various Klan groups went into steady decline. To boost membership, Robb figured the Klan, which called up images of backwoods bigots, needed a radical rebrand, so he set his group on a new course: a kinder, gentler KKK.

Robb's plan to attract a broader swath of the population included playing down some of the Klan's most iconic practices. Robb told members to keep their robes in the closet. The terrifying cross burnings were to be limited and called "cross lightings," reputedly an old Scottish tradition. Perhaps most ambitiously, he wanted his members to stop using the "n-word" in public.[2]

When author Jon Ronson caught up with Robb in 2000, on the eve of the KKK's annual National Congress in rural Arkansas, he found this early era of a more inclusive Klan awkward at best.

Following a series of speeches and workshops designed to maxi-mize Klan members' individual potential—led by his daughter-in-law, Anna—Robb used his keynote address to drive home his new direc-tion. He walked onto stage and held up a poster that said: "GET OUT NIGGER!" This, Robb said, is *stupid*. Instead of scaring people, Robb explained, the Klan needs to be seen as "knights in shining armor on the white horses."[3]

Not surprisingly, some hardline Klan leaders were underwhelmed by Robb's unorthodox behavior and his exhortations to Klansmen to get in touch with their feelings. A rumor began that, in order to soften the group's image, Robb had even publicly kissed a black baby.

For his part, Ronson was unconvinced of Robb's new tactic. The Klansman wanted to have his own television show "like David Let-terman," but Ronson thought, "Just being entertaining probably won't be enough. If Thom wants to become the voice of the Ku Klux Klan again, he's got to learn how to say the 'N word' entertainingly."[4]

But Robb stuck to his guns. After roughly twenty men had stepped forward during the ceremony for new members—the one night of the year when KKKers were still allowed to wear their robes—Robb asked the initiates: "Do we hate negroes?"

"No," repeated the new Klansmen. "We just love white people."

Robb's new direction was indeed promoting a certain kind of "white love." But it was a love born of the fear that if white people didn't stick together, their race would be wiped out within a generation or two.

The Klan had always portrayed itself as embattled. Its original purpose, immediately following defeat in the Civil War, was to push back against Northern occupation and newly emancipated African Americans, whose voting power had given control of Southern state governments to Republicans. The Klan responded with campaigns of terror and violence directed at the former slaves.

During the first few decades of the twentieth century, Klan member-ship was driven by propaganda—the film *The Birth of a Nation* idealized the hate group's origins—as well as paranoia about increased immigration, particularly from Catholic countries. KKK membership in the United States peaked at an estimated five million in 1925, roughly 4 percent of the country's total population.

In the decades immediately ahead, the Great Depression and a second world war heaped greater worries on the nation's plate, but the civil rights movement of the 1950s and 60s helped revive the Klan as a bulwark against a reputedly invasive federal government and outside agitators.

Robb's "new" direction of the early 2000s played off that same tried-and-true tactic: scaring whites into believing they were again under siege. But, during the 2000s, a unique set of political events, rapidly changing demographics, and the emergence of immigration as a divisive issue converged to create an excellent environment for Robb to put this plan in motion.

In 1970, the number of foreign-born US residents bottomed out at 5 percent of the total population—a century-long low—before beginning a steady march upward. By 2000, the number of foreign-born residents was approaching the level of the early 1930s, at about 11 percent, and climbing. By 2008, it was within a few percentage points of the twentieth-century peak.

However, the emotional impact of immigration was compounded in the Southern and rural states that surrounded Robb, areas where the KKK received a disproportionate amount of its support. The last time immigration levels had been this high, the overwhelming majority of immigrants had settled in big cities, where they created ethnic neighborhoods that included Chinese, Italians, Greeks, and Irish.

In the 2000s, the big states that already had established immigrant populations, like New York, Texas, and California, continued to get the largest number of new arrivals. But, largely drawn by labor-intensive agricultural work, a sizeable number of new immigrants headed for Southern and rural states. As a result, even small overall increases in immigrants made a much bigger relative impact. Between 2000 and 2012, for example, the foreign-born population of South Carolina shot up 87 percent—the single biggest percentage increase of any state. Alabama came in second, while Robb's home state of Arkansas was fifth with a dramatic 75 percent change.[5]

Over the 1990s and 2000s, South Carolina and Arkansas remained over 95 percent white or black, near historic levels, but the perception of immigrant-driven change was huge. In small towns near immigration employment hubs like meat-packing plants, residents saw Mexican restaurants and stores open for the first time. At the same time, kids who initially spoke only Spanish were enrolling in schools, something unheard of just two decades previously.

As this new "immigrant invasion" began unsettling white residents, Robb saw a prime opportunity to boost Klan membership. Simultaneously, certain sectors of the establishment media were handing Robb and other right-wing extremists a critical force multiplier.

In the first few years of the new millennium, however, immigration was on the back burner when it came to high-profile issues. Not that some people weren't trying. Colorado GOP representative Tom Tancredo worked hard to focus attention on the rising number of immigrants in the United States, but he was mostly a voice in the wilderness. The overwhelming focus was on the War on Terror. Just as important, there was a general bipartisan consensus on immigration. In the age of wedge politics, an issue that wasn't divisive was much less valuable—both to the major parties and cable news networks.

In a 2002 *Washington Times* opinion piece, Tancredo attempted to up the ante by tying immigration to the dominant issue of the day: terrorism. He warned that, after the next terror attack, a failure to pass tough immigration laws would leave national politicians with blood on their hands. The morning his article ran, Tancredo got a call on his cell phone while driving to the Capitol. He pulled over and got a tongue-lashing from GOP strategist Karl Rove who—unhappy he had conflated the two issues—told Tancredo "never to darken the door"[6] of the White House again. Despite the scolding, Tancredo held firm, and over the next few years, immigration become a divisive, and thus more politically useful, issue.

In 2001, when Gallup asked Americans how often they personally worried about illegal immigration, 52 percent answered either "a great deal" or "a fair amount," while 47 percent answered that they thought about the issue "only a little" or "not at all." By 2006, the worriers had reached 72 percent—up 20 percent. While American attitudes on immigration have always been complex, the Gallup poll made clear that, in a period dominated by terrorism, multiple ongoing wars, low unemployment, and a booming stock market, immigration was still a growing point of concern for many Americans.

The 2006 debate over comprehensive immigration reform was a clear catalyst for this abrupt shift in attitude. That year, the Senate passed a bipartisan bill that combined increased security for the US southern border with a path to citizenship for long-time undocumented residents of the US. Meanwhile, the House of Representatives passed a bill—supported by Republicans and opposed by most Democrats—that focused almost exclusively on immigration as a national security issue, with stricter enforcement and harsher punishments for immigrants in the United States illegally.

Because of their incompatibility, neither bill became law. But the failure marked a massive split in the way Democrats and Republicans viewed immigrants. According to a PEW research poll, in 2002, virtually the same number of Democrats and Republicans said that immigrants strengthened the country. Those numbers began diverging in 2006, and by 2010, only 29 percent of voters who identified as Republican said immigrants strengthened the country versus 48 percent of Democrats.[7] The gap has continued to widen even more dramatically since.

Once immigration became politicized, it was seized on by cable news, which exploited the issue in ways that played right into Thomas Robb's agenda. Fox News commentator Michelle Malkin incorrectly reported that a broad range of Latino activists were demanding that the southwestern third of the United States—or "Aztlan"—be returned to Mexico. Her sketchy analysis also appeared in a *Washington Times* article. Even worse, the *Times* article supported the massively exaggerated claim with a quote from a representative of the Federation for American Immigration Reform, a staunchly anti-immigration group with links to white supremacists.

On November 26, 2007, right-wing populist Patrick Buchanan appeared on Fox host Sean Hannity's show to discuss his latest book about the dangers of immigration. During the interview, Hannity validated the unfounded claim that immigrants crossing the United States' borders constituted the "greatest invasion in history."

At the same time came widespread media coverage of Census Bureau reports detailing the actual, rapid growth of the Hispanic population of the country. These same reports confirmed that whites would no longer be a majority in the United States by around mid-century, an event of apocalyptic proportions for white supremacists.

While immigration's rise in visibility during the 2000s wasn't enough for Tancredo to get much traction in the 2008 Republican presidential primaries, it worked perfectly for rebranding extremists like Robb. He wasn't worried about passing complex immigration bills or running for office. The establishment media's fearmongering over the issue stirred racial fear and economic anxiety. Robb could easily conjure up the specter of brown-skinned immigrant hordes overrunning white civilization. And he could do it without once using pejorative terms for African Americans.

By 2008, the increasingly high-profile and heated rhetoric around immigration created an environment in which, as the SPLC's Mark Potok explained, "hate groups have been able to grow remarkably quickly." By 2010, the number of KKK groups had surpassed the highest levels of the 1990s. In fact, immigration was a big enough winner that it fueled some of the most successful actions of other extremist right-wing groups in the early 2000s. Patriot groups, whose numbers bottomed out during the Bush presidency, rallied members to run militia patrols on the Mexican border.

Immigration fears, in turn, were part of much bigger project for rebranding the far right by portraying white Christian Americans as group under attack on multiple fronts.

In the early 1990s, several high-profile individuals including former Jack Kennedy adviser, Arthur Schlesinger, Jr., and Indian-born author Dinesh D'Souza published books highly critical of multiculturalism, a practice that encourages equivalent respect for multiple cultures within

American society. Since Anglo-European Christian culture had long been dominant in school curriculums, multiculturalism resulted in less Andrew Jackson and more Harriet Tubman. Just like recent immigration in Southern states, the curricular changes were minimal. But it could feel, and was certainly portrayed as, an attack on the country's Anglo-American roots. In the 2000s, the issue was picked up and mainstreamed by right-wing populist Pat Buchanan and other non-academics. Buchanan described multiculturalism as an assault on white identity in the same way that immigration was an assault on America's borders.[8]

Extremists like Robb took the criticism of multiculturalism, immigration, and changing demographics to its extreme conclusion. They weren't just national security issues or insults to traditional white culture but were perceived as existential threats to whites. Without drastic action, the result was clear: the complete disappearance of white culture and race. As Robb told it, the country was headed for "white genocide."[9]

Up until this point, Robb's drive to expand the Klan benefited from some uniquely modern capacities—particularly the fearmongering around immigration and multiculturalism on partisan cable news networks. But these issues were not, themselves, new. What was critical and novel was the white supremacist response to the perceived threat. Instead of dressing up in robes and burning crosses, the new Klan was going to play victim.

During his acceptance speech for the 2004 Jack London literary award, evolutionary psychologist Kevin MacDonald, whom the SPLC has called the "neo-Nazi movement's favorite academic,"[10] touched on the reputed clamor of Latino activists for a large section of the American Southwest to be returned to Mexico and the demographic inevitability of whites being a minority in the United States. He added a bit of anti-Semitic conspiracy theory, suggesting that multiculturalism is largely a result of Jews organizing ethnic interest groups to disenfranchise white Christians. Finally, he blamed the same academic left that promoted multiculturalism for "pathologizing" the "ethnic self-interest"[11] of European Americans. According to MacDonald, whites are not just a vulnerable group, but one unable or unwilling to mount a defense in the face of their near-certain demise. After establishing whites as victims of a Jewish conspiracy, MacDonald proposed a surprising solution: Zionism.

MacDonald, then a tenured professor at the California State University, Long Beach, proposed that whites emulate what he described as Jewish "hyper-ethnocentrism" by fiercely promoting their own self-interests and, ultimately, demanding their own, separate ethno-state along the lines of Israel.

Although white nationalists, including MacDonald, typically claim that segregating ethnic populations in their own states will prevent violence, it doesn't take much of an imagination to predict what dangerous forms this white "hyper-ethnocentrism" could take. And as if to squelch even that smidgen of doubt, in 2009, MacDonald joined the American Third Position—a group later renamed American Freedom Party, which was primarily comprised of neo-Nazis.

Despite his close association with skinheads, MacDonald's concepts were useful for mainstreaming far-right extremism. According to MacDonald, since white people were victims of immigration, shifting demographics, and multiculturalism, they should respond not with lynching but by unapologetically and fiercely celebrating their own culture, ethnicity, and race. They needed, as Robb would have it, not openly to hate black people but to love unabashedly white ones.

Robb and MacDonald were not the first to try to rebrand white supremacy around "white civil rights." Back in 1981, former grand wizard David Duke founded the National Association for the Advancement of White People (NAAWP), which met with some success. But as 2008 approached, white victimization, and the threat of "white genocide," was ready to take off.

When asked in an April 2008 interview which Democratic candidate he'd support if forced to, Robb took the long view, picking Barack Obama: "For the white nationalist cause, I think he'll be the best one for us. He might galvanize people. And then white people themselves might look upon this as a race war and begin thinking about their blood and their heritage again."[12]

In November of that year, Robb got his wish, and some white people responded just as he predicted. Stormfront and the white supremacist Council of Conservative Citizens had to upgrade their servers to deal with the spike in traffic to their websites.

While ugly incidents of hate and anger also followed, many of the leading figures on the extremist right saw a unique opportunity following Obama's election. A historic economic downturn, fear of jihadist attacks, a stalled war effort, and a sense among some whites that high immigration and multiculturalism were stripping them of their rights and country were already winning issues. The election of, as his critics made sure to call him, Barack *Hussein* Obama—an urbane, African American, liberal Democrat—seemed to combine and magnify all these threats.

As Todd Weingart, a leader of the hate group Nationalist Coalition, said, "If it was only immigration or the economy or a nonwhite running the country, there wouldn't be this interest. It's the combination that is getting people to stand up and get interested."[13]

With their eyes set on the mainstream, white supremacists followed Robb's lead. Don Black banned swastikas and other Third Reich symbols from Stormfront to avoid turning off first-time visitors to the hate site.

Speaking at a Klan event, a Stormfront moderator offered recruiting advice: Keep it subtle, at first. "Find a chink in their armor and make friends. If you are too radical, they won't listen."[14]

Similarly, the Detroit-based neo-Nazi National Socialist Movement (NSM) switched from Nazi brown shirts to black uniforms as part of what leader Jeff Schoep called a "modernization project."[15] Nonetheless, Schoep was not willing to embrace all the mainstreaming efforts within the white supremacist and neo-Nazi communities. The NSM, said Schoep, wasn't "trying to trick people; there are enough white groups now trying to soft-pedal people into joining."[16]

Thomas Robb, speaking at a Christian Revival Center and Knights Party event where his granddaughters' white nationalist duo Heritage Connection performed, had honed his message of white victimhood. "Why is it that when a black man wants to preserve his culture and heritage it's a good thing, and when a white person wants the same thing, we're called haters?"[17] he asked.

Victimhood turned out to be a popular pitch, but it was only the beginning. After 2008, Robb's brand of sanitized white nationalism merged with a much broader and less predictable online movement, which grew in ways he couldn't have imagined, eventually leaving him behind.

CHAPTER FOURTEEN

MAINSTREAM-ISM

Richard Spencer had a comfortable upbringing in a suburb of Dallas, Texas, in the 1990s. He attended St. Mark's, an exclusive prep school, where he was friendly with the one African American student in the class but was generally described as unremarkable by classmates.[1]

As he tells it, Spencer "self-radicalized" almost entirely at elite universities, including the University of Virginia, where reading Nietzsche's *Genealogy of Morals* had a "shattering" effect on him. He continued his intellectual journey toward extremism in graduate school at the University of Chicago, where a professor described him as a fascist, and during various stops in Europe, a continent with far more established extreme right groups.

After nine months as assistant editor at the right-wing the *American Conservative* magazine, Spencer was fired for holding views that were too extreme. He then edited the paleoconservative online Taki's Magazine, expanding it from primarily conservative and libertarian contributors to include writers like Jared Taylor, the editor of the white supremacist online magazine American Renaissance, who euphemistically fashioned himself a "white advocate" and "racialist." As Spencer's own politics definitively settled on white nationalism, he left the online magazine and started his own website, AlternativeRight.com.

Since then, Spencer's mission has been the same as his many academic racist forebears: making fascism acceptable, and even fashionable. The National Policy Institute (NPI), his think tank, is housed in Old Town Alexandria, just across the Potomac River from Washington, DC, where it occupies the top two floors above a chocolatier on a leafy street with colonial American charm. The NPI website looks more like the *New*

Yorker than Stormfront. It offers access to Radix Journal, "NPI's popular website for writings on culture, politics and society," and Spencer's own Washington Summit Publishers, which "produces books on culture, critical theory, and human biodiversity." He dresses neatly in sweater vests and suits while sporting the "fashy" haircut made originally popular among Nazi youth in the 1930s.

His politics, nonetheless, are a sanitized version of white supremacy increasingly advocated by the Klan, some neo-Nazis, and other less urbane hate groups. On an NPI training video, Spencer touches on all the white genocide talking points: "As long as whites continue to avoid and deny their own racial identity, at a time when almost every other racial and ethnic category is rediscovering and asserting its own, whites will have no chance to resist their dispossession."[2]

Spencer was a prime example of what, in 2012, academic Dr. Barbara Perry described as the "new, modern face" of the hate movement, which was repackaging itself and "attempting to move itself into the mainstream of United States culture and politics."[3]

Much of this repackaging was semantic branding. Spencer, who also dressed in a suit and tie, called himself an "identitarian," not a supremacist.[4] He claimed he left the PhD program at Duke to pursue a life of "thought crime."[5] But Spencer's most important contribution was popularizing and defining the term "alt-right"—a rebranding of the term "right-wing extremist."

Though it has never been a completely cohesive movement, what became known as the alt-right began to coalesce around 2008. Many future members of the alt-right had felt alienated from the Republican Party during George W. Bush's presidency. They rejected his neoconservative polices, the bipartisan consensus around free trade, and the multiple wars abroad. Many of these far-right figures, including Spencer, were so disgusted with Bush that, in 2004, they voted for Democratic candidate John Kerry or third party candidates out of protest. For them, the 2008 election had a double significance: not only did an African American Democrat win, but the Republicans had nominated John McCain, a foreign policy hawk who also supported bipartisan immigration reform. They were ready to burn the existing GOP to the ground.

Beginning in 2008, message boards like 4chan and reddit began experiencing rapid growth. Within a few years, though, they also saw a hardening of right-wing politics. In their early years, the communities had been rife with misogyny and pseudo-ironic racism, but they also shared an anarchist-libertarian insistence on absolute free speech. Above all, the boards celebrated an intense political free-for-all. During Obama's presidency, places like 4chan's main politics board drifted away from being chaotic online debating societies, coalescing around various reactionary, libertarian, and far-right ideologies.

The biggest single event marking this change was 2013's Gamergate controversy. The ferocious pushback against the positive reviews for a female programmer's unorthodox videogame was premised on the idea that "politically correct" or feminist forces were invading a masculine universe of first person shooter games.

Beyond all the vicious trolling and personal recriminations, Gamergate was essentially about mostly white males seeing themselves as victims of feminism, just as "identitarians" like Spencer saw whites as victims of multiculturalism. As a result, ironic, internet-savvy twenty-year-olds who wouldn't have been caught dead at a Klan rally joined a common cause with sanitized white supremacists. The meme machine joined the hate machine.

This same politics of male victimization defined another recruiting station for the alt-right, the huge network of blogs, message boards, and websites known as the "manosphere." Issues there could include "fathers' rights" advocates, incel groups—shorthand for "involuntarily celibate"—populated by men frustrated by their inability to find sexual and/or romantic partners, Men Going Their Own Way groups that discouraged relationships with women, as well as old-fashioned pickup artists. These often violently misogynistic groups were linked by the idea that feminism was their enemy. Many "manosphere" inhabitants saw the alt-right as a political vehicle to push back on the reverse-sexism that they claimed was lowering sperm counts and stripping men of their traditional roles.

By the time the term emerged into mainstream consciousness around

2014, "alt-right" referred to a loose coalition of academic racists, liber-
tarians, paleoconservatives, internet trolls, conspiracy theorists, misog-
ynists, anti-Semites, and white nationalists. But despite its ideological
spread, what bound the alt-right together was the belief that they were
all victims, whether of political correctness, globalization, multiculturalism, feminism, immigration, government overreach, massive Jewish
conspiracies—or all of the above.

The people associated with the group tended to hate both the earnest-
ness of the "Social Justice Warrior" left and "lamestream" conservatives.
They distrusted much of the establishment media. In fact, many had serious
doubts about the entire prevailing global economic and political order.

For the establishment media, the strange new political force was hard to
nail down. First, the alt-right was an unconventional coalition, largely
born on message boards and websites, that often manifested itself via
semi-ironic memes and inside jokes. It also presented many of the same
problems with covering internet phenomena that had plagued the establishment media for years and had only accelerated as social media itself
became a news source. In the limitless, deceptive online world, it was very
hard for a journalist to figure out exactly who was important and what
was to be taken seriously.

With traditional reporting stymied, some media decided to crowd-
source answers. An August 29, 2016 article in the *Washington Post* titled
"The alt-right, explained in its own words" consisted of combing through
tweets with the hashtag #AltRightMeans. The most popular consisted of
complaints about being victimized by ideological movements, including
feminism, multiculturalism, and political correctness. Other popular
tweets included attacks on 2016 Democratic presidential candidate
Hillary Clinton.[6]

Establishment news sources were accustomed to interviewing experts
or leaders of movements. The alt-right was too amorphous to work that
way, but Richard Spencer was very successful at promoting himself as an
authority. And for the *Washington Post*, interviewing a well-spoken, nicely
dressed man just across the Potomac River in Virginia was very convenient.

The *Post* ran multiple articles in which Spencer was given uncontested space to explain the alt-right movement. In a two-and-a-half-minute video titled "What is the alt-right?" mostly comprised of text and images, just two people speak on the subject. One of them, then-sixty-seven-year-old paleoconservative author Paul Gottfried, appears in a clip from a faded 2008 video. The other, is Spencer looking youthful, nattily dressed, and speaking directly to the camera.[7]

The decision to feature the two men makes sense, they are generally credited with co-creating the term in 2008, but no mention is made of this. Neither is the fact that Spencer was quoted in a 2013 issue of *Vice* saying his dream was a "white ethno-state"[8] or that, because Gottfried is Jewish, he would not be welcome in that nation. No experts offering a more critical view on the movement is provided. Perhaps in the spirit of being even-handed, much of the *Post's*—and other establishment media's—coverage of the alt-right left the impression that it was a non-threatening, if bigoted, emerging curiosity of American politics.

While this coverage may have been uncritical, it wasn't a straight publicity campaign like Breitbart's March 29, 2016 story titled "An Establishment Conservative's Guide to the Alt-Right." To the many critics of Breitbart, which was already closely associated with the alt-right, the generally positive tone of the article was unsurprising. But the lengths to which Breitbart went to explicitly sanitize the extremism rampant in the movement wasn't fully known until BuzzFeed News, a left-leaning news site, released emails detailing how the article was manufactured.

In early March 2016, Breitbart co-founder Steve Bannon assigned his high-profile provocateur Milo Yiannopoulos the prime job of explaining the alt-right to the world. Yiannopoulos's journalism consisted largely of emailing several right-wing extremists asking for their input. In an email to Andrew "weev" Auernheimer of the neo-Nazi Daily Stormer, Yiannopoulos said "Fancy braindumping some thoughts for me."[9] Yiannopoulos also contacted Curtis Yarvin, who had become famous for his searing "neo-reactionary" critique of liberal democracy and suggestion that monarchs and slavery would be part of a better social order. Yiannopoulos asked, "If you have anything you'd like to make sure I include." Yiannopoulos like-wise approached Devin Saucier, the editor of the online white nationalist magazine *American Renaissance*, for contributions. All three responded enthusiastically, and Yiannopoulos forwarded their thoughts, along with the Wikipedia entry for "alt-right," to his ghostwriter, Allum Bokhari, with instructions to "include a bit of everything."[10]

After Bokhari produced a first draft, Yiannopoulos allowed the white nationalist Saucier and the monarchist Yarvin to add line-by-line edits and suggestions. Yiannopoulos also requested input from Vox Day, a science fiction writer with a history of racist outbursts.

Though this was extremely sloppy journalism, the process became much more deceptive once Yiannopoulos shared a draft with his editors at Breitbart. They were generally enthusiastic, but, like Thomas Robb, wanted to avoid accusations of racism. They instructed Yiannopoulos to make the identifiable white supremacists seem marginalized within the broader movement. After being sanitized for explicit racism, the story went to upper management and back to the collection of neo-Nazis, white nationalists, antidemocracy advocates, and racists who were serving as unofficial editorial advisors. The final product read like ad copy for the alt-right, praising its youthful energy, its promise of "fun," and how its "fearsomely intelligent group of thinkers"[11] were terrifying establishment conservatives.

Throughout the article, readers are also reminded that the two authors on the byline—Yiannopoulos and Bokhari—are, respectively, a gay Jew and a mixed-race Pakistani. The article directly contended with—or, rather, defended against—the accusations of racism in the ranks of the alt-right. First, the authors drew a hard line between the reputedly harmless, lulzy ironic racism of trolls, and the actual racism of "1488ers" like the KKK and neo-Nazis. Then it belittles these groups, assuring readers that "there's just not very many of them, no one really likes them, and they're unlikely to achieve anything significant in the alt-right."[12]

Soon thereafter, the article uses the threat of the 1488ers it has just dismissed to make demands. If the establishment refuses to take the alt-right seriously, the article suggested, the extremists may convince many in the alt-right to join their violent revolution because "the bulk of their demands, after all, are not so audacious: they want their own communities, populated by their own people, and governed by their own values."[13]

The combined efforts of Breitbart editors and recognized far-right extremists had accomplished their goals: pumping up the excitement around the alt-right while denigrating the "scary" racists before suggesting that their program of ethnic cleansing was, actually, fairly reasonable. The bonus, however, was the wide-ranging coverage the article received in the establishment media. "It quickly became a touchstone," said BuzzFeed, "cited in the *New York Times*, the *Los Angeles Times*, the *New Yorker*, CNN, and *New York Magazine*, among others."[14]

Richard Spencer's speeches—"I am white, my life has meaning, my life has dignity"—and the appeals of other rebranded racists like Traditionalist Workers Party head Matthew Heimbach—"faith, family, and folk"—sound much like the appeal a Christian Identitarian might have made to suffering farm families in 1983. But by 2016, the alt-right's success in soft-pedaling, redefining, and sanitizing right-wing extremism was a completely different beast.

First of all, it looked different. Even Jeff Schoep, the leader of the neo-Nazi National Socialist Movement who had resisted "softpedaling" white nationalism, decided to remove the swastika from the group's imagery—replacing it with a Germanic Odal Rune also used by the Nazis. Schoep said the change would help American Nazis "become more integrated and more mainstream."[15]

Its messaging was also different. Schoep called his neo-Nazi group "not racist or neo-Nazi but pro-white civil rights."[16] Andrew Anglin, founder of the neo-Nazi Daily Stormer website talked about a "reboot of the White Nationalist movement."

Some extremists made names for themselves by hijacking academic language for the white supremacist cause. Nathan Damigo, a thirty-one-year-old veteran of such groups, ditched more overtly racist and anti-Semitic language in favor of phrases like "Cultural Marxism."[17] Damigo referred to writing the Identity Evropa symbol on a university chalkboard as a transgressive "thought crime." He produced a slick website decrying the idea that "our identities are mere abstractions to be deconstructed." Damigo's group targeted college students by demanding "safe spaces"—except that his safe spaces were for white students. His postering campaign, in which images of Grecian statues serve as backdrops for slogans like "Serve Your People" and "Our Future Belongs to Us," garnered national coverage from the establishment press.[18]

In the same spirit, Breitbart's guide to the alt-right had claimed the movement was "best defined by what it stands against." This was, however, an extensive list, ranging from feminists to intelligence agencies to liberal professors to Wall Street CEOs to Mitch McConnell and Nancy Pelosi. To bolster their war on the establishment, the alt-right borrowed terms from the margins of the internet that suggested everything you think you know is a lie.

For example, the term "sheeple," a combination of "sheep" and "people" that refers to the mindless herd, was used heavily on white supremacist websites like Stormfront a decade earlier. Approaching 2016, the term had migrated to the comment sections of establishment websites, with particular concentration on right-wing sites like Breitbart. It is most commonly used to dismiss people who agree with mainstream beliefs, although it could be a blanket attack on anyone with different politics. Some of the favorite terms of hardcore conspiracists—like "false flags" and being "red-pilled"—were also borrowed and increasingly mainstreamed by 2016. Those terms are, of course, extremely useful when painting the world as a massive illusion controlled by an evil cabal.

The more widely circulated these words and concepts, the easier it was to read seriously Daily Stormer articles like "Adolf Hitler: The Most Lied About Man in History," or listen to Richard Spencer tell you that everything you've been taught at school and by your parents is hogwash.

As the tools of the alt-right began eroding the mainstream arbiters of truth and its messaging of victimization spread, people with strong links to white supremacy were increasingly shameless—and successful at—dodging accusations of racism.

In 2015, a blogger published evidence that House Majority Whip

Steve Scalise had previously spoken at David Duke's white supremacist European-American Unity and Rights Organization, or EURO. Scalise, a Louisiana politician and former neighbor of Duke's, escaped political death by boldly claiming he had no idea about the group's connection to Duke or white supremacy.[19] For his part, Duke was given the opportunity to appear on both CNN and Fox News, where he claimed he had "never supported white supremacism" and that EURO was a group dedicated to "civil rights and preventing discrimination."[20]

Likewise, the white supremacist Council of Conservative Citizens (CCC), a group that has been supported by prominent right-wing commentators, such as Pat Buchanan and Ann Coulter, was drawn into the spotlight following the revelations that church shooter Dylann Roof considered the CCC website critical to his development as a white supremacist. The group issued a statement condemning the attacks, while adding that Dylann "had some legitimate grievances against blacks."

For this non-apology following the murder of nine African Americans in a prayer circle, the Council of Conservative Citizens' biggest punishment was having its PayPal link suspended. However, its content simply migrated to a site that sounded like a 1990s graduate-level media-studies thesis: Narrative Collapse—Derailing Media Agendas. The site, which was also accessible through the link "conservative headlines," pushed racially inflammatory stories primarily focusing on black-on-white crime under the guise of a news site.

Less than twenty years after Thomas Robb's awkward beginnings, right-wing extremism had been remarkably successful at sanitizing itself by appropriating the language of victimization, academic-left ideas of multiculturalism, and the Zionist project of an ethno-religious state. People and ideas that would have been shunted to the margins or dismissed altogether, like Richard Spencer, suddenly had a place in the mainstream political debate.

But Robb, and the Klan generally, were not among the beneficiaries of this sea change. In order to separate itself from accusations of violent racism, the Breitbart guide to the alt-right had dismissed the Klan and neo-Nazi skinheads as 1488ers. Even though white nationalists were among the article's editors, the extreme right's ugliest and most identifiable groups had to be publicly sacrificed to cleanse the broader alt-right. By 2016, the number of both neo-Nazi skinheads and KKK groups were in steep decline, replaced by crowds of young white men wearing white polos, khakis, and Spencer's fashy haircut.

The most revealing part of the 2016 *Washington Post* article analyzing responses to #AltRightMeans was the demographic data analysis of the over fifty thousand tweets. The vast majority of tweets using the hashtag did not originate with millennials or sexually frustrated incels, but with married white men forty to sixty years old. The alt-right—and its attitudes on gender, race, and multiculturalism—had moved well into the mainstream.[21]

Certain political and economic situations—a prolonged recession, stagnant wars in the Middle East, the nation's first African American president—set the backdrop for this sea change. But the alt-right could not have moved in from the political margins without the assistance of establishment media, national politicians, and some of America's largest corporations, like YouTube and Facebook. Despite the close relationship between the alt-right and America's mainstream, just about everyone outside the alt-right underestimated the depth and spread of the movement. By 2016, extremism was not just mainstreamed; it was ready to take over the establishment.

PART IV

UNCIVIL WAR

CHAPTER FIFTEEN

THE TROLL KING

Following defeat in the 2012 presidential election, a consensus developed among Republicans that they needed to be more inclusive. The party's core of aging white men was a diminishing percentage of the population. Just like white nationalists, the GOP foresaw a looming demographic death. However, its response—in terms of presidential candidates, at least—was just the opposite. Rather than double down on white maleness, the party's shining lights set out to attract new groups, especially the rapidly growing Latino voting bloc. As the early favorites for the 2016 Republican nomination announced their candidacies, they conspicuously pushed just those points.

In a speech at Liberty University, for example, Texas senator Ted Cruz's opening gambit was to ask the audience to imagine his father, a Cuban immigrant, "coming to the one land on earth that has welcomed so many."[1]

Florida senator Marco Rubio, speaking in his home state, explained that "I chose to make this announcement at the Freedom Tower because it is truly a symbol of our nation's identity as a land of opportunity,"[2] before playing up his Cuban parents and other immigrants who built the nation.

About a month later, former Florida governor Jeb Bush, whose wife is Mexican American, announced his candidacy at Miami-Dade College on a podium surrounded by a multi-ethnic crowd. "You know," he said, "I always feel welcome at Miami-Dade College. This is a place that welcomes everyone with their hearts set on the future. A place where hope leads to achievement and where striving leads to success."[3]

The next candidate to announce, businessman and reality television host Donald Trump, went dramatically off script.

"Our country is in serious trouble," Trump began. "We don't have victories anymore." In quick succession, he lamented the country's trade deals with China—"They kill us"—and Japan—a country we don't beat "at anything." Trump then turned to America's southern neighbor. "When do we beat Mexico—at the border? They're laughing at us. At our stupidity."[4]

The early favorites for the Republican nomination had all invoked hard-working people who had pulled themselves up by their bootstraps to build the greatest country on earth. As Trump described it, America was a disaster, Americans were getting kicked around by foreigners, and American leaders were incapable of doing anything about it.

Trump wasn't done with Mexico yet. "The US has become the dumping ground for everyone else's problems," he said. "When Mexico sends its people, they're not sending their best. They're sending people that have lots of problems. They're bringing drugs, bringing crime. They are rapists and some, I assume, are good people."[5]

Though Mexican immigrants were his favorite rhetorical target, Trump also latched on to other far-right extremist talking points. Following the San Bernardino, California, attack by a couple who pledged allegiance to ISIS, Trump called for a "total and complete shutdown of Muslims entering the United States,"[6] an idea that had been bouncing around white supremacist sites like Stormfront a decade earlier.

In July 2015, Trump invited Sheriff Joe Arpaio to a rally in Arizona. Arpaio, who had been dogged by Justice Department investigations throughout his tenure, was well known for reinstituting chain gangs, housing inmates in tent cities, and racially profiling Latinos. In 2007, after his department was compared to the Ku Klux Klan, Arpaio said it was an honor. In short, the sheriff was a poor choice for any candidate interested in appealing to minority candidates—especially Latinos. But Trump was ignoring conventional wisdom. It also appeared to be working. A few days after the rally with Arpaio, Trump overtook Jeb Bush in opinion polls.

Eight years after Tom Tancredo had tried to make a run at the presidency with a campaign based around immigration, Trump decided to try his luck. But Trump's staunch anti-immigrant stance was actually just part of his campaign's broader program, one that came straight out of the so-called "alt-right" playbook.

The fear of a huge wave of illegal immigration was just one of the factors the "alt-right" used in describing the alleged victimization of white, Christian males. The full list of supposed oppressors was enormous, but globalization, multiculturalism, feminism, media, intelligence agencies, Communists, liberals, Democrats, and most Republicans were prominently featured. By targeting these issues and groups, the alt-right had been incredibly successful at expanding the reach of right-wing extremist and conspiratorial ideas between 2008 and 2016. Not coincidentally, these were also some of Trump's favorite targets at his rallies. While the blustering businessman's campaign often seemed haphazard, it did have at least one consistent aim: testing how successful the alt-right had been at pushing radical fringe ideas into the mainstream.

During the rest of 2015, much of the country was simultaneously entertained and outraged by Trump, but members of the alt-right recognized his program early on. To them, he wasn't just a loudmouthed opportunist who had stumbled onto issues that resonated.

Nonetheless, many far-right extremists kept their support quiet initially, either expecting a Republican candidate for the presidency to disappoint them eventually by veering toward the center or because they thought the endorsement of identifiable racists might not help him. Not everyone stayed below the radar, however.

A few months into Trump's campaign, Matthew Heimbach, cofounder of the neo-Nazi Traditionalist Youth Network, went public with his approval. Although he doubted Trump would win, Heimbach thought that his campaign "could be the steppingstone we need to then radicalize millions of White working and middle class families."[7]

Toward the end of the year, an organizer for a KKK-affiliated group echoed this sentiment, saying that sparking up conversations about Trump was a good way to talk with strangers about issues important to white supremacy.[8]

Following Trump's June 2015 announcement of his candidacy, the *New York Times* had tried—and failed—to imagine a path to victory for him. By December, Trump had been leading in polls for five months and the newspaper was forced to re-evaluate him. Primary season hadn't begun, so Trump hadn't yet locked up a single delegate. His organization's ground game was considered somewhere between chaotic and nonexistent. He was an extremely nontraditional candidate, but it was also clear that Trump's success was not just a momentary glitch.

When sizing up Trump, the *Times* listed his massive media profile as one of his only political assets. Certainly, the reality TV host had used his media savvy to stand out from the crowded field. The *Times* article had also noted, again correctly, that Trump was the perfect candidate for an age in which news was shared virally through social media. But even given the expanded role of social media in 2016, the political consensus remained that Trump would eventually go too far, alienate too many people, and shock the nation's conscience.

In September of 2015, for example, Trump's campaign had run an Instagram ad that showed footage of a woman falling asleep next to Jeb Bush while he was speaking. The video, purporting to be an ad for a sleep aid, ended with white text that read: "Jeb, for all your sleeping needs."[9]

Over the top? Bush certainly thought so. During a debate a few months later, he shot back at Trump, "You're not going to be able to attack your way to the presidency."[10] Jeb Bush, though, had last run a political campaign in 2002, and a lot had changed since then. The combination of divisive and partisan cable news and websites, social media echo chambers, viral conspiracy theory videos, pseudo-ironic memes, and a historic lack of faith in the media was, in fact, the perfect platform for the most extreme candidate in the race.

Throughout his campaign, Trump borrowed openly from mainstream extremist alt-right ideas. But his success had much more to do with the new media environment that had allowed those extremist ideologies to mainstream in the first place. Trump was sixty-nine years old when he announced his candidacy, but he would have been more at home with the trollish millennials on 4chan than any of the younger, but more politic, candidates.

Within two minutes of announcing his presidency, Donald Trump made multiple false and questionable assertions, including that there were no Chevrolets in Japan and that Mexico was sending criminals and rapists into the United States. When fact checkers, including the independent PolitiFact, called him out on the claims, Trump simply repeated them more loudly.

Accounts of Trump's business dealings suggest he was a shameless and frequent liar well before his campaign began, but Trump was no longer reneging on promises made to subcontractors on his construction projects. He was running for public office under the full heat of media scrutiny. National politicians who are exposed for outrageous and verifiably false claims either resign, quietly walk it back, or pivot to a slightly different line of attack. Trump refused to play that game, and his claims that he was correct even in the face of actual evidence frustrated and outraged his opponents.

As the fourth estate, one of the media's most important roles is holding politicians and other powerful figures accountable, but it turned out that many Americans, fed a regular diet of conspiracy theories, viral rumors, and outright false and partisan claims from cable news and websites, had no interest in making Trump pay a serious political price for lying.

In fact, Trump's steadfast repetition of ridiculous falsehoods served to normalize a certain plasticity of fact around him while satisfying his base's emotional needs. Take his dogged insistence that thousands of people in a largely Arab part of Jersey City, New Jersey, were cheering as the World Trade Center came down across the river. He initially made the claim at a rally in November 2015. He doubled down a few days later on ABC's *This Week*, claiming, "I saw it. It was on television." He then pointedly added, "I know it might not be politically correct for you to talk about it." On NBC's *Meet the Press*, Trump again repeated: "I saw it. So many people saw it."[11]

First, by mentioning that something wasn't "politically correct," Trump automatically got a free pass from tens of millions of Americans who felt like they were also victims of a left-wing conspiracy to limit what they could say and think. Second, Trump knew better than most that, by 2015, the truth was as much a byproduct of individual emotional needs as anything else. By giving his supporters what they wanted to believe— that Muslims were a hateful threat to the nation—Trump validated their anger and fears.

In the end, Trump never walked the false claim back, and eventually, the flummoxed media stopped questioning him about it or mentioning it at all. Trump: 1. Media: 0.

The same month that the *Times* article analyzed Trump's surprising success, he became the only presidential candidate to appear on Alex Jones's online show. Trump told Jones, who had claimed that the 1995 Oklahoma City bombing, the 9/11 attacks, and the 2012 Sandy Hook elementary school shooting were faked by the government, "Your reputation is amazing. I will not let you down."[12]

Jones later claimed he was responsible for advising Trump to label the media the "true enemy" of the American people. Regardless of its origin, Trump was able to foment and leverage the widespread hatred of the media to put them on trial for being "unfair" to him. His cries of "fake news" allowed Trump to claim he was a victim of attacks from the liberal media elite, earning him the sympathy and support of conservatives who had spent years immersed in right-wing cable news and blogs.

What's more, in a conspiratorial extremist universe, it's a given that everyone you don't agree with is lying to you. Their belief is that the more that the media disagrees with and attacks you, the more correct you are.

Trump was a master of attention-hacking. Like Identity Evropa postering a college campus with white supremacist messages, Trump just wanted publicity. He calculated his tweets and pronouncements to dominate news cycles. Major TV networks and news websites gladly complied, providing him the equivalent of $5 billion in free earned media time in the year leading up to the election, more than twice what the Democratic candidate for presidency, Hillary Clinton, received.

And despite being repeatedly attacked by Trump both rhetorically and, at his rallies, physically, the establishment media continued to play the role it had taken on in the new media ecosystem: amplifying rumors that emerged on Facebook, reporting what searches were trending on Google, and analyzing and rebroadcasting outrageous tweets sent out by Trump. The media was also well rewarded financially for its nonstop coverage of Trump. All three major cable news networks showed huge returns in 2016, with CNN—a frequent Trump target—posting record profits.

Establishment media were, of course, aware that the previous few years had been full of extremist strife. In June 2014, Sovereign Citizens Jerad and Amanda Miller had murdered two police officers in a Las Vegas pizza restaurant. That September, survivalist Eric Frein shot two policemen, killing one. In June of 2015, Dylann Roof killed nine people in a church in Charleston, South Carolina. The next month, Muhammad Abdulazeez, an "all-American" young man, killed five members of the military in Chattanooga, Tennessee. In November 2015, Robert Dear, Jr., had opened fire on a Colorado Springs Planned Parenthood center, killing two civilians and a police officer. In December 2015, fourteen people were killed at an office party by Rizwan Farook and Tashfeen Malik, both adherents to ISIS.

But while many believed that the United States was an angry, unsettled place, the extremist attacks were considered just that: the acts of people at the margins of society. In a country where Barack Obama had been re-elected in 2012, it was hard to imagine that the support of a coalition of white nationalists, internet trolls, academic racists, KKK leaders, and opponents of multiculturalism and feminism would have much upside for a presidential candidate. Despite the *New York Times*'s insight into some of Trump's successes to date, establishment pundits didn't realize how radical the national political climate as a whole had become since 2008.

The dissolution of the mainstream was also evident, if somewhat less immediate, in the Democratic primaries. Instead of waltzing to the nomination as had been expected, former secretary of state Hillary Clinton faced a surprisingly strong challenge from a self-declared socialist—a term that had been used primarily as an insult in the past hundred or so years of American politics. By January 2016, socialism was preferred over capitalism by voters under thirty and, among self-identified Democrats, ran about even with capitalism.[13] Ideas that were formerly untouchably extreme were rapidly going mainstream.

Clinton operatives saw that Trump's antics—for example, his insults toward members of the military and his embrace of historic rival Russia— had left a huge gap in the political center. It was fine if Trump's positive comments about Russia played well with white nationalists—who regard it as the whitest country on earth—and his coarse, inflammatory rhetoric won over some rural, blue-collar Democrats who were sick of the system's hypocrisy. The Democrats would gladly trade those fringe constituencies in exchange for suburban independents and moderate Republicans. But the mainstream was a rapidly shrinking place and only one candidate was actively recruiting and borrowing from the extremists.

Over the course of 2016, Trump's links with most of the major players in right-wing extremism only tightened.

In January, he retweeted from the account @WhiteGenocideTm.[14]

In February, asked about robocalls supporting him voiced by academic white supremacist Jared Taylor, Trump responded with a weak non-endorsement, saying that he disapproved of the calls, but that the anger over violence being committed by illegal immigrants was legitimate. Trump's comments echoed the Council of Conservative Citizen's 2015 response that, while Dylann Roof shouldn't have murdered nine people in a prayer circle, he did have some legitimate grievances about black-on-white crime.

Trump also got the support of Jerry DeLemus, a former marine who founded New Hampshire Veterans for Trump. DeLemus had also played a major role in organizing the armed militias in the 2014 armed standoff at Cliven Bundy's ranch. Bundy himself voiced support for Trump as well.

In February, Trump retweeted a quote by Italian fascist Benito Mussolini: "It is better to live one day as a lion than 100 years as a sheep."[15] But that incident was overshadowed by one of the biggest scandal of Trump's candidacy.

On CNN, Trump was asked about the strong endorsement he received from former grand wizard David Duke. Trump claimed, "I don't know anything about David Duke, ok?"[16]

The next day, after media uproar, Trump blamed a bad earpiece, saying he didn't understand the question. The less-than-believable excuse did not stem the furor. A few days later, his spokesperson—not Trump himself—directly disavowed Duke.

Trump winked at white supremacists by not disavowing Duke immediately. To his more mainstream supporters, Trump's subsequent dubious claim of technical issues put a little distance between him and the KKK, while essentially calling the media stupid. All along, Trump trolled his opponents, reveling in the angry attacks leveled at him, while getting millions in free publicity as the episode played out over a week. Trump even earned the endorsement of the most successful propagator of pseudo-ironic racist bombast: the neo-Nazi Daily Stormer.[17]

In July, Trump delivered a dour acceptance speech for the GOP nomination. He ticked off the complaints of many "alt-righters," taking shots at globalism, the establishment, and immigration. He also reached out to Patriot groups and militias, claiming that his opponent in the general election, former secretary of state Hillary Clinton, would abolish the Second Amendment.

His continual bashing on Clinton and her alleged criminal activities were met by chants of "Lock Her Up!" Trump agreed, frequently saying that Clinton "has to go to jail"[18]—even though the FBI had already said there was no criminal case against her.

Trump wasn't running a big-tent operation. He pinned his hopes on rallying a hardcore base while turning the whole electoral process into entertaining but policy-devoid mudslinging. In the end, the election wasn't decided by who voted for the major-party candidates but by who didn't. In 2008, 1.4 percent of Americans cast their ballots for someone other than the two major party presidential candidates. In 2012, 1.7 percent did. In 2016, that number shot up to 5.7 percent.[19]

Trump's viability was also the result of maps that both parties had allowed to become extremely partisan in recent years. Up until 2000, much of the United States could be contested. Ronald Reagan won forty-nine states in 1984. In 1992, Bill Clinton won thirty-two states, including Arkansas, Georgia, and Louisiana. By 2016, only about a quarter of the country was contested by both parties. As a result, Trump didn't need to win a majority; he needed just enough people in a few swing states to get a victory.

Nonetheless, the morning of Election Day, Clinton was considered a 5–1 favorite over Trump.[20] The past two Republican presidents refused to support Trump. Just one major publication, the *Las Vegas Review-Journal*, supported him. He did, however, have the full-throated endorsement of *The Crusader*, a KKK newspaper, as well as that of Cliven Bundy, Jared Taylor, David Duke, Daily Stormer, and a whole host of other right-wing extremists.

Following Trump's shocking victory, the establishment media and political pundits churned out reasons for it—Bernie Sanders voters, Jill Stein voters, Russian interference, racism, sexism. Victorious white supremacists also chimed in. Richard Spencer claimed, "Trump's victory was, at its root, a victory of identity politics."[21] Jared Taylor said, "Make no mistake about it: we did this. If it were not for us, it wouldn't have been possible."[22]

On one hand, this was a ridiculous claim. Trump received nearly sixty-three million votes. The fact that, say, tens of thousands of white supremacists—most of them in safely red states—finally went to the polls didn't move the needle. But both extremists were correct in a different sense. Trump's election was only possible because it gave the salesman something seemingly unique to hawk: the successful alt-right project of mainstreaming extremism.

CHAPTER SIXTEEN

ANTI-ALL

In May of 2017, Richard Spencer led a nighttime protest against the planned removal of a prominent statue of Confederate General Robert E. Lee from a park in Charlottesville, Virginia. In July, a Klan-led protest in Charlottesville was met by large numbers of counter-protestors. After that, Spencer and another University of Virginia graduate named Jason Kessler planned a much larger rally. When Kessler applied for the permit, he described the so-to-be-infamous event's purpose as a "Free speech rally in support of the Lee Monument."

Compared to David Duke's all-but-canceled 2008 white nationalist conference in Memphis, the Unite the Right rally was a massive success, bringing together nearly one thousand people with white supremacist, white nationalist, anti-Semitic, and related hate-based ideologies. Duke told reporters covering the event that the protesters were "going to fulfill the promises of Trump" to "take our country back."[1]

But the rally was less a vindication of Duke than a sign that his run as the face of far-right racism was over. Richard Spencer, who had led several groups shouting anti-Semitic chants, saw his profile rise tremendously. The massive event had been promoted—largely online—by the innumerable websites in the "alt-right" universe. Most prominent among them was the Daily Stormer, the bombastic neo-Nazi news site created and maintained by two millennials—Andrew Anglin and Andrew "weev" Auernheimer—who had emerged from the troll subterranean web of comments boards typified by 4chan. In attendance were other new faces like Identity Evropa leader Nathan Damigo and Traditionalist Worker's Party leader Matthew Heimbach.

Protestors there also echoed the central theme of the alt-right and, later, Donald Trump's campaign: victimization. One of the participants, who gave his name only as Ted because he said he might want to run for political office someday, said he was from Missouri, and added, "I'm tired of seeing white people pushed around."[2] Though Klan-related groups attended, Unite the Right felt more like a coming out party for the alt-right.

Because Unite the Right belonged to the "alt-right," it definitively revealed the movement's fundamental ugliness. The alt-right had emerged as a political curiosity in 2016—a project that represented itself as the work of ironic, web-savvy millennials and well-spoken academic racists. While their rally included clean-cut young men from Vanguard America and Identity Evropa, it also attracted an ugly collection of neo-Confederates, neo-Nazis, and Klan supporters chanting racist and anti-Semitic slogans.

Still, despite the frightening images of men marching with Confederate T-shirts, neo-Nazi flags, and assault rifles, the worst damage was done by the sort of less threatening attendee associated with the alt-right. The day before the rally began, a twenty-year-old avid Trump supporter named James Fields, Jr., dropped off his cat at his mom's house and told her he was going to an alt-right rally. His mother, who tried not to discuss politics with him, said she thought it was a Trump—not a white supremacist—rally. She was surprised his views had gone that far right, claiming that her son had an African American friend.

Fields was photographed the next day with close-cropped hair, wearing a white polo shirt, and holding a shield—the de facto uniform of Vanguard America, a group associated with the alt-right and "white identity" that had hardened around neo-Nazism.

After the rally descended into mayhem and was declared illegal by local police, Fields drove his Dodge Challenger into a crowd of counter-protestors, injuring twenty-eight people and killing thirty-two-year-old Heather Heyer. The event's only fatality was committed not by grizzled-looking white-supremacist men toting semi-automatics, but by a clean-cut twenty-year-old with no known links to hate groups.

While it would be specious to say that Fields's violent extremist act was the result of online radicalization—he had exhibited violent and hateful behavior for years—it would likewise be disingenuous to claim that the alt-right universe that developed between 2008 and 2016 was marginal to his crime. Fields had spent years immersed in hateful online alt-right propaganda, which encouraged and focused his anger. This alt-right rally was the catalyst that pushed him to act out his impulses.

As a result of the fatal street violence in Charlottesville, the alt-right began to face a concerted pushback. Alt-right leaders were more likely to find themselves banned from the social media platforms that had been so critical to their rise, including Twitter, Facebook, and YouTube, as well as payment sites like PayPal. Just as importantly, media covering the alt-right was suddenly much more reluctant to use the movement's preferred terms (like identitarian, white advocate, and racial realist) in ways that distinguished the people and ideas from white nationalism or neo-Nazis.

Trump's election and the ascendant alt-right faced other types of backlash. Antifascists, or Antifa, are direct-action groups that trace their lineage back to Nazi-era Germany, although their most recent American relations are the anti-racist skinheads that began appearing in the 1980s. Today's Antifa exists as a hybrid between most modern extremists and nonviolent protest movements, such as Black Lives Matter. They are not a defined group but are a leaderless ideology that spawned a movement. In order to maintain anonymity, members of the group often wear black and cover their faces with bandanas or masks.

Antifa's goal—as its name suggests—is oppositional (i.e., antifascism). Antifa protest what they see as fascism—including racist, sexist, and homophobic behavior and politics—by "de-platforming" its practitioners. These efforts are both online, such as doxing right-wing extremists or hundreds of ICE employees by, for example, taking pictures of extremists at rallies and posting them online to identify them. Efforts are also done offline, by directly confronting attendees at right-wing rallies. While the group has traditionally been comprised of anarchists, Communists, socialists, and anti-racist skinheads, they have increasingly attracted members with more mainstream politics following Trump's election.

There is some disagreement exactly where Antifa fits into the world of extremist hate and terrorism. According to an article on Politico, Antifa is considered a domestic terrorist group by the Department of Homeland Security. However, the SPLC, while criticizing their violent tactics, has said they don't consider Antifa a hate group, an opinion for which the organization was vilified by some Republicans and right-wing websites as politically influenced.[3]

Perhaps surprisingly, Antifa shares its origin story and some of its techniques in common with groups like the Oath Keepers. Antifascists are motivated by the idea that if Nazis were more ferociously confronted in the 1920s and 30s, they would never have been able take over Germany. Stewart Rhodes, founder of the Oath Keepers, has long been convinced that if law enforcement and the military refused Hitler's orders, his power would have collapsed.

Likewise, both operate under the principle that law enforcement may not be up to the job of protecting Americans' freedoms. As a result, they carry weapons with them in the event of direct clashes. But while Oath Keepers carry assault rifles and wear bulletproof vests, Antifa typically have nothing more offensive than flag poles or homemade shields with bolts sticking out.

Both groups also played critical roles as unofficial police forces at the 2017 Unite the Right rally in Charlottesville. Despite the presence of hundreds of local and state police officers and members of the Virginia National Guard, the main rally on August 12 quickly devolved into widespread violence, with people hurling water bottles and spraying tear and pepper gas, while hundreds of others engaged in street fights.

The law enforcement on hand was roundly criticized for not doing its job. In one episode, a white nationalist protester wearing a bulletproof vest pointed a gun at a crowd of counter-protesters before firing a shot at the ground. He then reportedly turned and walked past a crowd of a dozen police officers who were standing behind a barricade ten feet away.

Complaints about law enforcement did not come just from counter-protesters. Rally organizer Jason Kessler said, "The police were supposed to be there protecting us, and they stood down."[4]

The 3%ers, Oath Keepers, and other militias that showed up with their paramilitary gear, assault rifles, and an announced mission to protect free speech rights were seemingly more effective. According to multiple attendees at the rally, the conspiratorial, anti-government militias essentially replaced the official law enforcement, which remained behind barriers even as fights broke out.

Antifa was also present in large numbers at the rally and were credited by members of an inter-faith group with saving their lives by fending off over a hundred neo-Nazis. According to multiple members of the clergy, they would have been killed without Antifa's intervention, while police and the National Guard stood watching.[5] Antifa's mission was not apolitical or peaceful, though. One member was captured on video punching Richard Spencer in the midst of raucous protest.

In the same infamous press conference in which President Trump equated the violence of neo-Nazis and white supremacists with that of counter-protestors at Charlottesville, he also labeled Antifa and related groups the alt-left. Trump had campaigned on victimization, somehow managing to be both the GOP frontrunner and under attack by his own party. Once he won the presidency and both houses of Congress, Trump needed to keep alive the narrative that he and his supporters were still victims.

With Black Lives Matter keeping a lower profile since 2016, Antifa emerged as the favorite target and villain of the right. Its members are consistently accused of suppressing free speech rights at pro-Trump, anti-Muslim, Patriot, and other right-wing rallies. Paradoxically, Antifa is blamed for being responsible for the violence at rallies, even as engaging in fights with Antifa members is a draw card for right-wing attendees. For the extremist right, Antifa is a win-win proposition.

The loosely bound movement has also become the subject of multiple far-right conspiracy theories. According to the SPLC, one theory claimed that Antifa "has become so vast, powerful and insidious that it threatens to overthrow the American government through an overnight revolution that entails the beheadings of white Christians."[6]

Another popular theory, propagated by Alex Jones, was that Antifa was going to start a civil war on November 4, 2017. Though the revolution never happened, a mass shooting at a Texas church the following day was immediately seized on by conspiracists as evidence of an unfolding plan. Oath Keepers' Stewart Rhodes warned his followers to expect a wave of left-wing terrorism aimed at conservatives, police, the military, and others. "Prepare yourselves," he said, "in case this does lead to a full blown civil war."[7]

Since Trump's election, angry divisiveness has become the only unifying feature of the nation's political landscape. On election night, tens of thousands of people protested across the country, from high-school students walking out of class to groups of people blocking freeways. In Portland, Oregon, up to four thousand people protested for six days. The incidents devolved into violence as some protestors smashed businesses with baseball bats, lit dumpsters on fire, and clashed with police who, in return, shot flash-bang grenades and tear gas and arrested over a hundred people.

The day after Trump's inauguration, half a million people marched in protest in Washington, DC—the city's largest ever rally—with hundreds of thousands joining in local protests across the country and world. The trollish online battles that had overtaken newspaper and website comment streams prior to 2016 played out on the streets of cities from Boston to Austin to Portland to Berkeley and Washington, DC.

The establishment press, like the *Washington Post* and *New York Times*, have run an average of at least one negative opinion piece on Trump's administration every day. The most consistent political goal of Democrats could be reduced to #resist and #impeach. In this feverish atmosphere, those opposed to Trump and the alt-right have also become more likely to engage in more extremist behavior. For example, during a May 2017 appearance on CNN, Democratic senator Ed Markey claimed that a grand jury was investigating Trump's collusion with Russia. It was a bombshell—and also untrue.

According to the *New Republic*, the rumor had been championed by a liberal blog known as the *Palmer Report*—a sort of left-wing Breitbart— and by anti-Trump Twitter personalities. What was clear was that the senator made the announcement without any sort of reliable reporting behind it. It's also clear that it was the sort of news that appealed to Democrats—probably including Markey—on an emotional level. Finally, a left-wing conspiracy theory had made it to the political mainstream!

A PEW research poll conducted in September and October 2018 showed, not surprisingly, that Democrats and Republican voters were massively separated on many of the biggest issues facing the country.[8] For example, only 10 percent of people who supported a Republican candidate thought that the way minorities were treated by the criminal justice system was a big problem, while 71 percent of people who supported Democratic candidates did—a 61 percent difference.[9] There were similar partisan discrepancies about the importance of climate change (61 percent), gun violence (56 percent), and the gap between rich and poor (55 percent).[10] Not surprisingly, there was also a 56 percent partisan gap over whether illegal immigration was considered a very big problem—an issue about which there had been much more bipartisan consensus before 2006.[11]

All of the division during the past year has sat very well with Trump. Many pundits thought he would have to switch course—to compromise and lower his rhetoric and act "more presidential"—once elected. But he has remained in an extremist world dominated by *Fox and Friends* and the few dozen people he follows on Twitter. Trump surfed into the White House on a wave of enthusiasm for an alt-right agenda of whitewashed extremism. But while his election was a symptom of that extremism, his presidency has also filled extremism's most obvious hole. He provides a public, charismatic leader around whom to unify. Partisanship begets partisanship. Extremism begets extremism. Where is this going?

CHAPTER SEVENTEEN

THE STATE OF THE UNION

The men spent weeks in a secluded cabin in Maryland, stockpiling arms and secretly training their unofficial militia. They knew their effort to violently take over a federal building might be a suicide mission but were convinced the time for political solutions was past. Their sacrifice, the men reasoned, would set off a violent insurrection—the only way to cleanse the nation.

This scenario sounds like the apocalyptic *Turner Diaries*-inspired fever dream of a modern right-wing extremist militia. But it actually describes the planning for radical abolitionist John Brown's 1859 raid on a US Army fort in Harper's Ferry, Virginia. Brown had hoped to seize arms and march down through the Appalachians, arming slaves in an insurrection that would eventually engulf the entire South.

Militarily, Brown's raid was a near complete failure but, just as his takeover of a federal building prefigured a modern militia's plan, the heated national debate that followed the raid sounds awfully familiar. Southern Democrats' reaction was a ferocious anger mixed with paranoia. The other side, which consisted mostly of Republican Northerners, thought Brown's effort was misguided, but more than few added that his plan to spark violent rebellion throughout nearly half the country was nonetheless righteous. Northern abolitionist and author Henry David Thoreau went so far as to say said that Brown had the "spark of divinity about him."[1] While Brown and his men were killed before inspiring any slaves to join them, the debate that followed his raid is itself considered a direct step toward the Civil War that broke out the following year.

Following the 2017 riots in Charlottesville, Virginia, the previously unthinkable specter of a second American civil war emerged for serious speculation. On August 14, the *New Yorker*'s Robin Wright asked: "Is America Headed for a New Kind of Civil War?"[2]

One of the national-security experts Wright interviewed, Keith Mines, who spent time with US Special Forces, the United Nations, and the State Department in the midst of multiple foreign civil wars, estimated that the US has a 60 percent chance of entering a civil war in the next 10–15 years. Other experts quoted put the likelihood of civil war at anywhere from a minimal 5 percent to virtually inevitable at 95 percent.[3]

The type of civil war these experts weighed in on would likely not resemble the formal military encounters seen at Gettysburg in 1863. The event would probably be closer to the Iraqi insurrection against US occupation, an ongoing and deadly campaign of political violence that required military intervention. The wide range of estimates revealed how hard it is to judge something that has no parallel in modern American history. Nonetheless, it's frightening that the question suddenly requires serious thought.

Of course, right-wing extremist groups have long thought—and sometimes acted—on the assumption that an apocalyptic clash was not just inevitable but desirable. The current gleeful anticipation of such an event across wide sections of the conspiratorial right is also concerning.

In June of 2017, the *Guardian* reviewed a number of right-wing pundits' claims that a type of civil war was inevitable or already ongoing, including columns appearing in the *National Review* and the *Federalist*. Many, like Pat Buchanan writing in the *American Conservative*, were using the term civil war somewhat metaphorically, but their language was still militant: "To prevail, Trump will have to campaign across this country and wage guerrilla war in this capital, using the legal and political weapons at his disposal."[4] Injected into the feverish, conspiratorial media ecosystem, such claims are just one step short of calling for actual violence.

A year later, on June 3, 2018, the right-wing conspiracy blog *Zero-Hedge* republished a speech called "The Modern Civil War is Being Fought Without Guns . . . So Far!" It was pure clickbait, but was also picked up by multiple similar sites, shared 4,600 times and garnered 250 comments, some pro-civil war and many confident of a right-wing victory.

On June 25, Iowa representative Steve King tweeted a picture of an encampment around an ICE office in Portland, Oregon, with the caption "America headed in the direction of another Harper's Ferry. After that comes Ft. Sumter."[5] Two days later, Gab, the right-wing social network, announced in a since-deleted tweet "Civil War 2.0 is going to be lit. Who has all the guns and grows all the food?"[6]

Alex Jones jumped on the bandwagon in early July, tweeting "BREAKING: Democrats Plan to Launch Civil War on July 4th."[7] Although he was roundly mocked, Jones's influence—remember that he provoked a listener to fire shots in a pizzeria based on rumors that it housed Democratic-controlled child trafficking ring—can never be completely ignored. Neither can the 2018 re-election of Congressman King, just a few months after predicting civil war.

Time magazine's May 11, 2015 black-and-white cover featured an African American man running down a Baltimore street with dozens of riot gear-clad police in pursuit. The text, "AMERICA, 1968 2015," was another comparison of the current United States with one of the most turbulent periods of its history. But some comparisons between the American tumult of five decades ago—which did not lead to civil war—and today suggest that the US is not actually going down the path of sustained, existential warfare. For all its divisiveness, today's level of public violence has nothing on the late 1960s and early 70s, with its multiple riots, assassinations, and the raucous protests against a disastrous war, all of which created the environment in which left-wing extremist groups like the Weathermen and Black Panther Party emerged.

Likewise, despite all the divisiveness and partisanship, there is no singularly irreconcilable issue like slavery. Abolitionists saw it as an unforgivable evil. Southerners believed that its destruction would mean tearing apart the entire economic and quasi-feudal cultural and social fabric of Southern life. The nation is much more integrated now, economically and socially. For most people, immigration, abortion, gun control, and other wedge issues have nowhere near the same overall impact as slavery did, particularly in the South.

But what is unique—and uniquely terrifying—about the United States today is that extremism, specifically right-wing radicalism, has entered the political mainstream more effectively at any time since at least the 1960s. Through the Trump administration and some members of Congress, it is directly connected to the levers of national political power. During his campaign and presidency, Donald Trump continually attacked national political institutions, including the legal system, elected officials and the media, encouraged violence and vigilantism, and repeatedly pushed back on democratic norms—including election results themselves.

In fact, many of the same factors that delivered the presidency to Trump—intractable political polarization, debilitated institutions, and extremely divisive media coverage—are cited by many historians, diplomats, and military experts as typical preconditions for civil war.

And, while a low-level civil war sounds better than a series of massive, bloody confrontations, it's also harder to know when you are slipping into one. Author Robert Evans wrote that Ukrainians he interviewed often described their civil war not as a defined event but a "bad dream."[8] Very few of them thought civil war was a possibility until bullets started flying. Likewise, in the midst of Lebanon's civil war, which eventually resulted in 120,000 fatalities, many people remained convinced that things weren't that bad. Though it lasted fifteen years, some people remained convinced it was always on the verge of ending.[9]

As they suddenly find themselves in a war, people act in ways they wouldn't have believed possible. David Kilcullen, a former state department employee focused on counterterrorism, describes debriefing captured insurgents in Iraq. The soldiers claimed that a form of "collective madness" came over them—they couldn't recognize their behavior during the war.[10] The dynamic sounds a lot like internet trolls' frenzied doxing attacks on harmless victims they don't know, except that instead of posting addresses and death threats, the soldiers cut off children's heads.

Another way to view post-2016 America is in terms of the process of radicalization. For example, the stabilizers critical to grounding individuals are now shredded on a national level. The sense the country is on a track to greater things is derailed. In July of 2016, multiple polls showed that between 60–80 percent of Americans thought the US was not headed in the right direction.[11] Likewise, any measurement of traditional religion's ability to bind the country shows precipitous slippage. In the past two years, attendance at churches, synagogues, or mosques has hit historic lows, as has the number of people saying that religion is very important in their lives.[12] Not only are marriage rates the lowest they've been in American history, but even the idea of what makes a family is divisive.[13] At the same time, other typical stabilizers like civic duty, education, and social networks have been increasingly captured by polarizing media and tribal online relationships. But how would we know if the toxic divisiveness in the United States was deteriorating into a situation that met the modern definition of a civil war? Based on the extremist activity we've seen to date, what might be possible trigger events?

In the days before the 2016 presidential election, Trump made clear that the only way he believed he could lose was if the system was rigged against him. He encouraged vigilante-like unofficial observers at polls. He said he would only accept the results if he won. And, even after winning the Electoral College majority, Trump insisted—possibly following the lead of Alex Jones—that his loss in the popular vote was the result of millions of non-citizens voting for his opponent, despite a lack of any evidence. Following the 2018 midterm elections, which produced a mixed result for the Republican Party, the president again made unfounded claims about vote fraud and encouraged states with close races to abandon legally mandated vote recounts.

By 2020, the combination of an incumbent president who has spent his first four years attacking democratic institutions, highly publicized claims of both voter fraud and culling, and a hyper-partisan and conspiratorial media ecosystem guarantees that large segments of armed right-wing extremists—and possibly left-wing and African American extremist groups—will be convinced that any electoral result they don't support is illegitimate. The election of Abraham Lincoln in 1860 all but guaranteed the Civil War. The election of anyone might pose a similar challenge 160 years later.

Another scenario involves the appearance of the Oath Keepers, 3%ers, and other heavily armed militias as private police forces at politically charged protests around the country. Through 2016, the groups occasionally usurped the traditional power of local police, but generally maintained that their role was to protect all Americans' constitutional rights from an encroaching government. Following the election of Trump, their mission has changed dramatically. Instead of keeping their assault rifles aimed at a reputedly dangerous US government, they have increasingly become a freelance right-wing security force.

In 2017, the Portland, Oregon–area Republican Party voted to accept the Oath Keepers' and 3%ers' offers to serve as security guards. For some reason, the local GOP apparently didn't think the local police were sufficient to protect its members from alleged Antifa violence.[14] In June of that year, the relationship between local police and unofficial militia security became even more blurred when a militiaman at a Patriot Prayer rally in Portland ended up assisting police in arresting a left-wing protestor.

In 2018, the Oath Keepers also organized a blatantly partisan protest outside of the Los Angeles offices of Democratic congresswoman Maxine Waters—and one that had nothing to do with protecting the Constitution. She had recently called for Americans to make members of Trump's cabinet feel unwelcome at restaurants and other public places. Oath Keepers leader Stewart Rhodes, who claims to be a fierce proponent of the Bill of Rights, claimed that Waters had overstepped her free speech boundaries and incited terrorist violence. In his press release, Rhodes also echoed administration talking points, including unfounded claims about Mexico exporting terror, rape, murder, and corruption to the United States.[15]

Today, the number of Patriot and militia groups is significantly lower than in 2015—this decline is a typical trend under Republican presidencies. But the drop-off in extremist groups is largely the result of a wholesale embrace of Trump's agenda. Why join a marginal group training in the woods when the president had taken on your agenda? Following the president's decision to send thousands of US troops to the Mexican border to intercept a migrant "caravan," Patriot groups and militias also sent out a call to arms. The military, however, considered the groups' decision to self-deploy a couple hundred members as unhelpful and potentially dangerous. A memo noted that, while most members cooperate with the military, there have been "incidents of unregulated militias stealing National Guard equipment during deployments."[16]

There are, however, two much larger dangers. First, that the presence of conspiratorial paramilitary groups becomes accepted—or even critical—to law enforcement activities throughout the United States. Second, that the president or other right-wing political figures decide to use the militias as private security forces to intimidate political opponents, expanding on the example of the Portland GOP.

In November 2018, after being asked about how police should handle a loud Antifa rally outside of right-wing journalist Tucker Carlson's house in Washington, DC, President Trump gave an inauspicious answer. According to him, the police didn't really have a role in dealing with the public disturbance. Instead, Trump suggested that Antifa was lucky that the opposition to them hadn't attacked them because they're "much stronger. Potentially much more violent. And Antifa's going to be in big trouble."[17]

As citizens, we accept that agents of the state have the monopoly on legal violence. But, today, that confidence is strongly divided along partisan lines. In 2016, 48 percent of Democratic voters expressed confidence in the police against 68 percent of Republicans. Among African Americans, that number bottomed out at 30 percent.[18] Among extremist groups, Antifa protestors frequently take oppositional stances against police presence, often accusing them of favoring right-wing groups and engaging in overly militarized and unconstitutional crowd control efforts.

The combination of declining police legitimacy among left-of-center groups and an increased use of militias as de facto security forces for mainstream right-wing groups is a troubling trend. The more public emergence of armed left-wing and African American groups—as in the late 1960s and 70s—to oppose right-wing militias and police is increasingly likely. In this case, the potential for serious, partisan violence would be high, and would quickly lead to rioting and further destabilization.

Another scenario envisioned by Robert Davis in the November 2016 issue of *Cracked* magazine is a civil war that breaks along rural and urban fault lines, as opposed to a North-South divide. This dynamic is most pronounced in the Western United States. Idaho and Montana have long histories of activity by neo-Nazis, white supremacists, millenarians, survivalists, militias, and other far-right groups. The Sovereign Citizen movement was born in neighboring Oregon and California. All three Pacific coast states have a large number of militias and other extremist right-wing groups, primarily in the interior and eastern portions of the states. But the big urban centers, Los Angeles, San Francisco, Portland, and Seattle, are among the most liberal cities in the country.

What's more, in many rural areas of the country, local police are outgunned by militia groups. Some militia groups explicitly cite the success of al-Qaeda in fighting the US military to a standstill in Afghanistan as a model. If even a handful of well-prepared militiamen in these areas decided to borrow these tactics, they could cause massive damage to the cities full of Democrats, liberals, minorities, and other supposed enemies.

Here's just one plausible scenario. US Interstate 5, which connects the major West Coast cities, stretches 1,400 miles through mostly sparsely populated areas. Tannerite is a widely available explosive that is essentially the same material used in WWII bombs. Logistically, it would be relatively easy for rural militias to plant powerful explosive devices along I-5, disrupting traffic and isolating the cities. Most importantly, in the United States, 90 percent of food is delivered by truck. If cities full of millions of people had their food supply disrupted, the resulting chaos would be massively destabilizing.

There is, however, a much more important issue than the plausibility of widespread and sustained civil unrest: what measures might push back the violent extremism that has more than a foothold in the nation's mainstream.

CHAPTER EIGHTEEN

KNOW THY ENEMY

In September 2012, the increase in violent domestic extremism was extremely troubling.

The previous month had been a busy one for violent extremists. A white supremacist killed six worshippers at a Sikh temple. Sovereign Citizens shot four sheriff's deputies, killing two. Four active duty US Army soldiers, who had formed a militia, began stockpiling weapons in an alleged plot to overthrow government. They were arrested after killing two other members whom they suspected were going to turn them in. And, a few blocks away in Washington, DC, a man non-fatally shot the security guard outside an anti-LGBT think tank.

Between 2008 and 2012, it was already clear that extremism was on the rise. There had been a combined 149 Patriot and militia groups in 2008. In 2012, that number hit 1360.[1] Meanwhile, there were 1,007 hate groups in 2012, the second highest number ever. As many of the report's predictions came to fruition, the government had taken little to no action to limit or even understand the threat.

So, on September 19, 2012, I gave testimony in front of the Senate subcommittee on Hate Crimes and the Threat of Domestic Extremism with the hope of changing this passive stance.

In 1999, the FBI released a report stating that "during the past 30 years, the vast majority—but not all—of the deadly terrorist attacks occurring in the United States have been perpetrated by domestic extremists."[2] Two years later, the World Trade Center went down and US intelligence agencies, law enforcement, and military scrambled to focus on the threat posed by agile, stateless Islamic terrorism.

The reorientation was necessary and had some successes. Intelligence agencies were better at communicating terror threats with each other and, through Joint Terrorism Task Forces, local law enforcement. The FBI and police developed good relationships with some local Muslim leaders. No more planes were hijacked. The military had all but destroyed al-Qaeda's operational ability. But the United States' massive counter-terrorism apparatus, which now dedicated the vast majority of resources on violent Islamic extremism, once again missed a growing threat.

In the eleven years since 9/11, Muslim extremists had carried out five fatal attacks in the United States, killing seventeen, including thirteen in a single incident in Fort Hood, Texas. In just the four years since the 2008 presidential election, domestic non-Islamic extremists had carried out many more attacks and killed more Americans. These attacks included, but were not limited to, shooting twenty-seven law enforcement officers, killing sixteen of them. The government's response, pushing almost all its resources into preventing extremist Islamic attacks, had been woefully inadequate.

Part of the problem was that government agencies hadn't even defined basic terms—like domestic terrorism—clearly or accurately. Take the case of an anti-tax zealot who killed an employee after crashing a small plane into an IRS processing center. Department of Homeland Security (DHS) Secretary Janet Napolitano said that the pilot "used a terrorist tactic . . . but he's not necessarily the member of a terrorist group . . . this is an individual who had his own personal issues and personal motives."[3] Meanwhile, the FBI never publicly disclosed whether the attack was considered terrorism, but Congress passed a resolution declaring the attack an act of terrorism. Everyone had the same facts, but there were three different answers about whether or not it was terror—the defining national security threat of the day.

Napolitano's statement also showed outdated thinking on what constitutes modern domestic extremism and terrorism. Since the 1980s, in part due to successful law enforcement efforts, domestic extremist groups began to adapt what white nationalist Louis Beam called a "leaderless resistance" strategy. Ideologies and conspiracy theories shared by neo-

Nazis, anti-Semitics, and white nationalists might guide the extremist, but he no longer operated as part of a large group like The Order in the early 1980s. In fact, rather than linking them with a group, contemporary domestic extremists can be better categorized according to their ideologies that inspire radicalization and motivate them toward violence.

The switch away from large, hierarchical groups had Beam's intended effect: making it harder for law enforcement to detect individual actors. It was also much more difficult to take down a whole organization at once.

The transition did have downsides for violent extremists. For example, it inhibited the most lethal capacities of actors who didn't already have training in, say, explosives. But the lone wolves were able to adapt. Over the past few decades, for example, readily available firearms replaced more complicated explosives as a weapon of choice. A mass shooting—or simply driving a vehicle into a crowd—required a relatively low level of training compared to blowing up a building.

By 2012, websites and social media also provided new tools for the self-training that Beam had called for in the 1980s. The transition from large groups to single actors was increasingly preferred by extremists across the political spectrum, including jihadists.

In other words, Secretary Napolitano's claim that someone couldn't be a terrorist or domestic extremist because they weren't part of large, well-delineated group that set off bombs was based on an extremely outdated model. We can't fight domestic terror if we can't identify it.

There were other deficiencies with the US government's response to terrorism, including a lack of basic authoritative reporting and analysis. The National Counterterrorism Center and US Department of State provided the law enforcement and intelligence communities with an annual summary of worldwide terrorism. But there was no longer an annual report summarizing domestic terrorism within the United States, exactly where it might have been most useful for law enforcement and domestic intelligence agencies.

Beginning in 1980, the FBI published a publicly available annual report entitled "Terrorism in the United States." Among other things, it included an array of terrorism stats, trends, FBI initiatives, and policy information that made it very useful for law enforcement threat assessment, as well as academia and the media. For unknown reasons, the FBI ceased publishing this report in 2005—just a few years before domestic extremist activity began spiking.

This lack of information is all the more damaging to efforts to understand and mitigate domestic extremism, because the FBI is the only federal agency with devoted multiple full-time resources to research and analyze domestic terrorist tactics, tradecraft, and emerging trends. However, as valuable as their expertise is, the FBI is limited to its law enforcement mission. In other words, it has to establish "probable cause" or "reasonable suspicion" of criminal activity prior to collecting, analyzing, and retaining information pertaining to domestic extremist activity. This means that the FBI's expertise is not used in, or available to, agencies that forecast and warn of domestic terrorist activity before it happens.

The intelligence capacities of other law enforcement agencies is also limited. They might use resources to monitor some aspects of domestic extremism, but only on an ad hoc basis. Unlike the FBI, they don't expend effort to develop subject matter specialists.

This has not always been the case. DHS had five analysts with subject matter expertise who were responsible for analyzing domestic non-Islamic extremist activity within the US. Although this group was dwarfed by DHS's Islamist extremist team, its specialized resources were essential to tracking, understanding, and predicting the rise in domestic extremism.

By 2012, however, even that skeleton crew had been disbanded. By September, a single analyst at DHS was responsible for monitoring the entire spectrum of domestic non-Islamic extremism, a category that includes animal rights groups, ecoterrorists, neo-Nazis, black nationalists, the KKK, Sovereign Citizens, militias, and Patriot groups.

The scope of this sole analyst was even more limited. In 2010, DHS chose to limit analysis work to three categories: violent environmental extremists, violent anarchist extremists, and violent skinheads. In other words, there was no analysis of threats from neo-Nazis, Sovereign Citizens, and other violent anti-government extremists.

Unfortunately, this decision was not based on either threat levels or the violent capabilities of a particular group. Rather, these three groups were selected for more political reasons. First, they were the only domestic extremist movements with a history of attacking critical infrastructure. Second, all three movements were transnational in nature, supposedly mitigating any intelligence oversight, privacy, or civil rights and civil liberties concerns. Finally, and most oddly, these movements had no history of infiltrating law enforcement—thus limiting the potential for future leaks. This type of decision-making meant virtually ignoring the real and developing threats at the time, like Sovereign Citizens, militias, and black nationalists. In other words, it was not the way to secure the homeland.

In addition to a general lack of expert information on extremism, law enforcement tends toward policing based on reports of suspicious activity. "Suspicious behavior" can be valuable, but it is too subjective a category around which to base a law enforcement policy. For one, behavior reports produce an enormous number of false positives. Since 9/11, responding to reports of suspicious activity has proven time-consuming and results in highly intrusive privacy and civil rights problems without being a very effective use of resources.

What is missing, again, is expertise on domestic extremism, particularly an understanding of how critical ideology is to extremists' future actions. While suspicious activity can be part of the overall equation in evaluating threats, it also needs to include an understanding of ideology, psychological factors, and—frequently—the precipitating life event(s) that precede violent extremist attacks. Combining these indicators will also likely reduce the number of false positives and resulting civil rights infringements.

Training in Behavioral Threat Assessment is also essential to the identification of problem individuals—before another incident like the Sikh temple shooting occurs. The law enforcement community appears to have neglected this effective analytical tool, choosing instead to emphasize suspicious activity reporting. The threat management methodology as a law enforcement tool has proven effective time and again, but it is not being used.

Unfortunately, neither my testimony—nor those of multiple experts from the FBI, DHS, and other intelligence operations—led to any of the much needed changes in the nation's lagging response to violent domestic extremism. The only meaningful change from this hearing was adding "Sikhs" to the FBI's hate crime reporting requirements.

Although the federal government wasn't taking action on the threats, law enforcement had noticed the uptick in activity. A 2014 University of Maryland national survey of state and local law enforcement officers found that Sovereign Citizens were the "top concern" for terrorist threats.[4] Jihadist-inspired terrorism ranked second, closely followed by militia/anti-government and white supremacist threats.

Two years later, the Center for Investigative Reporting reported that, between 2008 and 2016, there were nearly twice as many domestic terrorist attacks and plots as jihadist-inspired incidents. What's more, nearly half of the jihadist incidents were FBI sting operations.[5] Because they insert a motivated professional into the plot planning, sting operations are more likely to advance to the stage where an arrest can be made.

This massive disparity was indicative of the continued lopsided nature of US government counterterrorism and investigative resources. As the threat had grown since 2012, domestic non-Islamic terrorists continued to get far fewer resources—such as analysts, agents, informants, operatives—to analyze, assess, investigate, and prosecute. Fifteen years after the attacks of 9/11, government agencies had still not realized that the biggest threat the country faced was not jihadism.

In May of 2017, the FBI and DHS reported that white supremacist extremism posed a persistent threat of lethal violence, and white supremacists were responsible for forty-nine homicides in twenty-six attacks from 2000 to 2016—more than any other domestic extremist movement.

Three months later, in August, a Congressional Research Service report again highlighted the growing threat from domestic terrorists. As in 2012, the report detailed[6] the problems in law enforcement and intelligence gathering efforts, including the lack of an official domestic terrorist group list, overly broad and confusing federal definitions of "domestic terrorism," and insufficient resources allocated to the prominent threat.

Finally, in November 2017, three months after the fatal white supremacist and neo-Nazi rally in Charlottesville, Senator Dick Durbin introduced legislation that acted on these years of recommendations and warnings. The Domestic Terrorism Prevention Act took some good steps, such as requiring the offices already involved in monitoring and prosecuting domestic terrorism, such as the FBI and DHS, to provide the basic information needed to make informed decisions about combatting extremism. These groups had to issue joint annual congressional reports that assessed the domestic terrorism threat posed by white supremacists, analyzed the previous year's domestic terrorism incidents, and provided a public quantitative analysis of domestic terrorism-related assessments, investigations, incidents, arrests, indictments, prosecutions, convictions, and weapons recoveries. In other words, the bill would give senators and representatives a full reporting on what was happening on the ground in the battle against domestic extremism.

The bill also freed the limited resources used to track domestic terrorism from political interference. Instead, resources would be focused on the most significant threats, based on the number of domestic terrorism-related incidents.

Among other measures, the bill also encouraged better information sharing by requiring the Department of Justice and FBI to train and assist state and local law enforcement and help them develop plans to combat domestic terrorism activities in their jurisdictions.

Unfortunately, even in the wake of the Charlottesville tragedy, the bill had no chance of passing the Republican-controlled Senate. Even more discouragingly, the Trump administration has no interest in cracking down on right-wing extremists. In fact, it appears quite the opposite.

The current political climate is having a dramatic impact on right-wing extremism in America. When I wrote my 2009 DHS assessment about the rise of right-wing extremism, I never envisioned it would last ten years and beyond. I believe several factors have contributed to right-wing extremism thriving and growing under a Republican administration.

First, under Trump's administration, federal domestic terrorism training for state and local law enforcement, called SLATT, was canceled in October 2017 and is no longer funded. No other program has replaced it.

Second, soon after taking office, Trump's administration also abruptly canceled federal grant funding to two organizations that were working on countering violent extremism (CVE) by white nationalists. One of the award recipients, Life After Hate, was a nonprofit group devoted to helping people leave white supremacist groups. The other grant was supposed to be awarded to the University of North Carolina, which was developing media campaigns for young people directed at dissuading their peers from embracing white supremacy and other violent extremist ideologies. Trump's administration essentially narrowed the federal CVE grant funding to focus exclusively on Muslim radicalization threats.

Third, and more disturbing, Trump has mainstreamed right-wing extremist themes from the dark recesses of the internet into the general public. For example, building a southern border wall, banning travel from Muslim countries, and mass deportation of immigrants were ideas once discussed on white supremacist computer message boards merely ten years ago. Now, they are put forth as presidential policy recommendations. This sends a subtle signal to the far-right fringes that the president tacitly supports their radical political and social platforms.

Fourth, Trump often takes to social media to demonize his opposition with negative labels, which has the potential to push radicalized extremists over the edge into violence against such opponents. He's even forwarded false information on his Twitter account that originated with racist and conspiracy theory websites.

Finally, when the president uses terms such as "nationalist" to describe patriotism or refers to a Central American immigrant caravan migrating toward the US as "invaders," it resonates with right-wing extremists and has the potential to embolden them. When extremists hear the president say "nationalist," they hear "white nationalist." When he says "invaders," they equate that to a national-security threat. When Trump says "globalization," right-wing extremists hear "New World Order" or the Jewish conspiracy to control the world.

For these reasons, the lunatic fringe of the far right will continue to operate at a heightened level of activity for the next few years. Unfortunately, some will radicalize to the point of taking violent action. Even if Trump completely stopped his dog whistles and dehumanizing talk today, it will still take months, perhaps even years, to have a decelerating impact on right-wing extremist recruitment and radicalization activities.

Of course, even a really motivated government response to domestic extremism wouldn't squelch it out immediately. The conditions that gave rise to the current mainstreaming of radical ideologies have much to do with private media companies, the intricacies of the internet, and long-standing biases and paranoia. That said, even providing an accurate and consistent definition for domestic terrorism, reporting basic information on extremist activity to law enforcement, and providing a modicum of funding for expert subject matter analysis can make a very real difference. To look at what this could mean in the real world, let's revisit the investigation following the October 1, 2017 mass shooting in Las Vegas.

The shooter, Stephen Paddock, targeted a crowd of roughly 22,000 country music fans at the Highway 91 festival. In just ten minutes, he shot 1,100 rounds out of his room on the thirty-second floor of the Mandalay Bay hotel. It was the deadliest mass shooting perpetrated by a single gunman in US history, with 58 people killed and 546 injured. An hour later, Paddock was found dead in his hotel room.

In January 2018, the Las Vegas Metropolitan Police Department issued their definitive report on the incident. Based on 1,965 investigated leads, 21,560 hours of video, 251,099 images, and 746 legal notices filed, the reported stated that "nothing was found to indicate motive on the part of Paddock or that he acted with anyone else." The report also stated that "there was no evidence of radicalization or ideology to support any theory that Paddock supported or followed any hate groups or any domestic or foreign terrorist organizations."

This analysis fit into the general consensus about Paddock: a disgruntled middle-aged guy who snapped. But, to anyone with subject-matter expertise, the official report and some media coverage suggested a very different conclusion about Paddock's motives.

Paddock primarily grew up in Sun Valley, an underprivileged, economically depressed suburb of Los Angeles. He was the eldest of four sons. His father was a bank robber who was arrested when Paddock was seven.

A former middle school and high school classmate of his, Greg Palast, described Paddock as extremely smart, yet angry and resentful at his core.[7] Palast, a well-known investigative journalist, characterized Paddock as being closed-in, self-absorbed, and narcissistic, as well as having "a God complex." Palast suspected that Paddock was frustrated because his increased intellect did not immediately translate into opportunity, a conviction that possibly contributed to a lifetime of suppressed rage.

Richard Alarcon, a classmate, described Paddock as exhibiting anti-authority behavior early in life. "The thing that set Paddock apart," said Alarcon, "was his 'irreverence' toward authority."[8] Another credible witness corroborated Alarcon's recollection of Paddock's disrespect for authority, blaming it on his growing anger, resentment, and frustration.

Nonetheless, Paddock went on to graduate from high school and then Cal State, Northridge in 1977 with a degree in business administration. That same year, he got married, but was divorced by 1979. From a cone of radicalization standpoint, by the time Paddock was twenty-six, he likely had several weakened inhibitors, including family estrangement, an absent father, and a divorce. He also had several active destabilizers, including anger and resentment. But for the next thirty years, there was—as the Las Vegas police report stated—no evidence he was engaged in any extremist activities.

Paddock did, however, exhibit strong political leanings during that time. A real estate broker who helped Paddock sell multiple properties in California said he expressed a "dislike for taxes and the government—even selling off a series of buildings in California to move his money to the low-tax havens of Texas and Nevada." Bruce Paddock, Stephen's brother, recalled "how his brother used to do the family's tax returns and juice them so they would get back thousands of dollars in refunds."

Likewise, Adam Le Fevre, Paddock's brother-in-law, described Paddock as "animated about the government and the tax system." Paddock "was outspoken about the inadequacies and waste of the government," and "frustrated with the policy of government, in general."[9]

Le Fevre also recalled Paddock giving him a tour of his Nevada home, during which he made sure to point out his "gun room." Le Fevre said Paddock had an "obsession with guns." Paddock, Le Fevre claimed, also became very defensive when asked about the Second Amendment right to bear arms. "He was very strict and very firm on the fact that it's a right. It's the freedom of every American to participate, to own a gun and use it ... when need be." Paddock, who had acquired dozens of guns by 2016, "made it very clear he would have no part of gun ownership restrictions," said Le Fevre.

These three credible witnesses claim Paddock had espoused anti-government beliefs, including disrespect for tax law and contempt for government regulation and firearms laws, all of which correlate to right-wing ideologies. Further, right-wing extremists are the most likely to commit tax fraud. Militia members and other right-wing anti-government extremists are also much more likely to stockpile firearms and ammunition—and to loathe firearms regulation, restrictions, and laws. Neither far-left extremists, nor even homegrown violent extremists, such as ISIS and al-Qaeda supporters, are as likely to hoard weapons.

Of course, the fact that Paddock owned lots of guns and complained angrily about the government does not in any way mean he subscribed to a violent extremist ideology. However, the testimony of several other witnesses about Paddock's enthusiasm for conspiracy theories makes it more plausible. While these statements need vetting and additional confirmation, the claims—made by three unrelated witnesses—at very least tend to support one another.

One witness, a Las Vegas prostitute who spoke on condition of anonymity, said she "would spend hours drinking and gambling in Las Vegas" with Stephen Paddock, who she described as "paranoid" and "obsessive."[10] The twenty-seven-year-old female escort added that Paddock would "often rant about conspiracy theories including how 9/11 was orchestrated by the US government." A second witness reported to police that she saw a man resembling Stephen Paddock with another white male at a Las Vegas restaurant three days before the shooting. Both were reportedly overheard ranting about the 1992 standoff at Ruby Ridge and the 1993 Waco siege.

While these topics are fairly common in right-wing extremist circles, a third conspiracy theory may have direct relevance to the Las Vegas shooting. Another witness says he met Paddock in September 2017 at a Bass Pro Shop in Las Vegas, Nevada, to arrange the purchase of engineering schematics for an auto-sear, which is a gun part used to convert an assault rifle from semi-automatic to fully automatic. Paddock attempted to bribe the seller to manufacture the auto-sear for him. When the seller refused, Paddock reportedly became upset and made references to Federal Emergency Management Agency—or FEMA—detention "camps," Hurricane Katrina, gun confiscations, and other anti-government conspiracy theories as part of his rationale for needing the auto-sears.[11]

Another witness verified Paddock's conspiratorial interest in hurricanes. "He asked me if I remembered Katrina," the witness told Las Vegas police. Paddock reportedly stated "that [Hurricane Katrina] was just a dry run for law enforcement and the military to start kicking down doors and confiscating guns."[12]

A closely related theory, and one also pushed by Alex Jones's InfoWars, claims the government can create severe weather, like tornados and hurricanes, using technology at the High Frequency Active Aural Research Program (HAARP) at the University of Alaska. The rumors regarding HAARP, formerly a US Air Force facility, became so commonplace that, in August 2016, the university decided to hold an open house to show it couldn't control weather or human minds.[13]

With or without the weather control theory, the basics of the FEMA camp conspiracy theory are the same: FEMA is part of the New World Order, which is planning to declare martial law, will place Americans in designated concentration camps, and confiscate all guns. In addition, it will impose an adult curfew, and suspend constitutional rights during a government-created or "false flag" state of emergency. Such beliefs are widespread in conspiratorial Patriot and militia groups. In fact, they are very similar to Oath Keepers founder Stewart Rhodes's prediction about the future of America under President "Hitlery" Clinton.

If these witness testimonies are true, and they do need further confirmation, it's clear that Paddock had aligned himself with extremely far-right extremist conspiracy theories. That, in turn, is insightful and potentially critical for determining Paddock's possible motivation for the Las Vegas shooting attack.

Paddock's history of gun purchases provides other clues. From 1982 through September of 2016, he purchased twenty-nine firearms. These purchases consisted of handguns, shotguns, and one rifle. However, from October 2016 through September 2017, Paddock purchased over fifty-five firearms. What's more, most of these weapons were assault rifles of varying calibers, along with over a hundred firearm-related accessories like scopes, cases, bump stocks, and ammunition.[14]

The apparent disparity in his gun purchasing suggests that, instead of just snapping relatively soon before the mass shooting, something in October 2016 may have triggered Paddock to begin preparing for some sort of attack. Authorities have acknowledged that their investigation also uncovered an intriguing turning point in Paddock's life around this time, although they haven't revealed it.[15]

Based on Paddock's reported obsession with hurricanes and his gun purchasing history, it's significant that the month of October coincides with the peak of the Atlantic hurricane seasonal cycle. What's more, the 2016 Atlantic hurricane season was the first above-average hurricane season since 2012, producing fifteen named storms, including seven hurricanes and four major hurricanes. Of these storms, Hurricane Matthew, which occurred in late September and October 2016, was the strongest, costliest, and deadliest with 603 deaths—47 in the United States—and $15.1 billion in property damage.

The 2017 Atlantic hurricane season was even worse. Characterized as "hyperactive" and "catastrophic," it was the costliest hurricane season on record. It is one of only six years on record to feature multiple Category 5 hurricanes making landfall.

In other words, Paddock's massive hoarding of assault weapons began following the worst hurricane season in four years and his shooting took place immediately following an even stronger season. The connection between intense hurricane activity and the shooting occurred to one witness, who described Paddock as "fanatical." It "struck me odd was when he did the shooting it was right after those hurricanes . . . You know, I mean first it was Irma, then Maria, and I believe that's when he did the shooting. He was just saying the government's gonna crack down on everybody who owns weapons."[16]

Despite not having known associations with far-right extremist groups, Paddock's behavior—conspiratorial thinking, hoarding guns and other materials like bulletproof vests and tracer rounds—closely aligns him with survivalists and conspiratorial militia groups. In fact, following the shooting, Paddock received public approval of a survivalist online, who described Paddock as the perfect "Gray Man."[17]

A Gray Man, or Gray Neighbor, is a term used within the survivalist/prepper community to describe someone who blends into society, avoids attention, conducts their weapons stockpiling and other operational activities in secret, and, most importantly, remains elusive from detection by government authorities. Survivalist Kevin Felts notes that Paddock had no criminal record, political affiliations, no record of mental illness, and no incidents of violence. What's more, his friends and family never realized he was massing a huge cache of firearms.[18] So, while law enforcement found no evidence of extremist motivations, a known survivalist said Paddock possessed and practiced many of the skills and tradecraft of a true prepper.

There is one other reported similarity between Paddock and other extremists across the political spectrum: the conviction that they are the only one who can wake up the American people to what is happening, in an attempt to start another revolution or civil war. This belief is prominent in the comments and written testimony of violent extremists, including Timothy McVeigh, Dylann Roof, Micah Johnson, and, according to one witness, Stephen Paddock. "Somebody has to wake up the American public and get them to arm themselves," Paddock reportedly said. "Some sacrifices have to be made."[19]

It's also notable that when violent extremists and terrorists target groups, they aren't necessarily trying to kill all their presumed enemies at once, but to set off a larger chain of events. McVeigh, for example, wanted to start a race war. So, while the Oklahoma City bombing killed primarily white people, his larger goal was to provoke a violent government over-reach, which would lead to a *Turner Diaries*-type apocalyptic race war in which the federal government would be destroyed. It's possible that, by perpetrating a mass shooting on a primarily white crowd, the conspiratorial Paddock wanted to provoke the government into a similar overreach.

There are multiple potential motivations for a shooting attack—just a few of them include sociopathy, mental illness, racial hatred, revenge, and a quest for fame. Despite the official claims about Paddock having no motivation for the shootings, his known behavior, activities, and life's events suggest three possibilities: violent anti-government extremism, sociopathy, or other mental illness. Of those, the most likely is anti-government extremism with the other motivations probably contributing.

After careful consideration of all the available facts, circumstances, and allegations publicly available surrounding the October 2017 Las Vegas shooting attack, the most plausible scenario supports the notion that Stephen Paddock embraced right-wing anti-government extremism and conspiracy beliefs. These beliefs, combined with his firearms stockpiling, likely contributed to his motivation and mobilization for the mass shooting. Further, the 2016 and 2017 Atlantic hurricane seasons, along with the Georgia arrests, may have served as the "catalyst" for Paddock's mobilization toward violence and expedited the timeline leading up to the attack. If law enforcement can substantiate the veracity of the aforementioned witness claims, especially those related to Paddock's anti-government and conspiracy-minded views, then Paddock likely had an ideological motive for his shooting attack, thus meeting the definition of domestic terrorism.

This conclusion, of course, completely contradicts the Las Vegas police report that Paddock was neither an extremist nor terrorist. While all the facts and testimony have yet to be confirmed, his misclassification would fit all too well into the many errors and shortcomings in the current approach to combatting extremism and terror. Further, there may be political reasons to not officially classify Paddock's actions as "domestic terrorism." Doing so, would, once again, take away from the US government's perception of terrorism and call into question its counterterrorism strategy.

There is a strong tendency to see violent attacks by non-Muslim whites not as terrorism, but as the random acts of maniacs. This is compounded by the disproportionate amount of resources spent on combatting Islamic extremism and the media coverage that gives 4.5 times as much exposure to acts of alleged Islamic extremism versus alleged non-Islamic extremism.

There is also a real dearth of reporting provided to law enforcement about what extremism looks like today. While Paddock's lack of involvement with known extremist groups is significant, it's more important to note what specific ideologies he embraced and how critical those could have been to his motives.

To a law enforcement officer reviewing the details of Paddock's case, his complaints about the government might fly under the radar because he didn't attack a government building. His huge gun collection might signify a kind of individual violent paranoia. And his obsession with hurricanes and FEMA might just seem like the mutterings of a madman. But, if the law enforcement officer is trained to recognize the behavior of modern domestic terrorist threats, Paddock suddenly looks like an archetypal paranoid, right-wing survivalist who shot up a bunch of innocent people in the hope of creating violent government overreach.

But today, the intelligence and law enforcement communities don't receive the basic data and information about domestic extremism necessary to develop prevention strategies, new policies, possible legal remedies, and—perhaps most important of all—identification of potential warning signs to encourage public reporting to authorities.

Finally, there is no clear universal definition of domestic terrorism. If, upon review, Paddock did fit into that definition, his fifty-eight victims would be considered victims of domestic terrorism—making it a lot harder to justify the insufficient resources available to prevent it. Without proper analysis, information sharing, and definitions, the people Paddock killed will continue to be considered victims of random gun violence, a much harder category to target.

CHAPTER NINETEEN

LOVE THY NEIGHBOR

In February 2017, Cleveland Cavaliers all-star guard Kyrie Irving made a bombshell claim on ESPN: "This is not even a conspiracy theory. The Earth is flat."[1] It was ridiculous, outlandish and, because of his huge media profile, changed the history of science—at least in certain isolated locations. One of the many critics of the basketball player's reckless conspiratorial suggestion was a middle school teacher named Nick Gurol. As a result of Irving's comments, Gurol said some of his students refused to believe that the earth was, in fact, round.[2]

Over the next year, Irving responded with a string of evasive comments, first suggested that people do their own research, then later that he had been joking and misunderstood. In October 2018, he eventually apologized.[3]

Irving was, however, not the only celebrity to endorse an idea that, for over a century, has been synonymous with someone who is backward and out of touch with reality. The previous year, rapper Bobby Ray Simmons Jr, AKA B.o.B, tweeted a picture of himself on an icy landscape with the skyline from two cities peeking out over the horizon: "The cities in the background are approx . . . 16 miles apart . . . where is the curve ? please explain this."

Nor was Irving the most flamboyant flat earther. Over the past few years, a Californian named Mike Hughes has launched himself higher and higher across the Mojave Desert in a series of homemade rockets. He claims his ultimate goal is to get to an altitude where he can photograph the reputedly flat earth.[4]

Although scientists have known the earth was round since at least the days of the Ancient Greeks, suspicions to the contrary have never been fully extinguished. Sometimes suggestions that, say, the earth is a disc ringed by a range of Antarctic mountains were even advanced by members of the scientific establishment.

The Flat Earth Society was founded in the United States in 1956, eventually claiming thousands of members, but membership fell off—figuratively—in 2001 after its founder's death. But, as with so many other less innocuous-sounding conspiracy theories, social media and video platforms have revived flat earth beliefs.

In 2009, an American named Daniel Shenton resurrected the Flat Earth Society.[5] Google searches for "flat earth" have been spiking since 2015. In an April 2018 a YouGov poll, 2 percent of Americans claimed that have always believed the Earth was flat. A further five percent said they had thought the Earth was round but had recently had doubts.[6] There are, apparently, more Americans on the fence about whether the planet is flat than there are residents of Florida.

It's not so shocking, then, that Flat Earth Society conventions in the United States and UK have grown in recent years, drawing hundreds of people. It was also not much of a surprise that, when Mark Wilding, a correspondent for *Esquire*, attended the 2018 Birmingham, UK, flat earth conference, he found that nearly every flat earther "traced their conversion back to YouTube."

Stephan Lewandowsky, a psychology professor at Bristol University, also points to social media. "I don't think there is a belief absurd enough that you can't find 1,000 people sharing it on Facebook," said Lewandowsky. "No one realised what was going to happen. It's just a sort of tragic consequence that our cognitive vulnerabilities are amplified by social media."[7]

Accident or not, the planet is now stuck with a massive social and information network that was supposed to put the world's knowledge at everyone's fingertips but, instead, encourages people to ignore facts they dislike. Via Facebook forums, this same technological marvel also provides social reinforcement for their burgeoning but sometimes unpopular conspiracism—much the way it benefited ostracized white supremacists.

As harmless as some absurd fringe theories seem, the current web-fueled explosion in "alternative facts" and hidden realities is dangerous. In the case of the flat earth, advocates have to be willing to refute centuries—if not millennia—of mainstream, established science. And, today, this is a chore that many people find incredibly easy.

During a chatty back and forth on an NBA podcast, Kyrie Irving argued that, from his personal experience, the Earth seemed to be flat and that he was certain science was corrupt: "It's right in front of our faces," he said, "They lie to us."[8] Likewise, Mike Hughes told NPR that, although he understood the science-based engineering he used to build his rockets—"aerodynamics and fluid dynamics and how things move through the air, about the certain size of rocket nozzles, and thrust"—he didn't believe in science. "There's no difference," he said, "between science and science fiction."[9] Hughes, and others, seemed to view science as an *a la carte* tray of knowledge.

For the concluding event of the Birmingham conference, three PhD candidates in physics and astronomy had agreed to debate the attendees. The scientists, confident that their vast and specific knowledge would at least make some flat earthers reevaluate the arguments they had cobbled together off of YouTube, ended up completely shell-shocked by attendees' resilience.

The problem, of course, was that flat earth theory rests on the irrefutable antilogic of all conspiracy theories: any evidence contrary to one's position simply reveals an even larger conspiracy against one's privileged knowledge. So, instead of answering questions about orbital dynamics, the graduate students were assailed with questions like: "Why does NASA fake everything?"

They also encountered an unshakeable faith that not one astronaut had ever been to space, that there were strings visible in the "faked" NASA videos of space walks, and that the technology didn't exist to land an expedition on the moon in 1969. If sane, educated people can dismiss one form of established knowledge that flippantly, what else can they deny or choose to believe?

According to Lewandowsky, people who are exposed to conspiracy theories, even if they don't buy into them, are subsequently less likely to believe other official accounts of events. Kyrie Irving, for example, also claimed that President John F. Kennedy was killed by the Federal Reserve.[10] Of course, distrust of the banking establishment is often directed at, or a code word for, Jews. And truly steadfast resistance to establishment, consensus reality can also be a gateway to much uglier beliefs.

A featured speaker in Birmingham speculated that the North Pole may have given the Nazis access to Hollow Earth. A long-time popular YouTube flat earther named Eric Dubay described himself as fighting the New World Order, another stand-in for Jews. Later, Dubay made his anti-Semitism more explicit, posting videos promoting the "holohoax." In December 2017, he was banned from YouTube for hate speech.

Robbie Davidson, the organizer of the 2017 Flat Earth International Conference in North Carolina, even uses the tendency—belief in one theory increases the belief in additional theories—as a tactic to recruit nonbelievers to flat earther-ism. If they aren't convinced that the moon landing was faked, Davidson said, then "start with 9/11, see where they're at on that scale."

Even in the least hateful theory rests the bigger idea of conspiracism: the truth as we know it has serious holes. Indeed, a show of hands at the Birmingham flat earth conference revealed that, for example, only one attendee believed the US and other Western governments weren't involved in planning the 9/11 attacks.

However much scorn they heap upon these true believers, the media also can't keep away from these "kooks." Following the Birmingham conference, its organizer Gary John Heather appeared on a British morning show called *This Morning* with two other flat earthers. The three were met with staunch disbelief by the hosts and, via satellite hookup, their theory was called "drivel" by a well-known scientist.

Heather, of course, thought the event was a great success. By the measurements of conspiracists, he was right. As of February 2019, an edited clip of the show posted to YouTube has been viewed over 4.1 million times.[11] Heather was very happy to have the media do his most difficult job: exposing new viewers to his loopy conviction.

There is no moral equivalence between, say, flat earthers and rabid

Holocaust deniers, but there are meaningful similarities. The ideas and membership of both groups multiply rapidly because of the particular media ecosystem that has developed since 2008, in which social media carries the weight of truth that used to be reserved for textbooks.

This is the tattered state of mainstream truth and consensus around facts today. Rampant conspiracy theories and "alternative facts" permeate social media, establishment media, sometimes beginning with or being recycled by President Trump. The fantasy universes they inflate provide space for extremist ideologies to flourish. They justify baseless attacks on establishment institutions. At the most extreme, conspiracy theories may damage popular consensus so much that it is impossible for liberal democracy to exist.

The first really damning look at the power of social media over mainstream institutions didn't begin until after the 2016 election. Even then, it wasn't focused so much on the success of the alt-right or extremism, but more generally in hijacking the new media ecosystem as Russian interference in the 2016 presidential election. There continues to be debate over how much influence Russia hackers had in determining the ultimate outcome of the election. But the idea that a foreign intelligence operation could succeed in changing public opinion with a relatively cheap operation using American social media companies like Facebook and Twitter is stunning. It's also either a recognition of the power of social media or the fragility of US democracy.

Following the deadly 2017 Charlottesville Unite the Right rally, however, the reality of social media's essential role in spreading extremism became unavoidable.

There is no universal policy for what behavior will lead to being banned from a social media platform. What's more, doing so can create free speech concerns and hurt business. Despite dragging their feet, many companies have finally taken some useful steps to tamp down the spread of hateful extremism.

After banning relatively few high-profile accounts between 2011 through October 2016, Twitter went on a purge. Beginning in August

2017, David Duke was suspended, followed by alt-right activist Baked Alaska, the American Nazi Party, white nationalist Jared Taylor, Mathew Heimbach's Traditionalist Worker Party, Nordic Resistance Movement, and the alt-right leader of the Proud Boys, Gavin McInnes.

Facebook and Google, both slow to act despite their massive role in spreading extremism, also announced plans to ferret out fake news on their platforms. Facebook banned the Proud Boys. Reddit cracked down on some threads that were racist or misogynist. The neo-Nazi and white supremacist sites Daily Stormer and Stormfront had their accounts eliminated by web hosting companies.

Just as importantly, CNN pushed back on alt-right double speak, issuing a correction to a story about Richard Spencer that instead of "white rights activist," they were referring to him more accurately as a "white supremacist." The Associated Press likewise announced it will no longer use his illusive invention "alt-right," instead preferring "white nationalist."

Websites like snopes.com also continue to do the valuable service of attempting to debunk fake news. But, despite the site's high profile, it's hard to make a dent in the massive amount of fake or misleading information in circulation.

Probably the biggest name to suffer from an internet purge was Alex Jones. In 2018, in part because of his widely circulated claims that the Parkland High School shooting was a "false flag," Jones was banned from several social media platforms, including Facebook, YouTube, and his podcasts hosted by Spotify. But his ban also shows the limitations of online crackdowns.

First, YouTube has a relatively forgiving "three strikes" policy in which an account can be banned if it posts material that violates community guidelines three times in three months. This means that Alex Jones, InfoWars, or his other outlets could potentially post two dangerous and conspiratorial videos that are widely shared by YouTube's massive platform before being taken down, and then just post slightly less inflammatory material until those two strikes disappear in a few months.

This is exactly what happened in February 2018 when a video falsely accusing a Parkland high school student of being a "crisis actor" was viewed 200,000 times before YouTube removed it.[12] The problem for YouTube is that, in part because of their own video referral analytics, conspiratorial material is really popular. It simply goes against social media's business model to ban those videos that are most useful to spreading extremist ideas.

Even if you remove civil liberties concerns about infringing on free speech, the architecture of the internet simply resists shutting things down. Take, for example, efforts to remove Islamic extremist material. In 2018, eight European countries undertook a massive, coordinated operation to smash ISIS's online propaganda machine, what they called a "virtual caliphate."[13] Despite their efforts, the exercise soon turned into a game of whack-a-mole. One website, Amaq, kept on being taken down by providers but then reappeared at new addresses every few days. Both the internet and social media are set up to be incredibly accessible, so making new accounts is not hard. This made it relatively easy for Alex Jones to distribute his material under multiple names and accounts through podcasts, YouTube channels, Facebook pages, Twitter, and more. Permanently shutting down all of his outlets is a herculean task.

Not only is it easy to create multiple accounts, but there are also scores of alternatives to the highest profile social media apps. Eventually, the efforts of European law enforcement caused Amaq to move its content to Telegram, an encrypted messaging service popular with Islamic extremists. The efforts were able to cut back the effectiveness of ISIS's online recruiting activities—potential recruits couldn't just enter "ISIS" into a Google search bar. But encrypted apps like Telegram still allow already existing and core members to communicate and socialize. Similarly, far-right figures developed their own social media and web payment apps, like Gab, known as "Twitter for racists."

In April 2018, Facebook CEO Mark Zuckerberg told Congress that his company's artificial intelligence tools would help them take down ISIS and al-Qaeda related terror content almost permanently, by detecting duplicate sites soon after they create accounts. Even as Zuckerberg was speaking, though, other terror groups on Facebook included Boko Haram,

Hezbollah, and the Revolutionary Armed Forces of Colombia. What's more, Facebook's business model is designed around making it easy for its 2.2 billion global users to connect with groups they are interested in.[14] As a result, groups that were banned in one language could sometimes be located by searching in another. Because Facebook supports over a hundred languages, cracking down across all languages is a huge task.

More importantly, neither the infrastructure of the web nor the economics of media are going away. The beauty of the web is its massive reach combined with low entry barriers. In other words, not only can Stormfront reemerge on the dark web, anyone can start the next Daily Stormer.

The media's profit-motive also exists in constant tension with its public responsibility. And, despite being hated and distrusted by record percentages of Americans, the media is raking in profits off Trump. Not only have cable news networks boosted ratings by doing more Trump coverage, the traditional news broadcasts on NBC, CBS, and ABC have paid a price in ratings by doing the responsible thing: providing a wider range of stories like human interest, health, and local crime rather Trump 24/7.

Rather than trying to beat back the deluge of hate across the internet, a startup called Moonshot CVE is attempting to use social media's reach and analytics to counter the spread of extremism. The company has developed a platform targeting ads at potential ISIS recruits[15] by using artificial intelligence analysis of Facebook pages liked and Twitter accounts followed to predict likely targets of ISIS recruitment. It then uses Google's search advertising algorithms and YouTube to send counter-messaging to these same users. Given how powerful a role social media and the internet generally have played in the recent spread of extremism, this sort of technique will have at least some benefits. It may even prove more successful—and certainly less difficult—than continually kicking extremist content off the web.

Another way to combat extremism is both the simplest and most difficult: breaking down our tendency toward divisiveness and dehumanization by showing more love to each other.

Derek Black was born of white nationalist royalty. His godfather was David Duke, Grand Wizard of the Knights of the Ku Klux Klan. His father, Don Black, had succeeded Duke as grand wizard before starting Stormfront when his son was five years old. Derek Black quickly got involved in the family business. By the age of twelve, he had created KidsStormfront.

But Black has also learned from his father's failures, which included a botched white supremacist coup on the Caribbean island of Dominica and an unsuccessful run for mayor of Birmingham, Alabama. Black claimed that ever since he was a kid he thought white nationalist ideology could win elections "as long as it wasn't called white nationalism."[16] This intuition led the younger Black to play an important role in the alt-right rebranding of white nationalism. Following Barack Obama's election, for example, he convinced his dad to ban the racial slurs, swastikas, and threats of violence on Stormfront that might turn off first-time visitors.[17]

That same year, Black won an elected position on the West Palm Beach Republican committee, a role he used to push in what would become the main themes of the alt-right's sanitized white nationalism, including the impact of immigration, affirmative action, political correctness and the impending "white genocide." He also began to co-host a father-son white nationalist radio show on a local AM station. By his late teens, Black, with his thoughtful demeanor and lack of racial slurs, seemed certain to assume his role as a leader in the next generation of white nationalists.

Black's life took an unexpected turn in 2010, however, after he enrolled in Sarasota's New College of Florida, a liberal arts school three hours away. Exclusively homeschooled up to that point, the intellectually inquisitive Black was immersed in a new, diverse world. His father thought he was on a reconnaissance mission to an evil realm of multiculturalism. But Derek Black engaged his new surroundings with confidence and curiosity. He became friends with a Peruvian immigrant named Juan and dated a Jewish woman named Rose.

Black didn't feel he had to abandon his white nationalist beliefs, largely because he thought that segregating people by race wasn't inherently hateful or angry. But he didn't advertise them, either. Before long, though, he felt like he was occupying two different lives. Amazingly, he managed to keep them compartmentalized for a while. He would do his white nationalist radio show in his dorm room before heading off to class in the morning. He'd hang out with the grandson of a concentration camp survivor one day and former skinheads at home that weekend.

Then, inevitably, someone outed Black as a "white supremacist" on a college message board and his world collapsed. The post received hundreds of angry replies. Classmates jeered when Black walked by. A group of students even organized a school shutdown to demonstrate to him how unacceptable his hateful ideology was.

Black, who could have easily dropped out and returned to West Palm Beach, continued to attend classes. Then, an orthodox Jewish friend of Black's named Matthew Stevenson decided that shunning Black wasn't a productive reaction. He began to invite Black to Shabbat dinner every Friday. The dinners, awkward at first, were not intended as debates on white nationalism, but social events that allowed Black, Stevenson, and other students to engage other as people. To both of their surprise, Black and Allison Gornik, another student who sometimes attended Shabbat, eventually became involved romantically.

Over the next year, Black began to trust Gornik and his friends at Shabbat. He began to listen to her counter-arguments about race that he had previously dismissed as empty, left-wing rhetoric. Gornik and Black read academic studies about racial differences in IQ or crime rates together. Black, who considered himself logical and analytical, slowly admitted that some of arguments for white nationalism didn't hold together. He began to back away from the belief system he'd been brought up in. Black began to wonder if, in fact, nonwhite people were being discriminated against—and not the other way around.

Nonetheless, Black never completely abandoned the belief system he'd grown up with. Finally, during a road trip, Gornik angrily asked him how he thought the idea of a white homeland was going to be achieved nonviolently. When Black later put the question to his dad, he realized—finally—that immigrants, Jews, blacks, and others would be forced to leave, perhaps violently. "This country," Don Black told his son, "is on the verge of a reckoning."[18]

So was Derek Black. In 2012, he declined to attend the Stormfront conference. In January of 2013, he stopped doing his radio show. Later that same year, he finally cut his ties with white nationalism altogether in dramatic fashion: a letter posted on the SPLC website.

Afterward, his mother didn't want to talk to him. His dad—who thought his son had been brainwashed—tried, but there was too much ideological space between them. For his part, Black was disgusted with his previous life. He changed his name to Roland Derek Black and enrolled at a PhD program at the University of Chicago. He wanted to hide, but as Black watched Donald Trump's presidential campaign take off—with the candidate hawking the same sanitized racism he had spread for years—the former golden boy of white nationalism realized he had to speak out. Black denounced white nationalism in a *New York Times* op-ed and became a "reluctant public face of antiracism."[19]

Even as much larger trends—politics, media, economies, technologies, ideologies, conspiracy theories—play huge roles in spreading extremism, each radicalization also happens on a personal level. Black's radicalization process was unique in many ways, but it was still intensely personal.

The same is true of de-radicalization. Certainly, the shunning of Black by his classmates at a small liberal arts college had a personal impact. It may have helped him understand how hurtful white nationalism was to most of the student body. But, much more important—and difficult— was the trust and deep personal connection he had with the classmates who reached out to him. Although most extremists don't have the time and resources to debate white nationalism in a comfortable academic environment over months, factors such as trust, faith, kindness, and love play a role in almost every story of de-radicalization.

Another "former," as reformed neo-Nazis call themselves, named Tony McAleer was a high profile leader of the White Aryan Resistance. In the 1980s, he attended the first youth congress at the infamous Aryan Nations house in Idaho. Then, in 1991, his daughter was born and his slow exit from right-wing extremism began.

Four years later, McAleer was a single father with a newborn son as well, but the love and approval he received as a dad made the white power side of his life increasingly unattractive. What's more, his association with neo-Nazis was disrupting his life as a parent. His mom had to drop his kids off at preschool so they weren't shunned because of their dad.

McAleer's ongoing involvement with extremism was also limiting his ability to support his kids financially. Just as with Black, a deeply personal wedge developed between his extremist activities and his new life. Eventually, he decided he had to get out. Finally, during a professional self-development course, a Jewish mentor helped him to make his final exit.

Surveying the politically divisive world, McAleer asks for a "revolution in compassion."[20] He's worried that in the current political climate, the left will be just as guilty of dehumanization as the right, reducing the space for people to leave hate-based groups and ideologies.

Another ex-neo-Nazi, Frank Meeink, is most famous as the inspiration for the Edward Norton character in the movie *American History X*. Growing up in Philadelphia, Meeink was a prominent teenage skinhead recruiter and leader. Then, at age seventeen, he was sent to prison for kidnapping and torturing a rival skinhead leader. In jail, Meeink found that he had more in common with some of the African American inmates than the members of the Aryan prison gang he joined. After he got out of prison, Meeink was conflicted. He no longer agreed with neo-Nazi ideologies but was still part of the gang. His daughter had just been born, but her mother wouldn't let him see her. A Jewish man offered him the only decent job he could find, even though Meeink had a swastika tattooed on his neck.

Meeink's final turning point came as a result of the remarkable kindness shown to him by his Jewish employer during a long ride home from work. "[H]e kept telling me to stop calling myself dumb," something Meeink had not heard before. "After that day, I took my boots off, I was just done."[21]

Another former extremist, Maxime Fiset, was a Quebecois white nationalist organizer and leader between 2007 and 2012. He also began to question his extremist life after his daughter was born. Fiset decided he didn't want his daughter being around the sexism and racism pervasive among white nationalists.

As the member of a Montreal-based group that helps prevent radicalization, he advises against aggressive confrontation. Faced with staunch opposition, most people in the process of becoming radicalized, Fiset says, will just "harden their beliefs."[22] Instead, he recommends listening and asking questions. The goal is not to win arguments, but to instill doubt about the extremist ideas that are radicalizing them.

The same personal nature of de-radicalization is broadly true on the left as well. Ex-Weatherman Mark Rudd eventually turned himself in after years on the FBI most wanted list because he was tired of forcing his wife to move every year or two. No matter how deluded an extremist may be, their first step away from hate is almost always the result of trust, love and respect shown for them by others.

When discussing de-radicalization, some experts make the process sound like a 12-step program for alcoholics—a system in which success is dependent on the community support an addict perceives. Similar tactics—emotional connection and empathy—are also critical in treating suicidal people.[23]

In a completely different field, researchers are studying the possibilities of what amounts to a compassion drug. A so-far promising, but experimental, treatment for extreme cases of PTSD is the party drug MDMA, the psycho-active ingredient in ecstasy. The study followed the treatment of military veterans and first-responders who were too emotionally walled off to respond to traditional psychotherapy. During the test, one veteran said that he finally felt "the person inside the patient." MDMA, which is thought to create feelings of trust and openness, provided a chemically enhanced opening for traditional therapy sessions to begin.[24] But MDMA isn't so much a chemical solution to hate as an entry point for other forms of therapy.

On a local level, everyone can play a role in lowering the heated rhetoric and divisiveness that opens up space for extremism. A November 2018 *Washington Post* article details a liberal blogger named Christopher Blair who began creating fake conspiratorial right-wing stories during the 2016 election cycle as a kind of political satire.[25] He was shocked to find that, no matter how outrageous and implausible he made his articles, Trump supporters continued to read, like, and share them.

Before too long, Blair was making as much as $15,000 a month creating tall tales about California instituting Sharia law, Bill Clinton becoming a serial killer, and Barack Obama dodging the draft when he was nine. Typically, Blair allowed the stories to go viral before lowering the boom on the people who believed it, ending his posts with "congratulations, stupid."

But, after two years of letting people know they'd been had, Blair wasn't sure he'd changed a single person's mind. In fact, it would be shocking if he had. In today's media ecosystem, "truth" is a seriously devalued currency—part of the reason why the *Post* itself stopped publishing its "What was fake on the internet this week" column back in 2014.[26] Many people select what they want to believe based on emotional need, and those are same people who are inherently suspicious of fact checkers like the *Washington Post* and snopes.com. Most importantly, Blair didn't have anyone's trust when he told them they were wrong. In fact, he insulted them, making himself one more troll on the coarsened internet.

For all his desire to deflate conspiracism, Blair seems unlikely to do much but perpetuate the walling off of America. In fact, there is no fixed barrier between "extremists" and "normal people"—much less Democrats and Republicans. Likewise, extremists don't become so because they are lesser or worse people, but because of some unlucky combination of personality and experience. This doesn't mean they aren't responsible for their actions, but that they—like everyone—are capable of change. Not everyone could treat Frank Meeink with the compassion he needed to leave his neo-Nazi past behind, but everyone should accept that it can happen.

Likewise, extremists' often-hateful rhetoric doesn't arise unbidden. Today, what used to be called extremist ideology courses through mainstream websites, friends' Facebook feeds, and celebrity Twitter posts. The entire media ecosystem is even designed to create self-verifying tribal loops, essentially discouraging future extremists from confronting ideas that contradict their emerging belief system.

In this sense, the enemy is not them, but us: America's addictive social media, irresponsible cable news pundits, divisive political parties, unforgiving paramilitary culture, and an unbalanced economy with shortcomings that are easily exploited by extremists.

This is also how Micah Johnson, Muhammad Abdulazeez, and Dylann Roof came to be mass murderers. They were not double agents dedicated to an alien form of extremism. They were young men weaponized by contemporary America itself. Each was a neighbor looking for a place to pour their pain and frustration; their violent direction was not predetermined. With love and understanding, we can help to stop such violence from being repeated.

NOTES

INTRODUCTION: THE SECRET EXTREMISTS

1. Jennifer Emily, "Who Was Micah Johnson? A More Complex Picture Emerges," *Dallas Morning News*, July 2016, https://www.dallasnews.com/news/dallas-ambush/2016/07/10/shooters-journal-portal-madmans-mind.

2. "When Army Career Ended in Disgrace, Dallas Gunman Was Ostracized," *Chicago Tribune*, July 15, 2016, https://www.chicagotribune.com/news/nationworld/ct-dallas-gunman-micah-johnson-army-discharge-20160715-story.html.

3. Snejana Farberov, "FBI Recovers Chattanooga Gunman's 'Anti-American Diary' Which Reveals His Anger at the War on Terror, a Growing Dependence on Drugs and His Desire to Commit Suicide to Become a 'Martyr,'" *Daily Mail*, July 20, 2015, https://www.dailymail.co.uk/news/article-3168189/FBI-recovers-Chattanooga-gunman-s-disturbing-diary-talked-committing-suicide-martyr-struggled-addiction-debt.html.

4. Avery Wilks, John Monk, and Harrison Cahill, "Exclusive: Sharper Picture Emerges of Suspected Charleston Shooter Dylann Roof," *State*, September 19, 2015, https://www.thestate.com/news/local/crime/article35836482.html.

5. Richard Fausset, "Chattanooga Gunman Mohammod Youssuf Abdulazeez: 'Life Is Short and Bitter'" *New York Times*, July 16, 2015, https://www.nytimes.com/2015/07/17/us/chattanooga-shooting-suspect-was-ordinary-boy-neighbors-recall.html.

6. Ibid.

7. Emily, "Who Was Micah Johnson?"

8. Dylann Roof, "Dylann Roof's Manifesto," *New York Times*, December 13, 2016, https://www.nytimes.com/interactive/2016/12/13/universal/document-Dylann-Roof-manifesto.html.

9. "Dylann Roof's Friend: 'He Never Said Anything Racist,'" BBC, June 20, 2015, https://www.bbc.co.uk/news/av/world-us-canada-33209654/Dylann-roof-s-friend-he-never-said-anything-racist.

CHAPTER ONE: WE WANT THE BROKEN TOYS

1. "Skinheads USA Soldiers of the Race War Full Documentary," posted by Pawel Merlin, January 16, 2016, YouTube video, 10:58, https://www.youtube .com/watch?v=gSXYUoBxH-c&list=PL31YglUmKqu6g7fKT2ECsTtdH-ABaRt Jh&bpctr=1542768361.

2. Ibid.

3. Brentin Mock, "Former Followers Expose Neo-Nazi Skinhead, Former Klan Leader Bill Riccio for Sexual Harassment, Abuse," *SPLC Intelligence Report*, October 1, 2007, https://www.splcenter.org/fighting-hate/intelligence-report/2007/former -followers-expose-neo-nazi-skinhead-former-klan-leader-bill-riccio-sexual-harassment.

4. Ibid.

5. "Skinheads USA Soldiers of the Race War."

6. Dylann Roof, "Dylann Roof's Manifesto," *New York Times*, December 13, 2016, https://www.nytimes.com/interactive/2016/12/13/universal/document -Dylann-Roof-manifesto.html.

7. Ibid.

8. "Online Preachers of Hate: Anwar al-Awlaki, 'bin Laden of the Internet,'" *Telegraph*, June 7, 2011, https://www.telegraph.co.uk/news/uknews/terrorism-in -the-uk/8560438/Online-preachers-of-hate-Anwar-al-Awlaki-bin-Laden-of-the -internet.html.

9. Kathy Sawyer, "Turning from 'Weapon of the Spirit' to Shotgun," *Washington Post*, August 7, 1994, https://www.washingtonpost.com/archive/ politics/1994/08/07/turning-from-weapon-of-the-spirit-to-the-shotgun/ d5ba8384-de0a-4ee9-84ad-dd9983925a67/.

10. Frances Robles and Nikita Stewart, "Dylann Roof's Past Reveals Trouble at Home and School," *New York Times*, July 16, 2015, https://www.nytimes.com/ 2015/07/17/us/charleston-shooting-dylann-roof-troubled-past.html.

11. Matt Apuzzo, "Who Will Become a Terrorist? Research Yields Few Clues," *New York Times*, March 27, 2016, https://www.nytimes.com/2016/03/28/world/ europe/mystery-about-who-will-become-a-terrorist-defies-clear-answers.html.

12. Chip Berlet, "The Good, Bad and Ugly in Oregon Standoff Coverage," FAIR, January 15, 2016, http://fair.org/home/the-good-bad-and -ugly-in-oregon-standoff-coverage/.

CHAPTER TWO: A RADICAL ECHO, IGNORED

1. Joel Dyer, "The New Harvest of Rage," *Boulder Weekly*, October 27, 2016, https://www.boulderweekly.com/news/the-new-harvest-of-rage/.

2. Ibid.

3. Ibid.

4. *Rightwing Extremism: Current Economic and Political Climate Fueling Resurgence in Radicalization and Recruitment* (Washington, DC: Department of Homeland Security Office of Intelligence and Analysis, April 7, 2009).

5. Ibid.

6. Ibid.

7. "Dispute Led to Shootings in Pittsburgh," April 5, 2009, *New York Times*, https://www.nytimes.com/2009/04/06/us/06pittsburgh.html?ref=global-home.

8. "Shooter Wearing Bulletproof Vest Guns down 3 Pittsburgh Officers, Upset over Losing Job," Fox News, April 4, 2009, http://www.foxnews.com/story/2009/04/04/shooter-wearing-bulletproof-vest-guns-down-3-pittsburgh-officers-upset-over.html.

9. Michelle Malkin, "Confirmed: The Obama DHS Hit Job on Conservatives Is Real," *Michelle Malkin* (blog), April 14, 2009, http://michellemalkin.com/2009/04/14/confirme-the-obama-dhs-hit-job-on-conservatives-is-real/.

10. Ibid.

11. Ibid.

12. Ed O'Keefe, "Napolitano Defends Homeland Security Report on Right-Wing Extremism," *Washington Post*, April 16, 2009, http://www.washingtonpost.com/wp-dyn/content/article/2009/04/15/AR2009041503390.html.

13. "Bo Gritz," Southern Poverty Law Center, https://www.splcenter.org/fighting-hate/extremist-files/individual/bo-gritz.

14. "August Kreis," Southern Poverty Law Center, https://www.splcenter.org/fighting-hate/extremist-files/individual/august-kreis.

15. "Former Klansmen Tom Metzger and Bill Riccio Encourage Skinheads to Cooperate," *SPLC Intelligence Report*, October 19, 2006, https://www.splcenter.org/fighting-hate/intelligence-report/2006/former-klansmen-tom-metzger-and-bill-riccio-encourage-skinheads-cooperate?page=0%2C1.

16. "Once Popular Patriot Leader John Trochmann Now Leads 'Mail Order Militia,'" *SPLC Intelligence Report*, May 8, 2001, https://www.splcenter.org/fighting-hate/intelligence-report/2001/once-popular-patriot-leader-john-trochmann-now-leads-%E2%80%98mail-order-militia%E2%80%99.

17. Ibid.

18. "Real GDP Growth of the United States from 1990 to 2017," Statista, January 2018, https://www.statista.com/statistics/188165/annual-gdp-growth-of-the-united-states-since-1990/.

19. "Fewer Births and Divorces, More Violence: How the Recession Affected the American Family," Conversation, December 2, 2014, http://theconversation.com/fewer-births-and-divorces-more-violence-how-the-recession-affected-the-american-family-34272.

20. Peter Grüner and Marcus Brückner, "The OECD's Growth Prospects and Political Extremism," Vox CEPR Policy Portal, May 16, 2010, https://voxeu.org/article/global-crisis-and-political-extremism.

21. Glen Kessler, "When Did Mitch McConnell Say He Wanted to Make Barack Obama a One-Term President?" *Washington Post*, January 1, 2017, https://www.washingtonpost.com/news/fact-checker/wp/2017/01/11/when-did-mitch-mcconnell-say-he-wanted-to-make-obama-a-one-term-president/?utm_term=.9c1c885161d2.

22. "Trust in Government: 1958–2015," Pew Research Center, Washington, DC, November 23, 2015, http://www.people-press.org/2015/11/23/1-trust-in-government-1958-2015/.

23. "Congress and the Public," Gallup, Washington, DC, https://news.gallup.com/poll/1600/congress-public.aspx.

24. Mark Littler, "Rethinking Democracy and Terrorism: A Quantitative Analysis of Attitudes to Democratic Politics and Support for Terrorism in the UK," *Behavioral Sciences of Terrorism and Political Aggression* 9, no. 1 (2017): 52–61, https://www.tandfonline.com/doi/abs/10.1080/19434472.2016.1245211.

25. "Congress and the Public," Gallup.

26. "Confidence in Institutions," Gallup, Washington, DC, https://news.gallup.com/poll/1597/confidence-institutions.aspx.

27. "Right Track or Wrong Track," Rasmussen Reports, Asbury Park, NJ, January 21, 2019, http://www.rasmussenreports.com/public_content/politics/top_stories/right_direction_wrong_track_nov19.

28. Judy L. Thomas, "The Spotlight Dims on Ex-White Supremacist, Militia Leaders," *Ledger*, April 10, 2005, http://www.theledger.com/news/20050410/the-spotlight-dims-on-ex-white-supremacist-militia-leaders.

29. "Malik Zulu Shabazz," Southern Poverty Law Center, https://www.splcenter.org/fighting-hate/extremist-files/individual/malik-zulu-shabazz.

30. "Left-Wing Earth Liberation Front Advocates Extremist Agenda,"

SPLC Intelligence Report, May 8, 2001, https://www.splcenter.org/fighting-hate/intelligence-report/2001/left-wing-earth-liberation-front-advocates-extremist-agenda.

31. Barack Obama, "Transcript: 'This Is Your Victory,' Says Obama," CNN, http://edition.cnn.com/2008/POLITICS/11/04/obama.transcript/.

32. Bill Bradley, "AP Reports Nationwide Post-Election Racism," *Vanity Fair*, November 15, 2008, https://www.vanityfair.com/news/2008/11/the-national-press-is-no-longer-ignoring-small-town-racism.

CHAPTER THREE: THE GREATEST THING TO EVER HAPPEN TO HATE

1. "David Duke," Southern Poverty Law Center, https://www.splcenter.org/fighting-hate/extremist-files/individual/david-duke.

2. Ibid.

3. Chip Berlet, "When Hate Went Online," *Research for Progress* (blog), http://www.researchforprogress.us/topic/34691/when-hate-went-online.

4. Ibid.

5. "Louis Beam," Southern Poverty Law Center, https://www.splcenter.org/fighting-hate/extremist-files/individual/louis-beam.

6. Berlet, "When Hate Went Online."

7. "Tom Metzger," Southern Poverty Law Center, https://www.splcenter.org/fighting-hate/extremist-files/individual/tom-metzger.

8. Berlet, "When Hate Went Online."

9. Aristotle Kallis, Sara Zeiger, and Bilgehan Ozturk, *Violent Radicalization and Far-Right Extremism in Europe* (Istanbul, Turkey: SETA Publications, 2018).

10. Berlet, "When Hate Went Online."

11. "David Duke," Southern Poverty Law Center.

12. Karen Mock, *Human Rights and the Internet* (New York: Palgrave Macmillan, 2000), p. 142.

13. *Reference for Business: Encyclopedia of Business*, s.v. "Amazon.com: Forming a Plan," https://www.referenceforbusiness.com/businesses/A-F/Amazon-com.html.

14. Mock, *Human Rights and the Internet*, p. 142.

15. Ines von Behr, Anaïs Reding, Charlie Edwards, and Luke Gribbon, "The Use of the Internet in 15 Cases of Terrorism and Extremism," *Radicalisation in the Digital Era* (Santa Monica, CA: RAND Corporation, 2013), p. 17.

16. Mock, *Human Rights and the Internet*, p. 143.

17. "Harvard Law School Librarian Discusses Cyberhate," *SPLC Intelligence Report*, March 21, 2001, https://www.splcenter.org/fighting-hate/intelligence-report/2001/harvard-law-school-librarian-discusses-cyberhate.

18. Mock, *Human Rights and the Internet*.

19. "Harvard Law School Librarian Discusses Cyberhate."

20. Ibid.

21. Ibid.

22. John Kifner, "McVeigh's Mind: A Special Report; Oklahoma Bombing Suspect: Unraveling of a Frayed Life," *New York Times*, December 31, 1995, https://www.nytimes.com/1995/12/31/us/mcveigh-s-mind-special-report-oklahoma-bombing-suspect-unraveling-frayed-life.html.

23. Ibid.

24. Ibid.

25. "Deborah Rudolph Speaks out about Her Former Brother-in-Law, Olympic Park Bomber Eric Robert Rudolf," *SPLC Intelligence Report*, November 29, 2001, https://www.splcenter.org/fighting-hate/intelligence-report/2001/deborah-rudolph-speaks-out-about-her-former-brother-law-olympic-park-bomber-eric-robert.

26. Ibid.

27. Ibid.

28. Jeffrey Gettleman, "US Bomb Suspect's Picture of His Life in the Woods Draws Some Skepticism," *New York Times*, June 8, 2003, https://www.nytimes.com/2003/06/08/us/bomb-suspect-s-picture-of-his-life-in-the-woods-draws-some-skepticism.html.

29. Willem De Koster and Dick Houtman, "'Stormfront Is Like a Second Home to Me': On Virtual Community Formation by Right-Wing Extremists," *Information, Communication & Society* 11, no. 8 (2008): 1155–76.

CHAPTER FOUR: THE SOCIAL NETWORK'S NEGATIVE MIRROR

1. Ines von Behr, Anaïs Reding, Charlie Edwards, and Luke Gribbon, "The Use of the Internet in 15 Cases of Terrorism and Extremism," *Radicalisation in the Digital Era* (Santa Monica, CA: RAND Corporation, 2013), p. 19.

2. Aristotle Kallis, Sara Zeiger, and Bilgehan Ozturk, *Violent Radicalization and Far-Right Extremism in Europe* (Istanbul, Turkey: SETA Publications, 2018), p. 102.

3. Susannah Fox and Lee Raine, "Part 1: How the Internet Has Woven Itself into American Life," Pew Research Center, Washington, DC, February 27, 2014, http://www.pewinternet.org/2014/02/27/part-1-how-the-internet-has -woven-itself-into-american-life/.

4. Gary Rivlin, "Wallflower at the Web Party," *New York Times*, October 15, 2006, https://www.nytimes.com/2006/10/15/business/yourmoney/15friend .html?_r=1.

5. Associated Press, "Will Facebook Hold Out or Sell Out?" CNN, February 26, 2007, https://web.archive.org/web/20070324234412/http://www.cnn.com/ 2007/TECH/internet/02/26/next.big.deal.ap/index.html.

6. Tom Smith, "The Social Media Revolution," *International Journal of Market Research* 51, no. 4 (2009): 559, https://www.scribd.com/document/203686033/ The-Social-Media-Revolution.

7. Willem De Koster and Dick Houtman, "'Stormfront Is Like a Second Home to Me': On Virtual Community Formation by Right-Wing Extremists," *Information, Communication & Society* 11, no. 8 (2008): 1155–75.

8. Ibid.

9. Ibid.

10. von Behr, Reding, Edwards, and Gribbon, "Use of the Internet in 15 Cases," p. 26.

11. Brandon Griggs and John D. Sutter, "Oprah, Ashton Kutcher Mark Twitter 'Turning Point,'" CNN, April 18, 2009, http://edition.cnn.com/2009/ TECH/04/17/ashton.cnn.twitter.battle/.

12. "Twitter, Facebook and YouTube's Role in Arab Spring," *Social Capital Blog*, January 26, 2011, https://socialcapital.wordpress.com/2011/01/26/twitter -facebook-and-youtubes-role-in-tunisia-uprising/.

13. Carol Huang, "Facebook and Twitter Key to Arab Spring Uprisings: Report," *National*, June 6, 2011, https://www.thenational.ae/uae/facebook-and -twitter-key-to-arab-spring-uprisings-report-1.428773.

14. Kallis, Zeiger, and Ozturk, *Violent Radicalization*, pp. 104–105.

15. Ibid., p. 92.

16. Ibid., pp. 104–105.

17. Ibid., p. 92.

18. Ibid.

19. Graeme Wood, "What ISIS Really Wants," *Atlantic*, March 2015, https:// www.theatlantic.com/magazine/archive/2015/03/what-isis-really-wants/384980/.

20. Alessandra Masi, "ISIS Propaganda Magazine Dabiq for Sale on Amazon,

Gets Taken Down," *International Business Times*, June 10, 2015, https://www.ibtimes.com/isis-propaganda-magazine-dabiq-sale-amazon-gets-taken-down-1961036.

21. Matthew Rowe and Saif Hassan, "Mining Pro-ISIS Radicalisation Signals from Social Media Users," *Proceedings of the Tenth International AAAI Conference on Web and Social Media* (Menlo Park, CA: Association for the Advancement of Artificial Intelligence, 2016), pp. 329–38, http://oro.open.ac.uk/48477/1/13023-57822-1-PB.pdf.

22. Whitney Phillips, *This Is Why We Can't Have Nice Things: Mapping the Relationship between Online Trolling and Mainstream Culture* (Boston: MIT Press, 2015), pp. 164–65.

23. Tom Smith, "The Social Media Revolution," *International Journal of Market Research* 51, no. 4 (2009): 559, https://www.scribd.com/document/203686033/The-Social-Media-Revolution.

24. Rowe and Hassan, "Mining Pro-ISIS Radicalisation Signals."

25. von Behr, Reding, Edwards, and Gribbon, "Use of the Internet in 15 Cases."

26. Michael Cooper, Michael S. Schmidt, and Eric Schmitt, "Boston Suspects Are Seen as Self-Taught and Fueled by Web," *New York Times*, April 23, 2013, https://www.nytimes.com/2013/04/24/us/boston-marathon-bombing-developments.html?hp&pagewanted=all.

27. Tim Lister and Paul Cruickshank, "Dead Boston Bomb Suspect Poster Video of Jihadist, Analysis Says," CNN, April 22, 2013, https://edition.cnn.com/2013/04/20/us/brother-religious-language.

28. Cooper, Schmidt, and Schmitt, "Boston Suspects Are Seen as Self-Taught."

29. Ibid.

30. Lydia Warren and Louise Boyle, "'It Wasn't Blood . . . It Was Paint': Boston Bombers' Defiant Mother Launches Bizarre Defense of Her 'Framed' Sons," *Daily Mail*, April 25, 2013, https://www.dailymail.co.uk/news/article-2314663/Boston-bombers-crazed-mother-Zubeidat-Tsarnaeva-says-marathon-carnage-play-paint-instead-blood.html.

31. Alan Cullison and Pervaiz Shallwani, "Suspects' Mother Was Placed on Watch List," *Wall Street Journal*, April 26, 2013, https://www.wsj.com/articles/SB10001424127887324743704578447263803031592.

32. Michael Daly, "Terry Lee Loewen, the Mellow Kansas Man Who Allegedly Dreamed of Jihad," *Daily Beast*, December 16, 2013, https://www.thedailybeast.com/terry-lee-loewen-the-mellow-kansas-man-who-allegedly-dreamed-of-jihad.

33. Zlata Rodionova, "Paris Attacks Anniversary: 'Open the Door, I Am Here to Rescue You,' Isis Gunman Told Bataclan Survivor," *Independent*, November 12, 2016,

https://www.independent.co.uk/news/world/paris-attacks-one-year-anniversary
-bataclan-survivor-kelly-le-guen-isis-islamic-state-a7413901.html.

34. Caitlin Hu and Loubna Mrie, "ISIL Supporters Already Have a Hashtag for the Bloody Paris Attacks," Quartz, November 14, 2015, https://qz.com/549818/isil-supporters-already-have-a-hashtag-for-the-bloody-paris-attacks-underway/.

35. "Unit Sales of Sony PlayStation 4 Consoles Worldwide from 2013 to 2017 (in Million Units," Statista, October 2016, https://www.statista.com/statistics/651576/global-ps4-console-unit-sales/.

36. Andrew Griffin, "Paris Attacks May Have Been Arranged on a PlayStation 4, Reports Claim," *Independent*, November 16, 2015, https://www.independent.co.uk/life-style/gadgets-and-tech/news/paris-attacks-may-have-been-arranged-on-a-playstation-4-reports-claim-a6736231.html.

37. Ibid.

38. Thomas Brewster, "Sony Just Coughed Up PS4 Data to the FBI in a Kansas Terror Investigation," *Forbes*, February 14, 2018, https://www.forbes.com/sites/thomasbrewster/2018/02/14/sony-playstation-4-data-disclosed-to-feds-in-terrorism-probe/#41f9a5305c7f.

39. Ye Peiqun, "A Research of the Advantages of Internet Entrepreneurship Based on Microblog" (Xi'an, China: 6th International Conference on Information Management Innovation Management and Industrial Engineering, 2013), https://ieeexplore.ieee.org/document/6703211/.

40. "Former Klansmen Tom Metzger and Bill Riccio Encourage Skinheads to Cooperate," *SPLC Intelligence Report*, October 19, 2006, https://www.splcenter.org/fighting-hate/intelligence-report/2006/former-klansmen-tom-metzger-and-bill-riccio-encourage-skinheads-cooperate?page=0%2C1.

CHAPTER FIVE: 4CHAN AND THE RISE OF ANTI-SOCIAL MEDIA

1. Brian Raftery, "The 2009 Time 100 Finalists," Time, http://content.time.com/time/specials/packages/article/0,28804,1883644_1883653_1885481,00.html.

2. Monica Hesse, "A Virtual Unknown: Meet 'Moot,' the Secretive Internet Celeb Who Still Lives with Mom," *Washington Post*, February 17, 2009, http://www.washingtonpost.com/wp-dyn/content/article/2009/02/16/AR2009021601565.html.

3. Ibid.

4. Ibid.

5. Julian Dibbell, "Radical Opacity," *MIT Technology Review*, August 23, 2010, https://www.technologyreview.com/s/420323/radical-opacity/.

6. Hesse, "Virtual Unknown."

7. Jana Herwig, "Partial Transcript: Moot on 4chan and Why It Works as a Meme Factory," Digiom (blog), April 6, 2010, https://digiom.wordpress.com/2010/04/06/moot-on-4chan-and-why-it-works-as-a-meme-factory/.

8. Ibid.

9. Sean Michaels, "Taking the Rick," *Guardian*, March 19, 2008, https://www.theguardian.com/music/2008/mar/19/news.

10. Carrie Battan, "Is Vice Getting Nice?" *New York Magazine*, April 1, 2015, https://nymag.com/daily/intelligencer/2015/03/vice-getting-nice.html.

11. David Kushner, "4chan's Overlord Christopher Poole Reveals Why He Walked Away," *Rolling Stone*, March 13, 2015, https://www.rollingstone.com/culture/culture-features/4chans-overlord-christopher-poole-reveals-why-he-walked-away-93894/.

12. Ariana Eunjung Cha, "4chan Users Seize Internet's Power for Mass Disruptions," *Washington Post*, August 10, 2010, http://www.washingtonpost.com/wp-dyn/content/article/2010/08/09/AR2010080906102.html?hpid=topnews.

13. Fruzsina Eordogh, "Gamergate and the New Horde of Digital Saboteurs," *Christian Science Monitor*, November 25, 2014, https://www.csmonitor.com/Technology/Tech-Culture/2014/1125/Gamergate-and-the-new-horde-of-digital-saboteurs.

14. Willem De Koster and Dick Houtman, "'Stormfront Is Like a Second Home to Me': On Virtual Community Formation by Right-Wing Extremists," *Information, Communication & Society* 11, no. 8 (2008): 1155–76.

15. Ibid.

16. Kushner, "4chan's Overlord Christopher Poole."

17. Eordogh, "Gamergate and the New Horde of Digital Saboteurs."

18. Kushner, "4chan's Overlord Christopher Poole."

19. Ibid.

CHAPTER SIX: ATTENTION HIJACKING

1. Eli Langer, "The Five-Year Anniversary of Twitter's Defining Moment," CNBC, January 15, 2014, https://www.cnbc.com/2014/01/15/the-five-year -anniversary-of-twitters-defining-moment.html.

2. Ibid.

3. Samantha Grossman, "The Top 10 Things That Broke the Internet," *Time*, December 2, 2014, http://time.com/collection-post/3587943/things-that -broke-the-internet/.

4. Ibid.

5. Whitney Philips, *This Is Why We Can't Have Nice Things* (Boston: MIT Press, 2015).

6. Ibid.

7. Tara Golshan, "2 Big Takeaways from a Scandalous Report on Internal Breitbart Documents," Vox, October 5, 2017, https://www.vox.com/2017/10/ 5/16433172/buzzfeed-report-breitbart-documents-milo.

8. Joseph Bernstein, "Here's How Breitbart and Milo Smuggled White Nationalism into the Mainstream," BuzzFeed News, October 5, 2017, https:// www.buzzfeednews.com/article/josephbernstein/heres-how-breitbart -and-milo-smuggled-white-nationalism.

9. Angela Nagle, *Kill All Normies: Online Culture Wars from 4chan and Tumblr to Trump and the Alt-Right* (Portland: Zero Books, 2017), pp. 102–103.

10. Gabby Jeffries, "Gay Columnist Claims He Would Cure His Homosexuality if He Could," *Pink News*, October 2, 2015, https://www .pinknews.co.uk/2015/10/02/gay-columnist-claims-he-would-cure-his -homosexuality-if-he-could/.

11. Bernstein, "Breitbart and Milo."

12. Chris Mindock, "Milo Yiannopoulos filmed singing 'America the Beautiful' while White Nationalists gave Nazi salutes," *The Independent*, October 6, 2017, https:// www.independent.co.uk/news/world/americas/milo-yiannopoulos-nazi -salutes-video-karaoke-richard-spencer-white-nationalists-karaoke-bar-a7987486.html.

13. "Andrew Anglin," Southern Poverty Law Center, https://www.splcenter .org/fighting-hate/extremist-files/individual/andrew-anglin.

14. Ibid.

15. Ashley Feinberg, "This Is the Daily Stormer's Playbook," *Huffington Post*, December 13, 2017, https://www.huffingtonpost.com/entry/daily -stormer-nazi-style-guide_us_5a2ece19e4b0ce3b344492f2.

16. Ibid.
17. Ibid.
18. Ibid.
19. Ibid.
20. "Andrew Anglin," Southern Poverty Law Center.
21. Feinberg, "This Is the Daily Stormer's Playbook."
22. Ibid.

CHAPTER SEVEN: DEADLY FICTIONS

1. Herman Bernstein, *The History of a Lie* (New York: J. S. Ogilvie Publishing, 1921), pp. 22–41.
2. Ibid.
3. Ibid.
4. Ibid.
5. Ibid.
6. Ibid.
7. Ibid.
8. Ibid.
9. Ibid.
10. "Black Nationalist," Southern Poverty Law Center, https://www.splcenter .org/fighting-hate/extremist-files/ideology/black-nationalist.
11. Steven T. Katz and Richard Landes, *The Paranoid Apocalypse: A Hundred Year Retrospective of the Protocols of the Elders of Zion* (New York: NYU Press, 2011), p. 206.
12. Michael Slackman, "Bin Laden Says West Is Waging War Against Islam," *New York Times*, April 24, 2006, https://www.nytimes.com/2006/04/24/world/ middleeast/bin-laden-says-west-is-waging-war-against-islam.html.
13. Daniel J. Wakin, "Anti-Semitic 'Elders of Zion' Gets New Life on Egypt TV," *New York Times*, October 26, 2001, https://www.nytimes.com/2002/10/26/ world/anti-semitic-elders-of-zion-gets-new-life-on-egypt-tv.html.
14. David Lane, *Collection of Works of David Lane*, http://www.solargeneral .org/wp-content/uploads/library/collection-of-works-of-david-lane.pdf.
15. Ibid.
16. Ibid.

17. Ibid.

18. Ibid.

19. Michael Barkun, *A Culture of Conspiracy: Apocalyptic Visions in Contemporary America* (Berkeley: University of California Press, 2003).

20. Lane, *Collection of Works of David Lane*.

21. Ibid.

22. Ibid.

23. Ibid.

24. Ibid.

25. "The Murder of Alan Berg in Denver: 25 Years Later," *Denver Post*, June 17, 2009, https://www.denverpost.com/2009/06/17/the-murder-of-alan-berg-in-denver-25-years-later/.

26. Brett Barrouquere, "'Hail Bob Mathews:' Member of the Order Reminisces from Federal Prison," Southern Poverty Law Center Hatewatch, December 18, 2017, https://www.splcenter.org/hatewatch/2017/12/18/hail-bob-mathews-member-order-reminisces-federal-prison.

27. Ibid.

28. "David Lane," Southern Poverty Law Center, https://www.splcenter.org/fighting-hate/extremist-files/individual/david-lane.

29. Lane, *Collection of Works of David Lane*, http://www.solargeneral.org/wp-content/uploads/library/collection-of-works-of-david-lane.pdf.

30. Camille Jackson, "The Turner Diaries, Other Racist Novels Inspire Extremist Violence," *SPLC Intelligence Report*, October 14, 2004, https://www.splcenter.org/fighting-hate/intelligence-report/2004/turner-diaries-other-racist-novels-inspire-extremist-violence.

CHAPTER EIGHT: FALSE FLAGS AND THE END OF FACTS

1. Peter Fimrite, "Masked Man Enters, Attacks Bohemian Grove / 'Phantom' Expected Armed Resistance," *SFGate*, January 24, 2002, https://www.sfgate.com/bayarea/article/Masked-man-enters-attacks-Bohemian-Grove-2881742.php.

2. Rashah McChesney, "Alcoa Protestor Believes Obama Is an Alien," *Quad-City Times*, June 29, 2011, https://qctimes.com/news/local/article_91987a5a-a20e-11e0-9ed3-001cc4c03286.html.

3. Ibid.

4. Zack Beauchamp, "Alex Jones, Pizzagate Booster and America's Most Famous Conspiracy Theorist, Explained," Vox, December 7, 2016, https://www.vox.com/policy-and-politics/2016/10/28/13424848/alex-jones-infowars-prisonplanet.

5. "Alex Jones," Southern Poverty Law Center, https://www.splcenter.org/fighting-hate/extremist-files/individual/alex-jones.

6. David Weigel, "Alex Jones Celebrates Trump's Takeover of the GOP," *Washington Post*, July 18, 2016, https://www.washingtonpost.com/news/post-politics/wp/2016/07/18/alex-jones-celebrates-trumps-takeover-of-the-gop/?utm_term=.50cfe1b00370.

7. "Alex Jones," Southern Poverty Law Center.

8. Ben Popken, "As Algorithms Take Over, YouTube's Recommendations Highlight a Human Problem," NBC News, April 20, 2018, https://www.nbcnews.com/tech/social-media/algorithms-take-over-youtube-s-recommendations-highlight-human-problem-n867596.

9. Beauchamp, "Alex Jones, Pizzagate Booster and America's Most Famous Conspiracy Theorist."

10. Eric Killelea, "Alex Jones' Mis-Infowars: 7 Batsh*t Conspiracy Theories," *Rolling Stone*, February 21, 2017, https://www.rollingstone.com/culture/culture-lists/alex-jones-mis-infowars-7-bat-sht-conspiracy-theories-195468/former-fox-news-host-glenn-beck-is-a-cia-operative-114463/.

11. Michael M. Grynbaum, "Buckley vs. Vidal: When Debate Became Bloodsport," *New York Times*, July 24, 2015, https://www.nytimes.com/2015/07/26/movies/buckley-vs-vidal-when-debate-became-bloodsport.html.

12. Ibid.

13. Ibid.

14. Brian Stelter, "The Anti-Fox Gains Ground," *New York Times*, November 11, 2012, https://www.nytimes.com/2012/11/12/business/media/msnbc-its-ratings-rising-gains-ground-on-fox-news.html?pagewanted=1.

15. Amy Mitchell, Elisa Shearer, Jeffrey Gottfried, and Michael Barthel, "The Modern News Consumer," Pew Research Center, Washington, DC, July 7, 2016, http://www.journalism.org/2016/07/07/pathways-to-news/.

16. Jeff Bercovici, "Pew Study Finds MSNBC the Most Opinionated Cable News Channel by Far," *Forbes*, March 18, 2013, https://www.forbes.com/sites/jeffbercovici/2013/03/18/pew-study-finds-msnbc-the-most-opinionated-cable-news-channel-by-far/#71faab2e5f8c.

17. "American Rage: The Esquire/NBC News Survey," *Esquire*, January 4, 2016, https://www.esquire.com/news-politics/a40693/american-rage-nbc-survey/.

18. Jason Wilson, "Australia Still Has Time to Avoid the Worst, Says Alt-America Author David Neiwert," Guardian, August 31, 2018, https:// www.theguardian.com/world/2018/aug/31/australia-still-has-time-to-avoid -the-worst-says-alt-america-author-david-neiwert.

19. Jon Schwarz, "Fox News Has Done More to Incite Domestic Political Violence than Donald Trump," Intercept, October 30, 2018, https://theintercept .com/2018/10/30/fox-news-has-done-more-to-incite-domestic-political-violence -than-donald-trump/.

20. Shawn Langlois, "How Biased Is Your News Source? You Probably Won't Agree with This Chart," Marketwatch, April 21, 2018, https://www.marketwatch .com/story/how-biased-is-your-news-source-you-probably-wont-agree-with-this -chart-2018-02-28.

21. Angela Nagle, *Kill All Normies: Online Culture Wars from 4Chan and Tumblr to Trump and the Alt-Right* (Portland, OR: Zero Books, 2017).

22. Stephanie Mencimer, "PizzaGate Shooter Read Alex Jones. Here Are Some Other Fans Who Perpetrated Violent Acts," *Mother Jones*, December 12, 2016, https://www.motherjones.com/politics/2016/12/comet-pizza -suspect-shooters-alex-jones/.

23. Peter Kafka, "An Astonishing Number of People Believe Pizzagate, the Facebook-Fueled Clinton Sex Ring Conspiracy Theory Could Be True," Recode, December 9, 2016, https://www.recode.net/2016/12/9/13898328/ pizzagate-poll-trump-voters-clinton-facebook-fake-news.

CHAPTER NINE: PANTHERS, PATRIOTS, POLICE, AND SOVEREIGNS

1. Aaron Dixon, *My People Are Rising: Memoir of a Black Panther Party Captain* (Chicago: Haymarket Books, 2012), p. 58.

2. Ibid.

3. "What It Means to Have a Mass Base: A Lesson from Elder Aaron Dixon of the Black Panther Party," Medium, March 20, 2018, https://medium.com/ @BlackRedGuard/what-it-means-to-have-a-mass-base-a-lesson-from-elder-aaron -dixon-of-the-black-panther-party-4d2264a34f2f.

4. "Chicago's Black Police Charge: Killing of Panthers 'Assassination,'" United Press International, December 8, 1969.

5. Giovanni Russonello, "Fascination and Fear: Covering the Black Panthers,"

New York Times, October 15, 2016, https://www.nytimes.com/2016/10/16/us/black-panthers-50-years.html.

6. Michelle Alexander, *The New Jim Crow: Mass Incarceration in the Age of Colorblindness* (New York: New Press, 2012), p. 77.

7. John Kifner, "McVeigh's Mind: A Special Report; Oklahoma Bombing Suspect: Unraveling of a Frayed Life," *New York Times*, December 31, 1995, https://www.nytimes.com/1995/12/31/us/mcveigh-s-mind-special-report-oklahoma-bombing-suspect-unraveling-frayed-life.html.

8. Carey Goldberg, "Rampage in New Hampshire Kills 4 before Gunman Dies," *New York Times*, August 20, 1997, https://www.nytimes.com/1997/08/20/us/rampage-in-new-hampshire-kills-4-before-gunman-dies.html.

9. Robert Blechl, "Colebrook Shootings, 20 Years Later: Remembering the Victims and the Resiliency of a Small Community," *Caledonian Record*, August 19, 2017, http://www.newhampshire.com/Many-lessons-learned-from-1997-Colebrook-tragedy.

10. Ibid.

11. "Sovereign Citizens Movement," Southern Poverty Law Center, https://www.splcenter.org/fighting-hate/extremist-files/ideology/sovereign-citizens-movement.

12. Order, docket entry 102, February 12, 2013, *United States v. Kenneth Wayne Leaming*, case no. 12-cr-5039-RBL, US District Court for the Western District of Washington.

13. Ibid.

14. Leah Nelson, "Sovereigns in Black," Southern Poverty Law Center, August 24, 2011.

15. Mark Pitcavage, "The Washitaw Nation and Moorish Sovereign Citizens: What You Need to Know," Anti-Defamation League, July 18, 2016, https://www.adl.org/blog/the-washitaw-nation-and-moorish-sovereign-citizens-what-you-need-to-know.

16. "Moorish Sovereign Citizens," Southern Poverty Law Center, https://www.splcenter.org/fighting-hate/extremist-files/group/moorish-sovereign-citizens.

CHAPTER TEN: OATH KEEPERS, THREE PERCENTERS, AND STRANGE BEDFELLOWS

1. Justine Sharrock, "Oath Keepers and the Age of Treason," *Mother Jones*, March–April, 2010, https://www.motherjones.com/politics/2010/02/oath-keepers/.

2. Ibid.

3. Ibid.

4. "Elmer Stewart Rhodes," Southern Poverty Law Center, https://www.splcenter.org/fighting-hate/extremist-files/individual/elmer-stewart-rhodes-0.

5. Ibid.

6. Ibid.

7. Ibid.

8. Ibid.

9. Sovereign Citizens Movement, Southern Poverty Law Center, https://www.splcenter.org/fighting-hate/extremist-files/ideology/sovereign-citizens-movement.

10. Mark Pitcavage, "The Washitaw Nation and Moorish Sovereign Citizens: What You Need to Know," Anti-Defamation League, July 18, 2016, https://www.adl.org/blog/the-washitaw-nation-and-moorish-sovereign-citizens-what-you-need-to-know.

11. Kevin Carey, "Too Weird for the Wire," *Washington Monthly*, May 2008, https://washingtonmonthly.com/magazine/mayjunejuly-2008/too-weird-for-the-wire-2/.

12. Ibid.

13. Shaila Dewan and John Hubbel, "Arkansas Suspects Had Rage toward Government," *New York Times*, May 23, 2010, https://www.nytimes.com/2010/05/24/us/24arkansas.html.

14. Casey Sanchez, "Sovereign Citizens Movement Resurging," *SPLC Intelligence Report*, February 26, 2009.

15. Dewan and Hubbel, "Arkansas Suspects Had Rage."

16. David Mikkelson, "Did George H. W. Bush Resign from the NRA?" Snopes, December 23, 2012, https://www.snopes.com/fact-check/bush-nra-resignation/.

17. "Senate Acts to Ban Assault Weapons," *Chicago Tribune*, November 18, 993, http://www.chicagotribune.com/news/ct-xpm-1993-11-18-9311180157-story.html.

18. "American Gun Ownership and Hunting Rates at Record Lows, Survey Says," *Guardian*, March 10, 2015, https://www.theguardian.com/us-news/2015/mar/10/america-gun-ownership-hunting-rates-record-lows.

19. Kim Parker, Juliana Menasce Horowitz, Ruth Igielnik, Baxter Oliphant, and Anna Brown, "America's Complex Relationship with Guns," Pew Research Center, Washington, DC, June 22, 2017, http://www.pewsocialtrends.org/2017/06/22/the-demographics-of-gun-ownership/.

20. Neil Genzlinger, "Doomsday Had Its Day in the Sun," *New York Times*, March 11, 2012, https://www.nytimes.com/2012/03/12/arts/television/doomsday-preppers-and-doomsday-bunkers-tv-reality-shows.html.

21. "Glenn Beck's Apocalypse Survival Kits: An Instant Guide," *The Week*, October 20, 2012, https://theweek.com/articles/490063/glenn-becks-apocalypse-survival-kits-instant-guide.

22. David Neiwert, "'Doomsday Prepper' Arrested on Gun Charges in Washington State," Southern Poverty Law Center Hatewatch, January 21, 2014, https://www.splcenter.org/hatewatch/2014/01/21/doomsday-prepper-arrested-gun-charges-washington-state.

CHAPTER ELEVEN: THE TRAYVON EFFECT

1. Desiree Stennett, "O'Mara, Crump Agree: Social Media Playing Key Role in Trayvon Case," *Orlando Sentinel*, April 27, 2013, http://articles.orlandosentinel.com/2013-04-27/news/os-benjamin-crump-mark-omara-20130427_1_benjamin-crump-trayvon-martin-george-zimmerman.

2. Ibid.

3. Travis M. Andrews, "Black Dallas Police Officer Sues Black Lives Matter on Behalf of 'Christians, Jews, Caucasians,' Others," *Washington Post*, September 21, 2016, https://www.washingtonpost.com/news/morning-mix/wp/2016/09/21/black-dallas-police-officer-sues-black-lives-matter-on-behalf-of-christians-jews-and-caucasians-others/?utm_term=.3e811724c18c.

4. "Black Nationalist," Southern Poverty Law Center, https://www.splcenter.org/fighting-hate/extremist-files/ideology/black-nationalist.

5. "Police Officer Suspended after Branding Ferguson Protestors 'Rabid Dogs,'" *Telegraph*, August 23, 2014, https://www.telegraph.co.uk/news/worldnews/northamerica/usa/11052666/Police-officer-suspended-after-branding-Ferguson-protesters-rabid-dogs.html.

6. Chelsea Schilling, "2 New Black Panthers Admit Plot to Bomb Ferguson," WND, June 2, 2015, https://www.wnd.com/2015/06/2-new-black-panthers-admit-plot-to-bomb-ferguson/#et8P1vzXpxEw45yC.99.

CHAPTER TWELVE: "A FREE-FOR-ALL ARMAGEDDON"

1. Sarah Larimer and Abby Phillip, "Who Are the Oath Keepers, and Why Has the Armed Group Returned to Ferguson?" *Washington Post*, August 11, 2015, https://www.washingtonpost.com/news/morning-mix/wp/2015/08/11/who-are-the-oath-keepers-and-why-has-the-armed-group-returned-to-ferguson/?utm_term=.488fa6f2df25.

2. Ibid.

3. Jesse Bogan, "'Oath Keepers' Are Back on the Rooftops in Ferguson Despite St. Louis County Ordinance," *St. Louis Post Dispatch*, December 2, 2014, https://www.stltoday.com/news/local/crime-and-courts/oath-keepers-are-back-on-the-rooftops-in-ferguson-despite/article_18757380-b471-5a6f-848c-a4dfe9805ed6.html.

4. Ibid.

5. Ibid.

6. Adam Nagourney, "A Defiant Rancher Savors the Audience That Rallied to His Side," *New York Times*, April 23, 2014, https://www.nytimes.com/2014/04/24/us/politics/rancher-proudly-breaks-the-law-becoming-a-hero-in-the-west.html?smid=tw-share&_r=1.

7. Erin McClam and Pete Williams, "Kentucky Clerk Kim Davis Defies Supreme Court, Turns down Gay Couples," NBC News, September 2, 2015, https://www.nbcnews.com/news/us-news/same-sex-marriage-kentucky-clerk-defies-supreme-court-turns-down-n419351.

8. David Badash, "Kim Davis Won't Be Arrested Again Promises 'Patriot' Militia Group That Waged Cliven Bundy Standoff," New Civil Rights Movement, September 10, 2015, https://www.thenewcivilrightsmovement.com/2015/09/kim_davis_won_t_be_arrested_again_promises_patriot_militia_group_that_waged_cliven_bundy_standoff/.

9. Steven Nelson, "FBI Agents Weren't Posing as Militia, Ex-Fire Chief Clarifies," *US News and World Report*, January 14, 2016, https://www.usnews.com/news/articles/2016-01-14/fbi-agents-werent-posing-as-militia-ex-fire-chief-clarifies.

10. Chip Berlet, "The Good, Bad and Ugly in Oregon Standoff Coverage," FAIR, January 15, 2016, http://fair.org/home/the-good-bad-and-ugly-in-oregon-standoff-coverage/.

11. Tom Boggioni, "Militia Head Warns Feds: Don't 'Waco' the Oregon Occupiers Unless You Want a 'Bloody, Brutal Civil War,'" Raw Story, January 16, 2016, https://www.rawstory.com/2016/01/militia-head-warns-feds-dont-waco-the-oregon-occupiers-unless-you-want-a-bloody-brutal-civil-war/.

12. "Sean and Sandy Anderson 'Feel Like Hostages' in Oregon," February 10, 2016, YouTube video, 3:56, https://www.youtube.com/watch?v=nS8H94WrYGA.

13. "Oregon 'Standoff' Loser Sean Anderson Declares War on the United States," posted by Amelius Brown, February 8, 2016, YouTube video, 1:28, https://www.youtube.com/watch?v=WKetJB4W00M.

CHAPTER THIRTEEN: WHITE LOVE

1. "Terror on Trial: Who Was Timothy McVeigh?" CNN, December 31, 2007, http://edition.cnn.com/2007/US/law/12/17/court.archive.mcveigh2/.

2. Jon Ronson, *Them: Adventures with Extremists* (New York: Simon and Schuster, 2003), p. 179.

3. Ibid., p. 181.

4. Ibid., p. 200.

5. "Arkansas Demographics and Social," Migration Policy Institute, https://www.migrationpolicy.org/data/state-profiles/state/demographics/AR.

6. Derek Thompson, "How Immigration Became So Controversial," *Atlantic*, February 2, 2018, https://www.theatlantic.com/politics/archive/2018/02/why-immigration-divides/552125/.

7. Ibid.

8. Ibid.

9. "Thomas Robb," Southern Poverty Law Center, https://www.splcenter.org/fighting-hate/extremist-files/individual/thomas-robb.

10. "Kevin MacDonald," Southern Poverty Law Center, https://www.splcenter.org/fighting-hate/extremist-files/individual/kevin-macdonald

11. Kevin McDonald, "Can the Jewish Model Help the West Survive?" Kevin McDonald, http://www.kevinmacdonald.net/WestSurvive.htm.

12. "Inside USA – Rise of Hate," posted by Al-Jazeera English, April 19, 2008, YouTube video, 13:28, https://www.youtube.com/watch?v=Si4vbISz9D4.

13. Eve Conant, "Hate Groups Are Benefiting from Obama's Direction," *Newsweek*, April 24, 2009, https://www.newsweek.com/hate-groups-are-benefiting-obamas-election-77295.

14. Ibid.

15. Ibid.

16. Ibid.

17. Ibid.

CHAPTER FOURTEEN: MAINSTREAM-ISM

1. Graeme Wood, "His Kampf," *Atlantic*, June 2017, https://www.theatlantic.com/magazine/archive/2017/06/his-kampf/524505/.

2. "Richard Bertrand Spencer," Southern Poverty Law Center, https://www.splcenter.org/fighting-hate/extremist-files/individual/richard-bertrand-spencer-0.

3. Barbara Perry, "Button-Down Terror: The Metamorphosis of the Hate Movement," *Sociological Focus* 33, no. 2 (November 19, 2012): 113–21, https://www.tandfonline.com/doi/abs/10.1080/00380237.2000.10571161.

4. Wood, "His Kampf."

5. Ibid.

6. Caitlin Dewey, "The Alt-Right, Explained in Its Own Words," *Washington Post*, August 29, 2016, https://www.washingtonpost.com/news/the-intersect/wp/2016/08/29/the-alt-right-explained-in-its-own-words/?utm_term=.c95770fd4d8f.

7. "What Is the Alt-Right?" *Washington Post*, https://www.washingtonpost.com/video/politics/what-is-the-alt-right/2016/08/25/b275b12e-6aaf-11e6-91cb-ecb5418830e9_video.html?utm_term=.88b23404312c.

8. C. J. Ciaramella, "Some Well-Dressed White Nationalists Gathered in DC Last Weekend," *Vice*, October 30, 2013, https://www.vice.com/sv/article/kwpadw/some-well-dressed-white-nationalists-gathered-in-dc-last-weekend.

9. Joseph Bernstein, "Here's How Breitbart and Milo Smuggled White Nationalism into the Mainstream," BuzzFeed, October 5, 2017, https://www.buzzfeednews.com/article/josephbernstein/heres-how-breitbart-and-milo-smuggled-white-nationalism.

10. Ibid.

11. Allum Bokhari and Milo Yiannopoulos, "An Establishment Conservative's Guide to the Alt-Right," Breitbart, March 29, 2016, https://www.breitbart.com/tech/2016/03/29/an-establishment-conservatives-guide-to-the-alt-right/.

12. Ibid.

13. Ibid.

14. Bernstein, "Here's How Breitbart and Milo Smuggled White Nationalism."

15. Rob Beschizza, "White Supremacy Euphemism Generator for Journalists," Boing Boing, November 15, 2016, http://boingboing.net/2016/11/15/euphemisms.html.

16. Ibid.

17. "Nathan Benjamin Damigo," Southern Poverty Law Center, https://www.splcenter.org/fighting-hate/extremist-files/individual/nathan-benjamin-damigo.

18. Allie Conti, "An Alt-Right Group Is Trying to Recruit College Kids Like It's a Frat," *Vice*, September 12, 2017, https://www.vice.com/en_nz/article/paa7wk/an-alt-right-group-is-trying-to-recruit-college-kids-like-its-a-frat-vgtrn.

19. "David Duke," Southern Poverty Law Center, https://www.splcenter.org/fighting-hate/extremist-files/individual/david-duke.

20. "Exclusive: David Duke on Rep. Scalise Controversy," CNN, January 3, 2015, YouTube video, 7:41, https://www.youtube.com/watch?v=ZZWCBvl7iAw.

21. Caitlin Dewey, "The Alt-Right, Explained in Its Own Words," *Washington Post*, August 29, 2016, https://www.washingtonpost.com/news/the-intersect/wp/2016/08/29/the-alt-right-explained-in-its-own-words/?utm_term=.c95770fd4d8f.

CHAPTER FIFTEEN: THE TROLL KING

1. "Ted Cruz Announces 2016 Presidential Campaign (Full Speech)," ABC News, March 23, 2015, YouTube video, 0:30, https://www.youtube.com/watch?v=0YurHI-d3Dk&t=363s.

2. "Senator Marco Rubio Presidential Announcement Speech (C-Span)," C-Span, April 14, 2015, YouTube video, 18:27, https://www.youtube.com/watch?v=51jmJn8XwPQ&t=306s.

3. "Jeb Bush Presidential Campaign Announcement Full Speech (C-Span)," C-Span, June, 15, 2015, YouTube video, 28:51, https://www.youtube.com/watch?v=7w-bnAvrsds&t=321s.

4. "Watch Donald Trump Announce His Candidacy for US President," *PBS News Hour*, June 16, 2015, YouTube video, 46:33, https://www.youtube.com/watch?v=SpMJx0-HyOM&t=141s.

5. Ibid.

6. Jonathan Mahler, "Donald Trump's Message Resonates with White Supremacists," *New York Times*, February 29, 2016, https://www.nytimes.com/2016/03/01/us/politics/donald-trump-supremacists.html.

7. Ibid.

8. Peter Holley and Sarah Larimer, "How America's Dying White Supremacist Movement Is Seizing on Donald Trump's Appeal," *Washington Post*, February 29, 2016, https://www.washingtonpost.com/news/morning-mix/wp/2015/12/21/how-donald-trump-is-breathing-life-into-americas-dying-white-supremacist-movement/?utm_term=.0cce7e43ae0b.

9. Chris Cillizza, "Donald Trump's Troll Game of Jeb Bush: A+," *Washington Post*, September 8, 2015, https://www.washingtonpost.com/news/the-fix/wp/2015/09/08/donald-trumps-troll-game-of-jeb-bush-a/?utm_term=.bd35ee86dc91.

10. "Bush to Trump: You Can't Insult Your Way to the Presidency," CNN, December 15, 2015, YouTube video, 0:34, https://www.youtube.com/watch?v=HKQgrOV27X0.

11. Olivia Nuzzi, "Trump Still Hasn't Retracted His False Claim That He Saw Muslims Cheering on 9/11," *New York Intelligencer*, September 11, 2017, http://nymag.com/intelligencer/2017/09/trump-hasnt-retracted-claim-about-muslims-cheering-9-11.html.

12. Alexander Griffing, "Remember When Donald Trump Appeared on Alex Jones' 'InfoWars,'" *Haaretz*, August 6, 2018, https://www.haaretz.com/us-news/remember-when-donald-trump-appeared-on-alex-jones-infowars-1.5443723.

13. Catherine Rampell, "Millennials Have a Higher Opinion of Socialism than of Capitalism," *Washington Post*, February 5, 2016, https://www.washingtonpost.com/news/rampage/wp/2016/02/05/millennials-have-a-higher-opinion-of-socialism-than-of-capitalism/?utm_term=.c3fd776ecceb.

14. Kevin Drum, "Donald Trump's Love Affair with White Supremacists," *Mother Jones*, July 5, 2016, https://www.motherjones.com/kevin-drum/2016/07/donald-trumps-love-affair-white-supremacists/.

15. Ibid.

16. Melissa Chan, "Donald Trump Refuses to Condemn KKK, Disavow David Duke Endorsement," *Time*, February 28, 2016, http://time.com/4240268/donald-trump-kkk-david-duke/.

17. Rebecca Kaplan, "Donald Trump's Endorsers Still with Him after Proposed Muslim Entry Ban," CBS News, December 9, 2015, https://www.cbsnews.com/news/donald-trump-endorsers-still-with-him-after-proposed-muslim-ban/.

18. Jason Le Miere, "Trump Responds to Hillary Clinton 'Lock Her Up' Chants: 'Some Things Just Take a Little Bit Longer,'" *Newsweek*, August 3, 2018, https://www.newsweek.com/trump-lock-her-hillary-clinton-1056282.

19. Ed Pilkington and Adam Gabbatt, "How Donald Trump Swept to an Unreal, Surreal Presidential Election Win," *Guardian*, November 9, 2016, https://www.theguardian.com/us-news/2016/nov/09/how-trump-won-us-election.

20. "USA Presidential Election: 2016 Odds," OddsShark, November 10, 2016, https://www.oddsshark.com/entertainment/us-presidential-odds-2016-futures.

21. Mark Potok, "Year in Hate and Extremism," *SPLC Intelligence Report*,

February 15, 2017, https://www.splcenter.org/fighting-hate/intelligence
-report/2017/year-hate-and-extremism.

22. Ibid.

CHAPTER SIXTEEN: ANTI-ALL

1. Sheryl Gay Stolberg and Brian M. Rosenthal, "Man Charged after White
Nationalist Rally in Charlottesville Ends in Deadly Violence," *New York Times*,
August 12, 2017, https://www.nytimes.com/2017/08/12/us/charlottesville-protest
-white-nationalist.html.

2. Ibid.

3. Valerie Richardson, "Antifa Isn't a 'Hate Group,' Southern Poverty Law
Center Claims," *Washington Times*, December 2, 2017, https://www.washington
times.com/news/2017/dec/2/antifa-isnt-hate-group-southern-poverty-law-center/.

4. Stolberg and Rosenthal, "Man Charged after White Nationalist Rally."

5. Dahlia Lithwick, "Yes, What about the 'Alt-Left'?" *Slate*, August 16, 2017,
https://slate.com/news-and-politics/2017/08/what-the-alt-left-was-actually-doing
-in-charlottesville.html.

6. David Neiwert, "Far-Right Conspiracists Stir up Hysteria about Nonexistent
'Civil War' Plot by 'Antifa,'" Southern Poverty Law Center Hatewatch, November
13, 2017, https://www.splcenter.org/hatewatch/2017/11/13/far
-right-conspiracists-stir-hysteria-about-nonexistent-civil-war-plot-antifa.

7. Ibid.

8. Ibid.

9. Ibid.

10. Ibid.

11. Ibid.

CHAPTER SEVENTEEN: THE STATE OF THE UNION

1. Henry David Thoreau, "A Plea for Captain John Brown" (speech; Concord,
MA, October 30, 1859), http://avalon.law.yale.edu/19th_century/thoreau_001.asp.

2. Robin Wright, "Is America Headed for a New Kind of Civil War?,"
New Yorker, August 14, 2017, https://www.newyorker.com/news/news-desk/
is-america-headed-for-a-new-kind-of-civil-war.

3. Ibid.

4. Jason Wilson, "Are Rightwing Pundits Right That America Is on the Brink of a Civil War?" *Guardian*, June 22, 2017, https://www.theguardian.com/us-news/2017/jun/22/american-politics-civil-war-alt-right-left-wing.

5. William Cummings, "Iowa Rep. Steve King Says America Is Heading toward Another Civil War," *USA Today*, June 25, 2018, https://www.usatoday.com/story/news/politics/onpolitics/2018/06/25/steve-king-america-civil-war/733226002/.

6. Gab (@getongab), Twitter post, June 24, 2018 (since deleted).

7. Jennie Neufeld, "#SecondCivilWar: How a Wild Conspiracy Theory Became a July 4th Twitter Meme," Vox, July 5, 2018, https://www.vox.com/policy-and-politics/2018/7/5/17536556/second-civil-war-conspiracy-theory-july-4-twitter-meme.

8. Robert Evans, "6 Reasons Why a New Civil War Is Possible and Terrifying," Cracked, November 1, 2016, http://www.cracked.com/personal-experiences-2403-6-reasons-why-new-civil-war-possible-terrifying.html.

9. Nassim Nicholas Taled, *The Black Swan: The Impact of the Highly Improbable* (New York: Penguin, 2008).

10. Evans, "6 Reasons Why a New Civil War is Possible and Terrifying."

11. William Jordan, "Does "Right Direction/Wrong Track" Matter?" YouGov, August 13, 2016, https://today.yougov.com/topics/politics/articles-reports/2016/08/12/americans-are-unhappy-other-side.

12. Frank Newport, "Church Leaders and Declining Religious Service Attendance," Gallup, Washington, DC, September 7, 2018, https://news.gallup.com/opinion/polling-matters/242015/church-leaders-declining-religious-service-attendance.aspx.

13. Kim Parker and Renee Stepler, "As US Marriage Rate Hovers at 50%, Education Gap in Marital Status Widens," Pew Research Center, Washington, DC, September 14, 2017, http://www.pewresearch.org/fact-tank/2017/09/14/as-u-s-marriage-rate-hovers-at-50-education-gap-in-marital-status-widens/.

14. Katie Shepherd, "Multnomah County Republican Party Approves Oath Keepers and Three Percenters as Private Security," *Willamette Week*, June 30, 2017, https://www.wweek.com/news/2017/06/30/multnomah-county-republican-party-approves-oath-keepers-and-three-percenters-as-private-security/.

15. Chris Riotta, "Maxine Waters Urges Supporters Not to Counter-Protest Militia Group Targeting Her," *Independent*, July 19, 2018, https://www.independent.co.uk/news/world/americas/us-politics/maxine-waters-oath-keepers-protest-demonstration-los-angeles-california-militia-a8454846.html.

16.   Nick Miroff and Missy Ryan, "Army Assessment of Migrant Caravan Undermines Trump's Rhetoric," *Washington Post*, November 2, 2018, https://www.washingtonpost.com/world/national-security/army-assessment-of-migrant-caravans-undermines-trumps-rhetoric/2018/11/02/78b9d82a-dec0-11e8-b3f0-62607289efee_story.html?utm_term=.5cc29e5fb3b7.

17.   Bethania Palma, "Tucker Carlson's Claim about Protestors Damaging His Door Challenged," Snopes, November 16, 2018, https://www.snopes.com/news/2018/11/16/tucker-carlsons-claim-about-protesters-damaging-his-door-challenged/.

18.   Frank Newport, "US Confidence in Police Recovers from Last Year's Low," Gallup, Washington, DC, June 14, 2016, https://news.gallup.com/poll/192701/confidence-police-recovers-last-year-low.aspx?g_source=link_NEWSV9&g_medium=related_tile1&g_campaign=item_1597&g_content=US%2520Confidence%2520in%2520Police%2520Recovers%2520From%2520Last%2520Year%27s%2520Low.

CHAPTER EIGHTEEN: KNOW THY ENEMY

1.   Mark Potok, "The Year in Hate and Extremism," *SPLC Intelligence Report*, March 4, 2013, https://www.splcenter.org/fighting-hate/intelligence-report/2013/year-hate-and-extremism.

2.   Daryl Johnson, "Congressional Report Highlights Gaps in US Domestic Terrorism Policy," Southern Poverty Law Center Hatewatch, January 2, 2018.

3.   Spencer S. Hsu, "Napolitano Says Suicide Plane Crash Wasn't Related to Domestic Terrorism," *Washington Post*, March 10, 2010, http://www.washingtonpost.com/wp-dyn/content/article/2010/03/09/AR2010030903475.html.

4.   Jessica Rivinius, "Sovereign Citizens Perceived as Top Threat," START, July 30, 2014, https://www.start.umd.edu/news/sovereign-citizen-movement-perceived-top-terrorist-threat.

5.   Johnson, "Congressional Report Highlights Gaps."

6.   Jerome P. Bjelopera, "Shifting Homegrown Domestic Terrorism from Hate Crime and Homegrown Domestic Terrorism," CSR Insights, August 14, 2017, https://fas.org/sgp/crs/terror/IN10299.pdf.

7.   "Interview with Greg Palast: I Went To School With Stephen Paddock Grades 2–12," Jeff Rense Radio, October 16, 2017.

8.   "A Casino Regular, Quiet but Prickly, Unleashes a Rampage," *Seattle Times*,

October 6, 2017, https://www.seattletimes.com/nation-world/
a-casino-regular-quiet-but-prickly-unleashes-a-rampage/.

9. Adam Le Fevre, in email to Daryl Johnson, November 13, 2017.

10. Chris Pleasance, "'I Was Born Bad': Las Vegas Prostitute Who Romped
with Mass Killer Stephen Paddock Says He Enjoyed Violent Rape Fantasies and She
Reveals He Boasted He Had Always Been Evil," *Daily Mail*, October 8, 2017, http://
www.dailymail.co.uk/news/article-4959970/Vegas-prostitute-says-Stephen-Paddock
-enjoyed-violent-sex.html.

11. Enjoli Francis, "Las Vegas Gunman Made 'Anti-Government'
Rants, Sought to Have AR-15s Converted in Fire Fully Automatic: Witness,"
ABC News, May 18, 2018, https://abcnews.go.com/US/WorldNews/
las-vegas-gunman-made-anti-government-rants-sought/story?id=55244942.

12. Ryan Gaydos, "Las Vegas Gunman Stephen Paddock Ranted about FEMA
Camps, Waco before Concert Massacre, Witnesses Say," Fox News, May 17, 2018,
https://www.foxnews.com/us/las-vegas-gunman-stephen-paddock-ranted-about
-fema-camps-waco-before-concert-massacre-witnesses-say.

13. Eric Killelea, "Alex Jones' Mis-Infowars: 7 Batsh*t Conspiracy Theories,"
Rolling Stone, February 21, 2017, https://www.rollingstone.com/culture/
culture-lists/alex-jones-mis-infowars-7-bat-sht-conspiracy-theories-195468/
the-government-is-controlling-the-weather-118190/.

14. "LVMPD Preliminary Investigative Report 1 October Mass Casualty
Shooting," Las Vegas Metropolitan Police Department, January 18, 2018, https://
www.lvmpd.com/en-us/Documents/1_October_FIT_Report_01-18-2018
_Footnoted.pdf.

15. Scott Neuman, "Why Did He Do It? Authorities Still Baffled by Vegas
Shooter," NPR, October 5, 2017, https://www.npr.org/sections/thetwo-way/
2017/10/05/555864489/why-did-he-do-it-authorities-still-baffled-by-vegas-shooter.

16. Voluntary Witness Statement, Event-171001-3619, Las Vegas Metropolitan
Police Department, Clark County Detention Center, November 7, 2017, pp. 54–80.

17. Kevin Felts, "Stephen Paddock, The Perfect Gray Man," All Outdoor,
October 3, 2017, https://www.alloutdoor.com/2017/10/03/stephen-paddock
-perfect-gray-man/.

18. Daryl Johnson, "Lunatic Fringe: Survivalist Forum Praises Las Vegas
Gunman," Southern Poverty Law Center Hatewatch, October 9, 2017, https://
www.splcenter.org/hatewatch/2017/10/09/lunatic-fringe-survivalist-forum-praises
-las-vegas-gunman.

19. Voluntary Witness Statement, Event-171001-3619.

CHAPTER NINETEEN: LOVE THY NEIGHBOR

1. Mark Wilding, "Circle or Sphere? Inside the UK's First 'Flat Earth' Conference," *Esquire*, September 11, 2018, https://www.esquire.com/uk/culture/a22725244/inside-the-uks-first-flat-earth-conference/.

2. Avi Wolfman-Arent, "The Ongoing Battle between Science Teachers and Fake News," NPR, July 28, 2017, https://www.npr.org/sections/ed/2017/07/28/537907951/the-ongoing-battle-between-science-teachers-and-fake-news.

3. Lulu Morris, "NASA Responded to Rapper B.o.B's Flat Earth Plans," *National Geographic*, October 4, 2017, https://www.nationalgeographic.com.au/space/nasa-responded-to-rapper-bobs-flat-earth-plans.aspx.

4. "America's Flat-Earth Movement Appears to Be Growing," *Economist*, November 28, 2017, https://www.economist.com/graphic-detail/2017/11/28/americas-flat-earth-movement-appears-to-be-growing.

5. David Adam, "The Earth Is Flat? What Planet Is He On?" *Guardian*, February 23, 2010, https://www.theguardian.com/global/2010/feb/23/flat-earth-society.

6. Wilding, "Circle or Sphere?"

7. Ibid.

8. Mark Shanahan, "This Is What Kyrie Irving Said about the Earth Being Flat," *Boston Globe*, August 23, 2017, https://www.bostonglobe.com/lifestyle/names/2017/08/23/this-what-kyrie-irving-said-about-earth-being-flat/v7sNKtYS3SS1QX7s4S4ZaM/story.html.

9. Colin Dwyer, "'I Don't Believe in Science,' Says Flat-Earther Set to Launch Himself in Own Rocket," NPR, November 22, 2017, https://www.npr.org/sections/thetwo-way/2017/11/22/565926690/i-dont-believe-in-science-says-flat-earther-set-to-launch-himself-in-own-rocket.

10. Shanahan, "This Is What Kyrie Irving Said."

11. "Phillip Is Absolutely Baffled by the Men Who Believe the Earth Is Flat | This Morning," This Morning, May 2, 2018, YouTube video, 0:24, https://www.youtube.com/watch?v=erA3WQE9Zes.

12. Joan E. Solsman, "YouTube Bans Infowars' Alex Jones Channel," C-Net, August 6, 2018, https://www.cnet.com/news/youtube-bans-infowars-alex-jones-channel/.

13. Joby Warrick, "In Fight against ISIS's Propaganda Machine, Raids and Online Trench Warfare," *Washington Post*, August 19, 2018, https://www.washingtonpost.com/world/national-security/in-fight-against-isiss-propaganda

-machine-raids-and-online-trench-warfare/2018/08/19/379d4da4-9f46-11e8-8e87
-c869fe70a721_story.html?utm_term=.cfba4e517683.

14. Vernon Silver and Sarah Frier, "Terrorists Are Still Recruiting on Facebook, Despite Zuckerberg's Reassurances," Bloomberg, May 10, 2018, https://www .bloomberg.com/news/articles/2018-05-10/terrorists-creep-onto-facebook-as-fast -as-it-can-shut-them-down.

15. "Moonshot CVE, a Google-Backed Startup Is Using Internet Ads to Counter Online Extremism," Tech Startups, March 29, 2018, https://techstartups .com/2018/03/29/moonshot-cve-a-google-backed-startup-is-using-internet-ads-to -counter-online-extremism/.

16. Terry Gross, "How a Rising Star of White Nationalism Broke Free from the Movement," NPR, September 24, 2018, https://www.npr.org/2018/09/24/ 651052970/how-a-rising-star-of-white-nationalism-broke-free-from-the-movement.

17. Wes Enzinna, "Renouncing Hate: What Happens When a White Nationalist Repents," *New York Times*, September 10, 2018, https://www.nytimes .com/2018/09/10/books/review/eli-saslow-rising-out-of-hatred.html.

18. Ibid.

19. R. Derek Black, "Why I Left White Nationalism," *New York Times*, November 26, 2016, https://www.nytimes.com/2016/11/26/opinion/sunday/why-i -left-white-nationalism.html?module=inline.

20. Jason Wilson, "Life After White Supremacy: the Former Neo-Fascist now Working to Fight Hate," *Guardian*, April 4, 2017, https://www.theguardian.com/ world/2017/apr/04/life-after-hate-groups-neo-fascism-racism.

21. Mack Lamoureux, "Former NeoNazis Tell Us How They Finally Left the Movement," *Vice*, June 22, 2018, https://www.vice.com/en_us/article/59qeqa/ former-neo-nazis-told-us-how-they-finally-left-the-movement.

22. Ibid.

23. Mark Goulston, "Why People Kill Themselves—Part 2: It's Not Depression," Medium, June 10, 2018, https://medium.com/@mgoulston/ why-people-kill-themselves-its-not-depression-44113406ac79.

24. Eugene Rubin, "PTSD and Ecstasy: Science and Perception," *Psychology Today*, October 3, 2018, https://www.psychologytoday.com/intl/blog/ demystifying-psychiatry/201810/ptsd-and-ecstasy-science-and-perception.

25. Eli Saslow, "'Nothing on this Page Is Real': How Lies Become Truth in Online America," *Washington Post*, November 17, 2018, https://www .washingtonpost.com/national/nothing-on-this-page-is-real-how-lies-become-truth -in-online-america/2018/11/17/edd44cc8-e85a-11e8-bbdb-72fdbf9d4fed_story .html?utm_term=.1cfc08c66871.

26. Caitlin Dewey, "What Was Fake on the Internet This Week: Why This Is the Final Column," *Washington Post*, December 18, 2015, https://www.washingtonpost.com/news/the-intersect/wp/2015/12/18/what-was-fake-on-the-internet-this-week-why-this-is-the-final-column/?utm_term=.2c3de6fb809f.

INDEX